BARRIE PEPPER

BOOKS

50 *Great* Pub Crawls

Editor: Barrie Pepper

Cover design: McKie Associates 01604 497577

Cover photography: Tracey Sherwood

Maps: Perrott Cartographics

Managing Editor: Mark Webb

Printed by WBC, Bridgend, Wales

ISBN 1-85249-142-6

Published by CAMRA Books, Campaign for Real Ale Ltd, 230 Hatfield Road, St Albans AL1 4LW

CONTENTS

INTRODUCTION

Pub crawling has been an activity for as long as we have had pubs. The stages of stage coaching were pubs and a journey from say, Leeds to London in the eighteenth century would take three days with the start and finish, two overnight stops and a number of comfort stops for both passengers and horses in-between, all at inns, pubs and taverns.

These were the first long distance pub crawls. Later, from the industrial revolution onwards, workers would regulate their homeward journey after a hard worked shift by stops at pubs. An uncle of mine, a miner, told me how on pay day he would visit up to eight pubs on his way home from the pit. Knowing him, and my aunt, he would not have another drink for a week.

Many towns, particularly northern industrial ones, have what is known in many places as a 'stagger', which these days takes on the more dignified title of 'circuit drinking'. These are simply visits to a continual series of pubs without missing any out, often along one road. It probably means visiting some good pubs, some bad pubs and some indifferent ones. The fine art of pub crawling is to work out a route which allows you to visit a number of pubs, all selling good beers and, ideally, of some character and interest. And even better that the crawl should start and finish close to the same point and near to good public transport connections. Of course this is not always possible but this book attempts to give you a selection that comes close to the ideal. Occasionally you will find pubs marked in bold italics which means that they are in the 'try also' category. If you have time, call in, otherwise pass on.

Some of these pub crawls are in city centres, others are suburban, some are in country towns; one or two are in villages. And then there is a selection of unusual crawls: by train, by boat, by supertram and a couple of country rambles. Many of the crawls take you to places of interest other than pubs – castles, churches, stately homes, museums and even breweries. And there is a reasonable geographical spread, although I am conscious of the fact that certain areas are not covered too well. On the other hand there are some parts of the country where a group of crawls are close enough together to warrant thinking about short holidays and week ends pub crawling. Ideas for new pub crawls for another edition of this guide are welcome.

It is an irony that within weeks of signing the contract to edit this guide I started to feel the pains of osteoarthritis in my right knee. It is the sort of disease that doesn't get better. And then half way through the writing I undertook major heart surgery which was a great success but knocked my work back by six months. Therefore many of these pub crawls will remain either within my memory or will be far from attainment. However the pleasure of compiling the guide overcomes the albeit painful disadvantage of not being able to use it myself, but I hope it will give you, the reader, a great deal of pleasure and entertainment.

Barrie Pepper

BARRIE PEPPER is one of the country's best known beer writers and he has recently retired as Chairman of the British Guild of Beer Writers after seven years in office. This is his fourteenth book and his previous ones include Irish Pubs, The International Book of Beer, The Bedside Book of Beer and The Old Inns and Pubs of Leeds. He writes for What's Brewing, Pub Management Magazine, American Brewer, the Yorkshire Post and several other newspapers and journals. His other interests include sport and music and he enjoys good company and conversation in the convivial atmosphere of genuine pubs. He and his wife, Carolynne, who runs a beer shop, live in one of the leafier parts of Leeds.

Thanks Due

Thanks are due to the following for their help in compiling this guide book. They were either instrumental in suggesting and outlining a pub crawl or in some cases drafting one to my brief, in taking photographs and roughing out maps, or simply being helpful. There will be tangible 'thank yous' as well:

Dave Backhouse, Yvette and Neil Bacon, Roy Bailey, Gavin Brammer, Mark Bridges, Rob Buckley, Martin Butler, Andy Camroux, Alan Canvess, John Clarke, Pearl Claydon, the late Ivor Clissold, John Corcoran, Lucie Edginton, Peter Edwardson, Martin Ellis, Brian Glover, Spike Golding, Dave Haddon, Michael Hardman, John Holland, George Howie, Mark Hutchinson, Linda Hutton, Rhys Jones, Sean Kelleher, Jim Lawrie, Richard Lycett, the Northern Ireland Tourist Office, John McCloy, Charles McMaster, Susan and Fran Nowak, Chris Palmer, Ken Paris, Tracey Parker, David Pepper, Tim Proudfoot,

Roger Protz, Richard Putley, Jim Scanlon, the Severn Valley Railway Company, Andrew Shrigley, John Simpson, Gordon Small, Geoff Strawbridge, Martin Strawbridge, Chris Stringer, Karl Thomson, Rob Tough, Colin Valentine, Ralph Warrington, Nick Whitaker, John White, Drew Whiteley, Keith Wilson and Andy Wright.

And to members of the following branches of CAMRA: Abercolwyn, Aberdeen, Grampian and Northern Isles, Arun and Adur, Bridgenorth Sub Branch, Bristol and District, Burton upon Trent and South Derbyshire, Chester and South Clwyd, Derby, Edinburgh and South East Scotland, Exeter and East Devon, Gloucestershire, Herefordshire, High Peak and North East Cheshire, Hull and East Yorkshire, Kidderminster Sub Branch, Louth, Merseyside, North Sussex, Nottingham, Sheffield, South East London, South West London, Stockport and South Manchester, Sunderland and South Tyneside, Swindon and North Wiltshire, Tyneside and Northumberland, Walsall, West Lancashire and York.

Also to Mark Webb who kept me on the straight and narrow, David Perrott who drew some superb maps and Phillip Tordoff, Howard Bicknell and Jack Thompson who gave help that went far beyond the call of duty. I owe them all a few pints. And finally, I must single out for special mention my dear wife Carolynne for all her help, kindness and encouragement during the protracted preparations for this book. As usual, she was prepared to drive me to the pub. And back again.

Barrie Pepper

Stop Press

Sadly, a number of breweries have closed down since the editing of this book and information on the beers sold at certain pubs may be incorrect. Wherever Vaux and Wards beers are shown there will be other beers on sale. The same may apply to pubs selling beers from Morrell, Mitchell, Butterknowle, Ruddle and Morland. This does not change the quality of crawls affected. If you want to help save traditional breweries and beer styles then join CAMRA – call 01727 867201, email camra@camra.org.uk

ABERDEEN

Aberdeen, the Granite City, is an ancient town, receiving its first royal charter in the twelfth century, although the modern city with its handsome Union Street dates from 1806. It is Scotland's largest fishing port and home base of the North Sea oil industry. Twenty-five years ago there was little real ale here but plenty of good pubs. Now there is a lot of real ale and more good pubs than ever before. This circular pub crawl around the eastern end of the city starts at the bus and railway stations. One advantage of this crawl is that it can be cut if time is limited, for you are never very far from the start and finish. Most of the pubs on this crawl open all day, usually up to midnight. Variations are indicated.

Leave the stations and turn right along Guild Street towards the harbour. Pass two pubs and the Tivoli theatre, now closed after being sadly a bingo hall, and cross over Market Street at the traffic lights. Twenty yards along Trinity Quay there is the busy harbour on your right mostly packed with supply vessels servicing the oil platforms, the ferry terminal and the occasional fishing boat. On your left is **The Moorings (1)** built in 1870 on the former site of a sixteenth-century coaching inn with its mermaid pub sign remaining. It sells Caledonian Deuchars IPA and 80/-, Isle of Skye Red Cuillin and guest beers mainly from Scottish independent breweries. Toasties and snacks are available. This haven for Rock'n'Ale fans has one of the best rock juke boxes you'll find anywhere and with live bands most weekends this can make for a noisy pint; but it is well worth the effort. Three different colour schemes applied during a recent paint make-over are interesting for interior decorators!

Turn left as you leave the pub and follow Trinity Quay. Take the first left, Ship Row, a cobbled road which climbs past the Maritime Museum, housed in a new extension to one of Aberdeen's oldest buildings – Provost Ross House. Follow the road up the hill with the impressive clock tower looming on the sky line. The road bears right into Exchequer Row and a few yards on changes its name again to Castle Street where you'll pass the ***Tilted Wig***. Well worth a visit for its good beers, reasonably priced food and the comfiest bar

stools in the city. Just a few yards further on, situated on the corner of Castlegate, is **Old Blackfriars (2)**. Beers on sale are Belhaven 80/- and St.Andrews, Caledonian Deuchars IPA and 80/- with guests. It was twice voted local CAMRA Pub of the Year and is an excellent combination of old and new on a split level with the imaginative use of stained glass and of various relics including an ancient solid wooden door in the upper level. Great value food is served all day up to 9 p.m. (8 p.m. at weekends). It opens at 10.30 a.m. for coffee and newspapers, except on Sundays.

Top: *Moorings.* Bottom: *Old Blackfriars.*

The Castlegate is a large open paved area and is the site of the Mercat Cross. Admire the impressive Salvation Army Citadel, with its fairy-tale-like tower, at the eastern end of Castlegate. On the adjacent corner to Old Blackfriars is a former bank now converted into a Wetherspoon's pub called ***Archibald Simpson's.*** It offers a varied selection of beers, good value food and a long walk to the toilets! Walk west along Castle Street, passing the Tollbooth, now housing the civic history museum, and the Sheriff's Courts. Continue until you reach the traffic lights at the junction with Broad Street then turn right up Broad Street and admire the imposing gothic structure of Marischal College. At the next set of traffic lights the road changes its name to Gallowgate. Carry on along the road for 200 yards, passing another set of traffic lights until you reach the **Blue Lamp (3)** easily spotted by the very large Police lamp outside. There is a large, cavernous lounge, which hosts live bands usually on Friday and Saturday nights, and in which Caledonian Deuchars IPA and 80/- are sold. There is also a small intimate public bar which dispenses guest beers. Both the original 45s juke box in the public and the modern CD one in the lounge are free, dispelling the myth of the mean Aberdonian. Open till 1a.m. Friday/Saturday (must be in the pub by midnight).

Top: *Blue Lamp.* Bottom: *The Grill.*

Retrace your steps down Gallowgate until you reach the second set of traffic lights and turn right down Upper Kirkgate. Cross over and walk down Flourmill Lane to take a look at Aberdeen's oldest building Provost Skene House, described as the 'Jewel in the City'. Continue to the end of the lane and turn right into Netherkirkgate. Take the footpath between Marks and Spencer and the underpass. The footpath comes out into a piazza and opposite is St Nicholas Lane where the **Prince of Wales (4)** is located. One of the first things you will notice as you enter this pub is the length of the bar counter – the longest in Aberdeen. It is adorned with a bank of eight handpumps, backed by two fine old gantries, from which Draught Bass, Caledonian 80/-, Theakston Old Peculier, Tomintoul XXX and guest beers are sold. The Draught Bass and beers from a selected Scottish brewer are usually on offer at a special price. There is good value food every lunch time until 2 p.m. On Sundays it opens at 11 a.m. (no alcohol till 12.30 p.m.) serving an all-day Scottish breakfast (forget any thoughts of slimming diets). Regular folk music sessions are held on Sunday evenings.

From here turn right and walk to the end of St Nicholas Lane, then use the steps on Correction Wynd to climb to Union Street. Walk 50 yards west past St Nicholas Churchyard and take the first right up Back Wynd, then turn left into Little Belmont Street, where **Cameron's Inn (5)**, known affectionately as Ma's, and Aberdeen's oldest pub is located. The beer range varies but it usually sells Orkney Dark Island and guest beers. The snug as you enter on the right is probably the oldest, unspoilt bar in Aberdeen, with a serving hatch to order beer. At the back is a large modern lounge where meals are served at lunch times and early evenings. Real ale is available in both bars, but the snug is the recommended place to sample the local atmosphere with your pint.

Right next door to Ma's is the ***Old Town School***, a Hogshead pub. This is worth a quick visit to see the city's only gravity dispensed beer and to pop up to the balcony to have a look into the 'cellar'. On leaving, turn right towards Belmont Street and left back on to Union Street. Turn right, crossing over Union Bridge, although you'll hardly notice that you are on a bridge thanks to the skills of the city architects more than 200 years ago. On your right you can see the imposing His Majesty's Theatre in the distance. Walk past the statue of Edward VII at the junction with Union Terrace and carry on walking west until just before you reach the splendour of the Music Hall with its pillared entrance, at which point you have the cobbled South Silver Street on your right. Walk north across Golden Square, passing the statue of George, Duke of Gordon, who was the first Colonel of the 92nd Gordon Highlanders. Continue into North Silver Street and there, underneath the Bon Accord Auction Saloons, you will find the cellar bar **Under The Hammer (6)**. This pleasant, one room wine bar is handy for His Majesty's Theatre. Table candles add to the intimate atmosphere where you can occupy a table and try the varied food on offer. Also, it is perfectly acceptable to stand at the bar and consume your pint. Caledonian Deuchars IPA and a guest beer are on offer. The bar does not open until late afternoon except on Saturdays when it opens at 2 p.m.

Retrace your steps to Union Street and almost opposite you is **The Grill (7)** which is very handy during concert intermissions at the Music Hall. Boddington's Bitter, Caledonian 80/-, McEwans 80/- and a guest beer are sold at this superb example of an Edwardian pub with unique wood-panelling and high ceiling spoilt only by the strip lighting. A variety of good value snacks are served and there are discounts for pensioners. It has an amazing range of malt whiskies. This was one of the original men-only bars but now there are ladies toilets at ground floor level whilst stairs have been cleverly built where the gents used to be, leading to new downstairs facilities.

Leave The Grill by the back door and cross the street to ***Macandrews.*** This was Aberdeen's first Scottish theme bar. The concept is not as bad at it sounds, for the theme was that it only sold beers from Scottish breweries. Walk south down Crown Street passing the flamboyant old Post office building until you have the Brentwood Hotel on your left. **Carriages (8)** is in the cellar of the hotel. This is a very friendly busy bar with ten handpumps dispensing a usually excellent choice of guest ales as well as Boddington's Bitter, Caledonian Deuchars IPA, Castle Eden Ale, Courage Directors and Flowers Original. There is also a range of bottled Belgian and German Weisse beers. Food is available in the bar with a separate restaurant open in the evening. The bar closes in the afternoons.

Retrace your steps north up Crown Street and turn right into St John's Place. Turn left into Crown Terrace following the signs 'To Bridge Street', then walk down the flight of steps to South College Street from where the bus and railway stations are only about 100 yards away.

ARUNDEL

This historic small town is dominated by its magnificent castle, home to the Duke of Norfolk. The Museum of Curiosity is worth visiting to see an amazing collection of Victorian whimsy. Bus number 702 from Brighton, (via Worthing and Littlehampton) or from Portsmouth take you to the Bus Station which is a good place to start the crawl. Train travellers on the Brighton to Portsmouth line should change at Ford. From the station walk along The Causeway, past The Arundel Park Hotel, (no real ale), crossing the busy A27 at the pedestrian lights, and into town.

The **Swan Hotel (1)**, is a large white Victorian building, situated on the corner of High Street and River Road. This lively pub is the brewery tap for Arundel Brewery although it is not owned by them, and sells the full range of its current portfolio, together with one or two guest ales. There is only the one bar, which makes it an ideal meeting place. A good selection of food is available in the bar and there is a restaurant attached. On leaving The Swan turn left past The Red Lion and the tourist information centre, then left again along Tarrant Street until you reach, on your left, **The Eagle (2)** on the corner of the mouth-wateringly named Brewery Hill. It is a popular and basic pub with one large bar and an annexe. The beers on sale are Draught Bass, Fuller's London Pride and Courage Directors Bitter.

A little further along Tarrant Street, on the corner of Kings Arms Hill, you should not be entirely surprised to find The **Kings Arms (3)** This is an old established free house dating from 1625 and was the local CAMRA branch pub of the year in 1997. It is certainly one that you should not miss. There are two bars with a range of four ales, always in excellent condition. Regular beers are Fuller's London Pride and Young's Special and Hopback beers are usually available. The accent is on beer so the food menu tends to be basic. There is often Morris dancing on summer evenings.

Leave The Kings Arms and walk up the hill. It is short but has an increasing gradient, then cross Maltravers Street and ascend Parsons Hill, turning left at the Roman Catholic

Top: *Drinking in view of the castle.*

Bottom: *Swan Hotel.*

Cathedral continuing along London Road to **St Mary's Gate Inn (4)**. The sign on the pub misleadingly proclaims 'Free House' on what is in fact a Hall and Woodhouse pub selling Badger beers. The beers are well kept, the pub is friendly and popular with diners. It was built in 1525 as a farm dwelling and is well worth visiting for it's historical significance.

On leaving what most folk call the Mary Gate aim for The White Hart; by going back into town along London Road towards the castle and then down the High Street alongside the imposing castle walls. It is a fair walk from the Mary Gate and you may be tempted to try ***The Norfolk Hotel (5)*** and ***The Red Lion (6)*** on the way. The Red Lion is a strange 'A' shape with an island bar which sells Ind Coope Bitter, Young's Special and Ansell's Bitter which are usually well kept. The Norfolk is cosy, oak panelled pub selling three real ales although it is not primarily a cask ale orientated bar.

Cross the river at Queen Street and **The White Hart (7)** is on your immediate left. It is a free house and the range of beers is constantly changing. The only general rule is that they tend to sell Gales during the winter months and a wider choice in the warmer weather. (Hop Back Summer Lightning sometimes.) The bar is very comfortable and the hosts friendly. First impressions might say that the decor is a bit fussy or overcrowded with bric-à-brac, but the quality of the beer soon compensates for this. Rational people might at this point decide to stagger back to the starting point. If you do not fall into this category, or only drink halves, and enjoy a mile walk, then turn right as you leave the White Hart, go over the bridge and right again, following Mill Road to its end. You will pass Swanbourne Lake which is a wild bird sanctuary (although Southern Water does its best to prevent this in summer) before reaching **The Black Rabbit (8)** to enjoy another selection of Hall and Woodhouse's Badger beers, usually Dorset Best, Dorset IPA and Tanglefoot as well as a house beer – Black Rabbit Bitter. This pretty riverside pub – the only one in Arundel – is one mile from the town centre and the walking time is up to twenty minutes. A more picturesque route, affording dramatic views of the castle is along the riverbank, but this is less direct, and will double the walking time. It is also not recommended at night.

Below: *St. Mary's Gate Inn.*

BATH

Bath is a city of mainly Georgian elegance with many well-preserved buildings including the eighteenth-century Assembly Rooms, the Guildhall, the fashionable terraces, Bath Abbey and the Roman Baths. The cultural quality of the city is reflected in its pubs, as you shall see.

From Bath Spa railway station or the bus station head up through the centre of the city to the **Old Green Tree (1)** in Green Street. This is a charming three-roomed pub and both the wood-panelled front and back rooms are non-smoking. The Uley Brewery brews a house beer and others include Pitchfork from the RCH brewery and Wickwar BOB and a porter. The pub does not open until 7 p.m. on Sundays.

From Green Street cross over Milsom Street into Quit Street and then to **Hatchets (2)** in Queen Street. This is a very popular genuine free house with the beers always changing – even on a daily basis – but they are always well kept, well served and reasonably priced. Go back to Milsom Street. and head up to the traffic lights at the bottom of Landsdown Road hill. If you feel like a brisk walk then make your way up the hill to the **Old Farmhouse (3)**, a lively Wadworth house with a single horseshoe bar and superb views over the city. Look out for the portrait of the landlord on the pub sign. Apart from Wadworth ales there are also Butcombe Bitter, Draught Bass and Abbey Bellringer and behind the pub you'll find the home of Abbey Ales, Bath's only brewery. Then downhill via Guinea Lane to **The Star (4)** (see below).

"Oh! Who can ever be tired of Bath?"

Jane Austen

If you are not feeling energetic then miss out the Old Farmhouse and stroll direct along the Paragon to The Star, a classic city-centre two-roomed pub full of atmosphere. Draught Bass is served from glass pitchers filled by gravity from the cask. Other beers include Exmoor Ale, Wadworth 6X and a guest ale.

A hundred yards away at the top of Walcot Street is the **Hat and Feather (5)** a noisy pub that is popular with aging

hippies who come for the live music and students who dominate the table football machine. Drinks include Courage Bitter and Directors, Smiles Best Bitter and Cheddar Valley cider.

Down from the Hat and Feather in Walcot St. is **The Bell Inn (6)** an open plan bar which is renowned for it's live music (folk, jazz and rock) and a excellent range of beers which include Courage Bitter and Directors, Exmoor Gold,

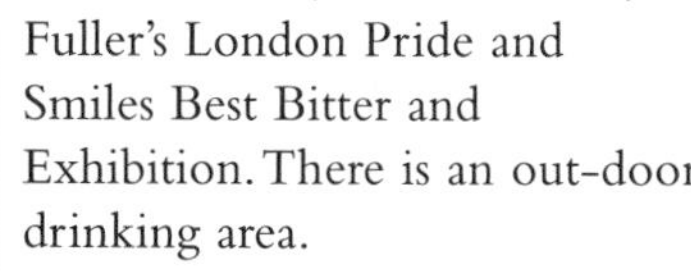

Fuller's London Pride and Smiles Best Bitter and Exhibition. There is an out-door drinking area.

Make your way to Saracen Street and the **Pig and Fiddle (7)**. This is an Ashvine outlet that has been recently refurbished and extended. Very lively and popular with the twenty-somethings of Bath. It is just the place to be on a balmy summer evening and the right place to end a crawl by trying Ashvine Bitter, Challenger and Hop and Glory as well as a guest beer and Thatcher's (no relation) cider. It's downhill from here to the stations.

Top: *The Old Green Tree.* Bottom: *The Star Inn.*

BELFAST

Belfast is one of the great Victorian cities, an important port, with an industrial base in shipbuilding and manufacturing industries particularly textiles and importantly linen. Start the crawl from the Europa Bus Centre. Go through the Great Northern Mall into Great Victoria Street and facing you are the first two pubs on the crawl. To the right is the **Beaten Docket (1)** a modern, lively pub with a public bar on the ground floor and a comfortable lounge and restaurant upstairs. There is a no smoking area and children are welcome. It has what is probably the best selection of real ales in Northern Ireland including Draught Bass, Cains FA, Caledonian Deuchars and IPA, Timintoul Laird's Ale and guests. There is live music on Friday and Saturday evenings. Next door is the **Crown Liquor Saloon (2)** one of the best known and best loved pubs in Ireland. It is owned by the National Trust and managed for them by Bass Ireland. It was built in 1826 as the Railway Tavern to service the fledgling Belfast to Lisburn line and its new name came in 1885 when it was rebuilt to the design of the owner's son by Italian craftsmen who were in Belfast to build churches. And a century later the Trust gave it a sympathetic restoration to its present glory. John Betjeman tagged it 'a many-coloured cavern' and his description is easy to understand. Take your time to admire it from the tiled exterior with its ornate columns and splendid iron gates to the magnificent bar with its glorious tiled backdrop that faces ten private snugs or 'confessionals' as they are called. The Crown is one of the great gin palaces of the world. It sells Draught Bass and a fine selection of wines and spirits and the food has a high reputation. The Crown saw through the troubles with a few scars yet many famous folk continued to come; so ask to see the visitors book just to find out who they were. Make your reluctant departure and turn right into Great Victoria Street passing the Europa Hotel and the Grand Opera House into College Square and fork right into King Street. Turn right at Castle Street and left at Chapel Lane and then right into Bank Street where you will find ***Kelly's Cellars (3)***. This is marked as a try also entry simply because you are unlikely to

"I was born in Belfast between the mountain and the gantries

To the hooting of lost sirens and the clang of trams."

Louis Macneice

Top: *Kelly's Cellars.* Bottom: *The Crown Bar.*

find real ale on sale here. However you will not be disappointed so seize the moment. It was built in 1720 and is the oldest continuously licensed premises in Belfast. It has a wealth of history and played its part in the 1798 insurrection when men like Wolfe Tone, Thomas Russell and Henry Joy McCracken met and plotted here. Famous visitors abound, particularly sportsmen. From golf there have been Dai Rees the winning Ryder Cup captain and Fred Daly the only Irishman ever to win the Open Championship; boxers such as Floyd Patterson and Sonny Liston; and great footballers: Matt Busby, Bill Shankley and Stanley Matthews along with the rest of the Blackpool team that won the 1953 FA Cup. There were entertainers too: Wilfred Pickles, G H Elliott, Sir John Martin Harvey, Guy Mitchell and Buck Alec who signed himself as 'the world's greatest lion tamer.' Today's customers are journalists and lawyers and 'the plain people of Ireland'. There have been changes over the years at Kelly's Cellars but the essential atmosphere remains along with the barrel seats, whitewashed walls and archways as old as the pub. Food is available at lunch times with a basic menu downstairs and more variety on the first floor. There is music, either traditional or blues, at the weekends when a later opening is allowed.

Continue along Bank Street turning right into Royal Avenue and left into Castle Place and finally left into Lombard Street for the **Monico Bars (4)**. You are now in the heart of the busy shopping area of the city. There is a small snug at the front that is popular with the racing fraternity and a larger bar at the back with a number of enclosed cubicles. It is well decorated with mirrors and wood prints. Cains FA from Liverpool is on regular sale along with some guest beers. Food is available at lunch times.

Close by is our next stop. Carry on to Rosemary Street and on the right is Winecellar Entry and **Whites Tavern (5)**. This pub dates back to 1630 and is one of the oldest in Belfast. It was once a warehouse and the exposed beams give it real character. It sells Cains FA and occasional guest beers. The home-cooked food at lunch times is good value.

Retrace your steps to Rosemary Street and turn right into Bridge Street and then left into High Street. After the Hipark Centre turn right and go to the junction with Victoria Street and **Bittles Bar (6)**. This unusually shaped bar is friendly and very welcoming. It is tasteful decorated and most comfortable. There is a fine collection of water-colours of views of the city and Belfast's characters. It sells Draught Bass and Worthington White Shield in bottle and food is available at lunch times.

Not more than a hundred yards away in Victoria Square is the **Kitchen Bar (7)**. This cosy and much loved pub dates from 1859; before that it was a boarding house for young ladies working at a nearby department store. For its first 130 years in business it was run by the Conlon family who created a famous relationship between the pub and the Empire Theatre which stood next door. Many famous stars trod its boards and the Kitchen Bar was the entertainers' pub. Charlie Chaplin appeared at the Empire as a young man, and so did Marie Lloyd, Lily Langtry, Will Fyffe, George Formby and many others. The walls of the pub are covered with theatre posters. The long narrow bar at the front is the popular place to be and the Parlour bar behind is a touch more upmarket with many theatre memories on its walls. The food here is filling – good helpings of Irish stew for example – and there is a good choice of drinks. There are cask beers from the Scottish Courage stable and also guest ales from a 'cellar' that is two floors up. There are regular beer festivals. You are now about ten minutes walk away from the starting point and perhaps another visit to the Crown!

Below: *Kitchen Bar.*

BRIDGNORTH

Bridgnorth is one of the most idyllic market towns in Shropshire with some fine historic buildings including a tower that leans steeper than that of Pisa. And it is well supplied with good pubs. This crawl takes in eight of the best pubs in the town including four that are in the *Good Beer Guide*. Be warned that many of the pubs close during the afternoon. The only train access into Bridgnorth is by the Severn Valley Railway for which a separate crawl is included elsewhere in this book. Trains from Kidderminster and Bewdley run at weekends in winter and through the week from the end of May to the beginning of October. Bus services to the town run from several surrounding towns and it is best to seek advice from the companies (Midland Red 01952 223766 and Go Whittle 01562 820002). Bus termini are indicated on the crawl.

This is a circular crawl and can be joined at any point but for convenience the Severn Valley Railway station is used as the starting point. Leaving one of the great delights – the Railwayman's Arms – until the end, walk down to Hollybush Road to the **Hollyhead Inn (1)**. It shares a car park with the railway. This tastefully renovated pub was once called the George Hotel and has a small bar and comfortable lounge with a separate dining area. There are many exposed beams and a cosy open fireplace. A patio at the front is served direct from a hatch to the lounge bar. Cask beers on sale include Draught Bass, Fuller's London Pride, Boddington's Bitter and a guest ale. Meals are served at lunch times and there is a separate restaurant. Children are welcome and the pub is disabled friendly. Overnight accommodation is available.

Continue along Pound Street up to its junction with Salop Street, turn left and opposite is the **Bell and Talbot (2)**. This is a 250-year-old former coaching inn retaining many features of its former brewhouse at the back. There are open log fires in two of the three attractive bars that sell Banks's Mild and Bitter, Cameron Strongarm and Marston's Pedigree. There is good food with evening meals until 8.30 p.m. but no meals on Sundays. This is a Mecca for live music with varying styles played on four nights including Irish on

Above: *The Railwayman's Arms.*

Sundays. A mural in the alleyway shows musicians, staff and customers. There are bedrooms to let. It is disabled friendly.

Retrace your steps into Whitburn Street and on the right is the **Carpenters Arms (3)**. This single-roomed pub dates from 1888. There is no jukebox. Burtonwood James Forshaw's Bitter and Buccaneer beers are on the handpumps. Food is available both at lunch times and early evening. The pub is wheelchair accessible.

Turn right out of the Carpenters Arms along Whitburn Street turning left at High Street and pass through the historic North Gate with its museum. It is the only one of five gates of the town's original fortifications that remains. On the left is the **Bear Inn (4)**, a regular entry in CAMRA's *Good Beer Guide* that is listed as a building of architectural and historic interest. There are two characterful bars without juke boxes or fruit machines in which Batham's Mild and Best Bitter, Boddington's Bitter, Ruddle's Bitter and a constantly changing guest beer are sold . The Bear is renowned for its excellent food and is noted in Sue Nowak's guide *Good Pub Food* as serving food of special interest or merit. Gourmet nights on Thursdays need advance booking (01746 763250). High standard accommodation is available. Buses leave from here to Ludlow and from the nearby Golden Lion to Ludlow and Kidderminster.

Return through North Gate into High Street and on the left find the **Harp (5)**. This black and white faced building has been little altered since it was built. It was originally a wines and spirits retailer licensed as the Harp Stores. The pub is very popular particularly with younger folk and there are two rooms with a central bar selling Banks's Mild and Bitter and Marston's Pedigree. The use of electric pumps for Banks's beers is a standard practice in line with company policy; however it is real ale (cask beer). Food is available at lunch times. The Harp is one of the few pubs in Bridgnorth that is open all day.

Continue along High Street turning left into Cartway bearing sharp right and on your left is the **Black Boy Inn (6)** which is known locally as the Blackie Boy thought to indicate that a former landlord was a chimney sweep who employed young boys to climb inside chimneys to clean them. It was first licensed in 1790. It has a bar and lounge with some old photographs of the town and a beer garden that commands wonderful views over the low town and the River Severn and in which families are made most welcome. Banks's Mild and Bitter and Marston's Pedigree beers are on sale. Meals are served Monday to Saturday lunch times and weekday early evenings. There is disabled access.

Top: *Bear Inn*. Bottom: *Town Hall.*

Proceed down Cartway into Underhill Street and turn left into Bridge Street to cross the river. Immediately on the right is the **Black Horse Hotel (7)** which is also known as 'Bentley's'. It was built about 1800 and first licensed in 1810. The name is taken from the colour of a horse stabled here in 1879 that is said to have gone on to win the Grand National but there is some doubt about its name. The stables remain however. There is a good selection of real ales including Banks's Mild and Bitter, two house beers: Black Horse Best Bitter and Shire Bitter (in truth Morrells Varsity and Graduate) and a guest beer. There is a front bar, lounge and separate no smoking restaurant. No meals are served on Sunday evenings. Accommodation is available and there is access for the disabled. Buses leave from nearby to Wolverhampton, Madeley, Telford and Wellington.

It is a fair old walk now to the final stop but it is very picturesque. Return across the bridge and turn left along Underhill Street passing the caves and the information board at the foot of the cliff. The caves once stored locally brewed beers before they were bottled and transported by river. Follow the road round and up New Road and then cross the footbridge to the railway station.

The **Railwayman's Arms (8)** is the former waiting room and is on the platform of the northern terminus of the Severn Valley Railway. This is another regular entry in the *Good Beer Guide* and is the home of the Bridgnorth branch of CAMRA. In addition to selling Batham's Best Bitter there are three regularly changing guest beers from small independent breweries and a good range of malt whiskies. The bar is full of railway memorabilia or railwayana as the aficionados call it. More about the Severn Valley Railway can be found on the crawl along that line, which also features in this book.

Below: *The Harp.*

BRISTOL

Bristol is a seafaring city that grew over several centuries on a natural harbour in the River Avon. Over the years it has served the wool, slave and wine trades amongst many others. Isambard Kingdom Brunel's association with the city continues in many ways: the Clifton Suspension Bridge, the docks which he redesigned, the Great Western Railway and ships including the SS Great Britain which is now in its original dock. There are also many wonderful old buildings with the cathedral which began life as a twelfth century Augustinian abbey particularly outstanding. It was here that the phrase 'paying on the nail' originated.

This is a linear crawl that starts from Bristol Temple Meads railway station and finishes at Bristol bus station, or the Centre. Or it can just as easily start at the bus station, take all the directions in reverse and finish back at the railway station – the choice is yours! Both ends are linked by frequent bus services.

"There were three sailors of Bristol City

Who took a boat and went to sea.

But first with beef and captain's biscuits

and pickled pork they loaded she."

William Makepeace Thackeray

Bristol Temple Meads railway station, one of Brunel's greatest achievements, was built during the construction of the Great Western Railway. Walk down the station approach, and cross the busy main road at the bottom. Immediately across the road, you will see the **Reckless Engineer (1)** a wooden floored alehouse well noted for its support of local and regional real ale breweries. Between two and five traditional beers are normally available, and the pub is usually open all permitted hours, although it may close on Saturday afternoons depending on football fixtures. There is occasional live music – a CAMRA membership card guarantees free entry!

From here go back across the road bearing left across the roundabout towards Victoria Street. Once there look for the **Kings Head (2)** on the right hand side. This was described as a 'friendly Victorian Gem' in the *Good Beer Guide*, and is well worth a visit. It has a superb snug, and dispenses beers from the Courage and Bass/Worthington range.

Turn right, and carry on walking into nearby Temple Street, noting Temple Church with its leaning spire (Bristol's answer to the Leaning Tower of Pisa!) on the right. Once in Temple

Street, look carefully for the **Cornubia (3)**, which is set back on the left hand side, opposite the fire station. It only reopened to the public in 1996, after many years as the hospitality pub for the nearby Courage Brewery. It is a small pub, with sometimes restricted opening hours, so do check first. Four ales are normally on sale, usually from local independent brewers. There is a small and popular restaurant where booking is essential (Tel: 0117 925 4415).

On leaving the pub, keep left along Temple Street, and then turn right (taking care to avoid any fire engines!), into Counterslip, leading over the river (known as the Floating Harbour) into Passage Street. Almost immediately on your left, you will then see the aptly named **Bridge Inn (4)**. This takes beer from the Bath Ales brewery, as well as Courage, and has been a *Good Beer Guide* regular for many years. It also claims to be Bristol's smallest bar, as you will see!

After enjoying a pint here, you now have a ten minute walk in front of you. Turn right and retrace your steps back across the river, but keep straight on, passing Courage's Bristol Brewery. At the junction with Victoria Street, turn right, and cross the river again at Bristol Bridge, then bearing left into Baldwin Street. On the right, you will soon notice the **Old Fish Market (5)** – Fuller's first pub in Bristol, and one of their first anywhere outside London. It opened in 1997 and has been tastefully decorated inside. It sells the full range of Fuller's beers and some guest ales from time to time.

Turn left on leaving here, and you will soon come across steps on your left leading up to the St Nicholas Market area. The market itself offers stalls selling a very wide range of products – great to browse in if you want a break from the serious business of drinking. A path leads straight through the market area, and ends up in the pedestrianised area of Corn Street. This is one of the oldest parts of Bristol, and is famous for the term 'pay on the nail', where traders from the Corn

Exchange settled their bills. The 'Nails' themselves – four bronze pillars – can still be seen.

From here, look left, and you will see a road. Walk into this from the pedestrianised area, and you will see one of Bristol's finest pubs on the right, the **Commercial Rooms (6)**, owned by J D Wetherspoon. It was extensively and very expensively (costing well over £1 million) renovated from a gentlemen's club. It won the English Heritage/CAMRA award for refurbishment in 1996. It is a large pub, which can get very busy in the evenings, and stocks the usual range of ales that the company is well known for at competitive prices. There are occasional beer festivals.

Next door on the right is a try also entry the ***Wig and Pen* (7)**. This is another recent conversion, and it's worth popping inside to view the interior. A range of beers mainly from Morlands is on sale. Like the Commercial Rooms this can get very busy at weekends.

From the Wig & Pen, turn right, and then right again into St. Stephen's Street, which leads into the wide expanse that is the Centre. Keep to the right, and a short distance away on the right is the **White Lion Hotel (8)**. This is a small pub selling a range of ales often from regional and independent brewers where you can watch the hustle and bustle of the traffic circulating the one way system (a bus spotter's paradise!).

On leaving the White Lion, bear right, and then cross the Centre at the pedestrian lights. Bear to the right and you will arrive at the **Three Sugar Loafs (9)** a split level pub, selling beers from the Moles range. Opposite the pub is an excellent fish and chip shop.

Between the pub and the chip shop are the Christmas Steps. Walk up these, noting the range of antique shops and antiquarian booksellers on either side. At the top of the steps cross straight over Colston Street and walk up Lower Park and one minute's walk will bring you to the **Ship (10)** which sells a range of ales which usually includes beers from independents and regionals. Many nautical artefacts are on display in this two level pub.

Then retrace your walk to Colston Street, and cross over it, before bearing left and walking for a couple of minutes. You will then see the **Smiles Brewery Tap (11)** on your right. This is a wonderfully designed pub which serves the full Smiles range and occasional guest beers. When originally opened, the bar area was the size of the pub – very small! It is only in the last few years that it has been expanded to give much needed room. The brewery is right behind and below the pub.

The crawl is now at an end. If you turn left out of the pub and walk back down Colston Street, you will come back to the Centre, from where most Bristol First City Line bus services depart, as well as some country First Badgerline services. You can catch buses back to Temple Meads station from several locations. Or you can turn right on leaving the Brewery Tap into Upper Maudlin Street (passing the large Bristol Royal Infirmary on the left) then right into Lower Maudlin Street, bearing left for the Bus Station proper. If you are doing the tour in reverse, buses depart next to the Reckless Engineer pub for the Centre and Bus Station.

BURTON UPON TRENT

Nowhere in the world is better known for its brewing heritage than Burton upon Trent. Towns like Milwaukee, Pilsen, Munich and Copenhagen are small fry in comparison.

This crawl takes you through the industrial heart of the town past the two giant breweries (now both owned by Bass) to pubs of great character where beers from all the town's breweries – and further afield – can be tasted. A visit to the town should, if possible, include the splendid Bass Museum.

Say, for what were hop-yards meant,

Or why was Burton built on Trent?

Or many a peer of England brews

Livelier liquor than the Muse,

And malt does more than Milton can

To justify God's ways to man.

A E Housman

The best place to start from is the railway station. Unfortunately, whichever way you follow this crawl a certain amount of backtracking is involved, but it's well worthwhile. From Burton station turn right down Station Street to the first stop on the corner of Mosley Street: **The Roebuck (1)** which is known locally as the 'Ale House'. It stands opposite the former Ind Coope brewery now known as Bass 'C'. The Bass brewery is Bass 'B'. And before you ask whatever happened to Bass 'A', 'C' is for Carlsberg-Tetley and 'B' is for Bass! The beers include: Greene King Abbot, Draught Burton Ale, Marston's Pedigree, Morland Old Speckled Hen, Tetley Bitter and guests which are usually from a small independent brewer. The single bar is popular with brewery workers. Breweriana and related prints and artefacts are displayed on the walls. There is bar billiards and piped music – sometimes a little too loud! The pub is a regular entry in the *Good Beer Guide*.

Turn right along Station Street to the **Devonshire Arms (2)** which is a Grade II listed building. There is a small front bar and a large, comfortable lounge. This recently became the third tied house of the Burton Bridge Brewery and its trade and reputation is building up steadily. On sale are three Burton Bridge beers (usually Bridge Bitter, a dark beer and perhaps the monthly special) and Draught Burton Ale. Of particular note is the 1850s town map by the lounge bar which shows the locations of many of Burton's lost breweries.

Continue along Station Street and look through the railings on the right at the Bass (B!) brewery to see an unusual foun-

Top: *Thomas Sykes.* Bottom: *Coopers Tavern.*

tain made up entirely of metal beer casks. Back track and turn left into Cross Street and proceed to **Coopers Tavern (3)** on the right. This is a traditional ale house with a counterless back tap room. Stillaged casks (cooled in summer), barrel tables and a 'top bench' seat in the corner are all of interest. The tap room oozes character but can get smoky and the less traditional lounge is a retreat from the fug. Draught Bass, Hardy and Hanson's Best Bitter and Classic and Marston's Pedigree are sold. There is good, reasonably priced, wholesome food served in a very friendly environment.

From here go to the junction with Moor Street and then turn right and walk a hundred yards or so to the **Black Horse (4)** which is an honest-to-goodness, two-roomed local. The basic bar is dominated by a pool table and darts and other pub games played by the enthusiastic locals. The lounge is cosy with old photographs of the locality on the walls. The pub is one of the best (consistently good) Pedigree outlets in Marston's home town.

Cross the road and walk straight ahead past the roundabout into Anglesey Road until the **Thomas Sykes (5)** is reached. The pub is situated on the site of the former Everard's Brewery, part of which then became the now sadly defunct Heritage Brewery Museum. The pub is in the former stables and wagon sheds of the brewery. It comprises two high-ceilinged rooms with stable fittings and breweriana, wood benches, cobbled floors and is truly atmospheric. Beers on sale are Draught Bass, Marston's Pedigree and Owd Roger and two guest beers. The now derelict brewery was built in1880 by Thomas Sykes of Liverpool and was owned by Everards between 1898 and 1984. It was a fine example of a tower brewery and now it stands pitifully in its present ruinous state. Note the Goat Maltings behind the brewery buildings with the eponymous weathercock.

Back track down Anglesey Road, across the roundabout turning right into Moor Street and left up Mosley Street which returns you to Station Street. Turn left into Borough Road and pass the railway station then right into Derby Street. The final call **The Alfred (6)**, is on the left about five to ten minutes walk from the station. This is Burton Bridge Brewery's second tied house. It sells a wide variety of their beers including XL, Bridge Bitter, Porter, Festival Ale, seasonal beers and a guest. It has spartan, bare boards though it is full of character with pleasant seating and a raised eating lounge. A games room with bar billiards, table football and other games is at the back. Families are welcome and budget-priced bed and breakfast is available.

Top: *Black Horse.*
Bottom: *Alfred.*

BURY ST. EDMUNDS

An historic market town named after the last king of East Anglia. There is much of interest including the cathedral, the Athenaeum – a one time centre of the town's social life, a Georgian theatre, a Queen Anne mansion and a museum in a twelfth century flint and stone building. And then, of course, there are the pubs. The crawl provides a visitor with a pleasant tour of most of the historic sites.

Start from the public car park behind **The Fox (1)** with a footpath through to the pub. This is a fine pub, full of character, and claims to be the oldest in the town. Originally it consisted of only the rear part with its superb oak panelled room but it has since been expanded. It sells Greene King ales (IPA, Abbot and seasonal ales) and has a reputation for good food.

Leave The Fox and walk via Mustow Street following the old abbey wall turning left into the Abbey Gardens for a pleasant stroll with views of the Cathedral (soon to have a new tower) exiting by the Abbey Gate into Angel Hill. Turn left at gate and go past the front entrance of the Cathedral, viewing Norman Tower (bell tower) before turning right into Churchgate Street thence to the **Queen's Head (2)**. This is a free house with a Victorian facade on an older building. A popular pub with younger folk. Quite large with a patio and conservatory at the rear. Adnams Bitter and Broadside, Nethergate IPA and frequently changing guest beers are available along with a limited food menu.

From here turn into Bridewell Lane which is typical of this part of the town with many fine timber framed buildings, – a house named The Blackbirds was formerly a pub. Turn left into Tuns Lane (yes, a pub called the Three Tuns occupied No 44 Crown Street) and then right for views of St Mary's church and Great Churchyard, continue along Crown Street. passing the ***Dog and Partridge*** (interesting front bar if you have time to linger) with Greene King brewery premises on either side until you enter Westgate Street. Opposite is the Theatre Royal, the only theatre in the country owned by the National Trust. The Georgian auditorium is open for viewing

when no performance is on. Continue to the right along Westgate Street, passing the recently closed maltings, to the **Rose and Crown (3)**, an unspoilt town pub owned by Greene King. There are two bars and an off-sales area between them. The public bar is described as "a down-to-earth gem". IPA, Abbot, XX Dark (mild) and seasonal beers are available along with good value food and accommodation. Very popular with brewery staff.

From the Rose and Crown enter Whiting Street and walk towards the town centre, passing several more fine timber framed buildings on the way. Cross Churchgate Street viewing the Essex boarded ***Mason's Arms*** on the right and carry on to the top of Whiting Street, then turn left towards the imposing Corn Exchange, and neatly tucked away to the right you will find the country's smallest pub, **The Nutshell (4)** in The Traverse. This is one not to miss so do not go on Sundays for both this and the next entry will be closed. Its uniqueness is registered in the Guinness Book of Records. Yet another Greene King house selling IPA and Abbot. It is full of curios including a mummified cat found interned in a wall during alterations.

Top: *Queen's Head.* Bottom: *The Nutshell.*

Leaving the Nutshell with the Corn Exchange on your left, follow the pedestrianised Traverse to **Cupola House (5)** reputedly the oldest town house in Bury. It has fine oak panelling to admire, and a superb cupola on top. Yet another Greene King pub with IPA and Abbot on sale. Good value food with early morning breakfasts available on market days.

Carry on from the Cupola House along The Traverse to enter the Cornhill which is Bury's busy market place on Wednesdays and Saturdays. The handsome Moyses Hall in the corner to the right houses a fine museum of local treasures. Follow along the extended market area going right into the Buttermarket and enter the top of Abbeygate Street

Top: *Angel Hotel.* Bottom: *Cupola House.*

from where you can see the Abbeygate at the bottom of the hill. Walk down Angel Hill and turn right to enter the **Angel Hotel (6)**. This is the last surviving town hotel. It is vine covered and the superb building dominates Angel Hill. It has all the facilities of a first class hotel including the prices! Adnams Bitter and a guest beer are on sale. The Angel has Dickensian associations – he gave readings here and used it as a location in Pickwick Papers.

From the Angel retrace your steps through the Abbey Gardens to the car park but beware the gardens are closed from dusk so an alternative route skirting round the abbey to the left of the Abbey Gate may be necessary.

CAMBRIDGE

There is much to see in this ancient city, not only the colleges but the museums, the churches, the Backs and the Botanic Gardens. The pub crawl starts at Cambridge bus station in Drummer Street in the centre of town. It is the depot for National Express coaches and the pick-up and drop-off point for the bus circular to the railway station.

Begin by following Emmanuel Street down to St. Andrew's Street turning left with Emmanuel College on your left. You will pass ***The Castle (1)*** owned by Greene King – a pub with a limited range of real ale and a rather cramped and dingy interior but with a colourful history. There is an interesting story though about how Doctor Barnes, a senior university tutor, introduced a "shag tax" penalising any freshers found in flagrante delicto with a £20 fine. The Sherwoods, the university's drinking society, was banned by this same tutor and the landlord of the Castle announced that its members were welcome to seek refreshments at his establishment. Since then there has been a tradition of hanging photographs of the current years membership of the society on the pub's walls.

We were walking the whole time – out of one college into another...I felt I could live and die in them and never wish to speak again.

Mary Lamb

The first choice is the **Fountain Inn (2)** in Regent Street. Housed within a Victorian building, it has a traditional wooden interior with bare wooden floorboards. It has one long bar running three-quarters of the length of the pub and an open plan seating area. The front of the pub has a large traditional leaded bay window that gives great views onto the street at the passing scene and to the University Arms Hotel opposite. The selection of real ales is good with Theakston Best Bitter, XB, Old Peculier, Courage Directors, Charles Wells Bombardier and two guest ales together with a good selection of bottled beers including Duvel, Czech Budvar, Marston's Owd Rodger and some wheat beers. The atmosphere is lively with friendly bar staff – this place is popular with the students particularly those from Downing College next door. Food is served up to 7 p.m. with a selection of snacks, pies and puddings – the pies are famous and include Beef and Ale, Lamb and Rosemary and Creamy Vegetable and Herb.

From the Fountain carry on down Regent Street passing Downing College on your right and then either continue along Regent Street and go down an alley way into the **Hogshead (3)** or go down Regent Terrace to get to the Hogshead by the entrance in Parker's Piece. This pub has a cellar bar with a large seating area and another large bar and seating area upstairs. It has a view across Parker's Piece – a large green area in the centre of Cambridge which is popular in the summertime for lazing around on or for flying a kite. It is common land where residents can tether a goat. The interior is of a traditional barn decor. It is quite spacious and whilst it can get busy it is never really crowded. The staff are very friendly and the selection of ales is good – Adnams, Young's Special, Black Sheep, Brains, Marston's Pedigree, Morland's Old Speckled Hen, Brakspear Bitter, Wadworth 6X, Atomsplitter from the local City of Cambridge brewery and at least three guest ales.

Top: *The Tram Depot.* Bottom: *Champion of the Thames.*

Now time for a pleasant stroll across Parker's Piece – weather permitting – to its east corner following East Street past the Police and Fire Stations. On the right you pass the Zion Baptist Church and Anglia Polytechnic University which houses the Mumford Theatre. Turn left into Dover Street and visit the **Tram Depot (4).** This is a single bar pub with mezzanine style seating upstairs. The bar itself is fairly small and it gets very busy on Friday and Saturday nights. Beers on offer are Old Original and Tiger Best from Everards and guests often include Gale HSB and one of Adnams range. There is a reasonable selection of food served until 9 p.m.

Walking from the Tram Depot turn left into Adam and Eve Street and take the second right into Prospect Row for the **Free Press (5)** where a friendly welcome awaits you.

This *Good Beer Guide* listed pub claims to be the only completely no-smoking pub within a 100 mile radius. The Free Press dates from the 1840's and today has a policy of no games, music or interference with the proper occupation of drinking. Beers available are Greene King Abbot and XX dark and True Blue from the City of Cambridge brewery and other guests. Food is served at lunch times and in the evenings although last orders for food are at about 8.30 p.m. dependant on how busy they are. On Saturday lunch times it is crowded for lunch so finding a seat may be difficult. There is also a snug called the Lloyds Room that the landlord claims he has fitted 61 people into – you will be amazed! There is a small beer garden.

Move along into Orchard Street for the **Elm Tree (6)**, a small bar with a front room feel, fish tanks and wallpaper but a lively atmosphere and friendly people. There is live jazz on Monday and Thursday evenings. There are bar billiards and games such as Risk! and chess available upon request. The beers include Adnams Broadside, Badger Tanglefoot, Wells Eagle and Bombardier. Filled baguettes are available at lunch times. There is a newly opened patio garden.

A slightly longer walk of maybe ten minutes from the Elm Tree takes you down Orchard Street, turning right into Emanuel Street. You will pass the Wesley Methodist church – an impressive building – and on the corner by the roundabout ahead is King Street where the **St Radegund (7)** is located. This pub is quite spacious and the atmosphere is relaxed – maybe somewhat boisterous in the evenings. Regular beers are Fuller's London Pride, Adnams Bitter and Shepherd Neame Spitfire plus a guest. Have a look at the graffiti on the ceiling. A *Good Beer Guide* entry.

Carry on down King Street passing some alms houses that were built in 1880 to **The Champion of the Thames (8)**. This has a affable, gentleman's club feel to it with dark wood panelling and leather sofas. It sells Greene King XX Dark Mild, IPA and Abbot beers and there is food at lunch times. According to a large sign on the front:

"This house is dedicated to those splendid fellows who make drinking a pleasure, who reach contentment before capacity and who, whatever the drink, can hold it, enjoy it and still remain gentlemen."

It could be a fitting quote to end the pub crawl! And if you wish you can take Milton's Walk alongside Christ's Pieces back to the bus station. However, if you are still up for one more then ***The Bun Shop (9)*** is worth a look. This is still on King Street and boasts a tapas bar, a cocktail bar and a 'fine ole Irish bar' all in the same building. Food is served all day up to 10 p.m. and there is a reasonable selection of drinks to finish the walk on – Greene King Abbot and IPA, Tetley Bitter and Young's Special.

CHESTER

The walled city of Chester's history begins with the Romans who established a legionary fortress on the banks on the River Dee in 76 AD. The famous Rows – two levels of shops – are well worth seeing and are unique to Chester. Visitors should also search out the Roman Amphitheatre and garden, St Werburgh's Cathedral and take a walk along the walls. The street layout of the old Roman town remains intact and the city centre is free from intrusive traffic. Chester is a thriving and attractive business, shopping, tourist and administration centre.

Start the crawl at the railway station. Chester General station is probably the grandest of Chester's Victorian buildings. It was built between 1847 and 1848 and the main station building is of Italianate style. Take the free bus which runs regularly (remember to keep your ticket) from the station to the Town Hall. Tucked in the corner of town hall square, beside the Forum shopping arcade entrance is the **Dublin Packet (1)** pub selling good Greenall beers plus a guest. Chester Cathedral is close by with its breeding Ravens. This is the only city centre in England where Ravens breed, having nested here for five years after taking a break of more than 300 years.

"The tortuous wall...wanders in narrow file between parapets smoothed by peaceful generations...with rises and drops, steps up and steps down, views of cathedral tower and waterside fields, of huddled English town and ordered English country."

Henry James

From the 'Dublin Packet' turn right and walk along Northgate Street passing Weinholt's bakery on your right towards The Cross, this is the very centre of Chester and is where the four original Roman roads met. Carry on down Watergate Street passing number nine, 'God's Providence House', the only house to survive the plague in the late seventeenth century, and number eleven now 'Watergates', which dates from 1744 and has a crypt from 1180. Continue along Watergate Street until you reach **Ye Olde Custom House (2)**, a seventeenth century pub selling well kept Banks's Bitter and Mild, Marston's Pedigree and Head Brewer's choice. This pub has an oriel window which dates from 1637. Come out the pub and walk along the alley immediately beside the pub, continue along Weaver Street passing the florist on your right, cross over the road and con-

Top: *Falcon*. Bottom: *Bear and Billet.*

tinue along Whitefriars. At the end turn right and you will immediately see the **Falcon (3)**, a well preserved sixteenth century pub serving Samuel Smith's Old Brewery Bitter and basic bar food. There is live jazz on Saturday lunch times. It is owned by a trust which renovated it in 1980 and is leased to Smith's. It has a fascinating history and a leaflet is available to fill you in. For a period around 1878 it was a temperance house – The Falcon Cocoa House!

Turn right out of the pub and continue down Lower Bridge Street take note of "Tudor House' on the opposite side, said to be one of the oldest buildings in Chester. ***The Olde Kings Head (4)*** is worth a look in. This sixteenth century pub, which was a coaching house on the Holyhead route, serves Greenall beers. Continue along Lower Bridge Street until you reach the **Bear and Billet (5)**. This pub was built in 1644 and has a very colourful history. It's name is derived from the time when Russian sailors billeted there and left their vessels guarded by Bears armed with sticks. Regular beers are Lees Bitter, one from the Theakston range and at least one guest.

From here, cross the road and walk alongside the River Dee a little way until you reach the 'Recorder Steps' erected in1700 which take you up onto the walls, turn right and walk until you reach a fingerpost which directs you to Eastgate; continue until you see the **Albion (6)** on your left. Go down the steps or the ramp and enter this little Victorian gem selling Greenall Bitter and Mild, Cain's Bitter and a guest beer all in excellent condition. Good traditional food is served up to 8 p.m. except on Mondays. There is memorabilia of the Great War on display. The Albion is a long standing *Good Beer Guide* entry.

Continue along Park Street passing the Nine Houses on the left – these are genuine mid-seventeenth century almshouses and in 1969 they were restored from near dereliction with six remaining of the original nine. At the end turn right into Pepper Street then cross Souters Lane to the pedestrian crossing and note the Roman Amphitheatre on your right. Cross over at the lights and make your way up St Johns Street until you come to a T-junction, from here you have two choices.

1. Turn right along Foregate Street passing the main shops until you come to the subway, take the City Road path and continue along here until you reach the Mike Melody antique shop. Go down the steps towards the canal and you will come across **Old Harkers Inn (7)**, a converted canalside Victorian warehouse. It sells Timothy Taylor Landlord, Fuller's London Pride, Boddington's Bitter and guest beers. There is good value food with burgers particularly praised.

From Harkers turn left and walk along the canal until you come to Seller Street, then turn right and cross over the canal and continue to the junction with Milton Street where the **Union Vaults (8)** is on the corner. It is a friendly local selling Plessey Bitter and Greenalls Bitter and it has folk music on Sunday evenings. Continue along Milton Street to the **Mill Hotel (9)**. This hotel bar (accommodation is available) is welcoming and lively and sells an extensive and continually changing range of beers mainly from independent brewers. The house beer comes from Coach House brewery. It serves a good choice of reasonably priced food both at lunch times and in the evenings. To return to the station, walk back to Seller Street and at the Union Vaults turn left into Egerton Street and continue as far as Crewe Street which you should follow round until it reaches City Road and the station.

Below: *Albion.*

2. Turn left at the junction and pass under The Eastgate, taking note of the second most photographed clock in England after Big

Ben. The Eastgate was built in 1768-69 and the Jubilee clock was added in 1897-9. Continue until you reach the National Westminster Bank, a handsome classical building from the middle of the nineteenth century and one of the finest in Eastgate Street. Beside the bank are some steps, climb these and walk along the row until you reach the **Boot (10)** which sells Samuel Smith Old Brewery Bitter and has a reputation for good food. It is another fine, historic pub with a fascinating history. At times it has been a Royalist meeting place during the Civil War, a Victorian brothel, a coffee house and a 1920s gambling club. There is a leaflet available with all the detail.

From here continue to walk along the row toward The Cross and turn right into Northgate Street back towards the Town Hall Square. The free bus runs from here back to the railway station.

CIRENCESTER

There are many reasons for visiting Cirencester. It stands on the edge of the Cotswolds and is rich in history which dates back to the Romans who made it the second most important town in Britain. The town's museum has many important relics and mosaics, and there is an amphitheatre on the edge of the town. Although the countryside around Cirencester is notable for a profusion of Roman roads, the town itself has shrugged off the Roman influence in its roads which are mainly gently curving, even to the extent of a curved Market Place. Dominating one end of this is the magnificent fifteenth-century parish church with its soaring tower looking more like a cathedral. Not least of Cirencester's attractions are the pubs as you shall see.

The town's railway has long since disappeared, although there is still a station at Kemble, three miles outside Cirencester, on the Swindon to Gloucester line and a typically infrequent country bus service takes you from there into the Market Place. More convenient public transport is available from the National Express buses which stop in the London Road outside the Beeches car park from where we start our tour. For those driving, this car park is found almost immediately on your left as you drive into Cirencester from the roundabout on what has newly become the A435 and the main access to the town from the new by-pass.

The first stop is the **Waggon and Horses (1)** in London Road just a few yards towards the town centre. If you arrive by bus in the Market Place, then pick up the tour at the second pub and make this your last stop. This is a picturesque eighteenth-century pub with an interesting display of cameras and pump clips. Friendly and efficient with separate restaurant and an outdoor drinking area in a small courtyard. It sells Courage Best Bitter, Fuller's London Pride, Marston's Pedigree, Theakston Best Bitter and Inch's Harvest cider and serves lunch time and evening meals.

From London Road turn down Dyer Street and into the Market Place, always an impressive sight, but more so on Mondays and Fridays which are market days. Our next goal

Top: *Corinium Court Hotel.* Bottom: *Waggon & Horses.*

is the **Golden Cross (2)** in the wonderfully named Blackjack Street This is a gimmick-free pub relying on friendly and efficient service and good company – appealing to all ages. There is a full size snooker table and a skittle alley. It is an Arkells tied house selling 2B, 3B and the company's seasonal ales with food at lunch times. There are two letting bedrooms including a family room. A few doors away is the fine tiled frontage of the award-winning butcher Jesse Smith. On the other side is the excellent Corinium Museum, and across the road is the massive yew hedge of Cirencester House. For those feeling unchallenged by the relatively short stroll around the pubs, Cirencester Park is nearby in Cicely Hill.

Go through Coxwell Street; past the antique shops of Dollar Street and walk down the gently curving Gloucester Street to the **Nelson Inn (3)** a seventeenth-century pub with a strong nautical theme – the lounge bar is in the form of a man o' war, not nearly as bad as it sounds! It sells Wadworth 6X and a guest beer from Whitbread's selection. Meals are served at lunch times and weekend afternoons.

Turn back to the **Corinium Court Hotel (4)** which is closer to the town centre. This is an upmarket hotel with charming courtyard and garden entrances and a small flagstone bar which opens out to a smart comfortable lounge. There is an attractive walled garden and a separate restaurant with meals at all sessions. The bars close during the afternoons. Beers on tap are Hook Norton Best Bitter, Old Hooky and seasonal beers and Wadworth 6X. There are sixteen letting bedrooms all en-suite.

Leaving Gloucester Street, a detour takes you past the picturesque remains of the medieval St John's Hospital and into the Abbey Grounds. The only memory of the abbey is the

Norman arched North Gate by the main road but the lawns and lake bring welcome variety to the uninterrupted pavements of the usual pub crawl.

Return to the town centre with another short detour up Castle Street. Turning left through the archway next to Oddbins brings you into the Brewery car park – the site of the old Cirencester Brewery. Further on down Cricklade Street go past the old brewery maltings. The buildings have been superbly restored but for dwellings rather than for barley.

The Twelve Bells (5) in Lewis Lane is possibly Cirencester's jewel with a superb selection of beers and food. It is a beer drinker's haven lovingly resurrected by the owner. There is a lively front bar and quieter panelled rooms at the back. The beer range varies but there are always five on sale including two session beers from a local brewery. Good value, high quality food is served lunch times and evenings.

Turn right and then right again into Tower Street and left into the Avenue to Chester Street and the **Oddfellows Arms (6)**. This is a sensitively refurbished back-street local to which some gentle changes are promised. Beers include Greene King IPA and Abbot and guests. There is a family room and a garden. Lunches are served every day but it is advisable to book for Sundays.

Return up Chester Street, along The Avenue and Victoria Road back to London Road and our starting point and the Waggon and Horses for those who started at the second stop. Or even for those who have been here before.

Above:
Golden Cross.

DERBY

Derby has had many royal favours. George III gave it the right to use the Crown insignia for porcelain made there. Queen Victoria upped this to Royal and the present Queen declared it a city on her Jubilee visit in 1977. There were many silk mills here and the coming of the Midland Railway works in the mid nineteenth century and Rolls-Royce in 1908 gave Derby a firm industrial base. It is a pleasant city with many parks and a good selection of pubs.

One Tuesday in January 1997 a CAMRA survey recorded 86 different draught beers on sale in Derby. You should be luckier: the usual score is more than one hundred. The big choices are to be found in the half-a-dozen specialist pubs. Pubs owned by the big operators are less adventurous.

Start at the railway station, or train station, as the locals call it. There is a bit of a walk after the first two pubs, so try one and save the other for the return journey. Turn right along Railway Terrace. The housing block on the left is the world's first estate for railway workers, built for the Midland Railway in 1841 by Francis Thompson. At the end of the block on Station Approach is the flat-iron shaped **Brunswick Inn (1),** the world's first railway inn, built to serve the railway cottages as well as providing accommodation for the new breed of horseless travellers. It is now a free house providing a wide range of ales – as many as seventeen – including those from its own brewery which opened in 1991. There are no-smoking and children's rooms; lunch time meals are available upstairs in a time honoured tradition and the pub serves snacks all day. A beer festival is held at the end of September.

Follow the same direction and cross what used to be a bridge over the Branch Canal, to the **Alexandra Hotel (2)** in Siddals Road. The present building which dates from around 1870 is run by Tynemill Inns and houses a pleasant two-roomer selling Bateman's beers, Marston's Pedigree, a wide range of guest beers and a perplexing number of bottled, continental beers. It is open all day and serves lunches and snacks. There are four, reasonably priced, letting bed-

rooms and the breakfasts are described as 'substantial'. Continue along Siddals Road on a road which became very busy after the railway opened in 1835, as the quickest route out of town, though its ten pubs must have slowed down some. The area on the left was crammed with mean houses built round courtyards, interspersed with silk and other mills. Cross Traffic Street using the pelican crossing and continue ahead into Morledge.

Top: *Alexandra Hotel.* Bottom: *Brunswick Inn.*

The traffic roundabout on your right is believed to be the site of Derby Castle. Morledge is the old cattle market area. The bus station on the right is a nice example of 1930s design, but will soon be swept away for something more utilitarian. On the left is the Foal and Firkin (was the White Horse) which is not part of our crawl. Cross Albert Street, walk through the sunken garden into the Market Place, dominated by the Guildhall on the left (1842) and the modern Assembly Rooms, venue for the Derby Beer Festival which is held in mid July.

Cross the Market Place diagonally and take the street to the right (Iron Gate). The pub on the corner – temporarily called Lafferty's – was part of a large coaching inn called the George, which housed some of the '45 rebels on the last night of their march to London. They got as far as Swarkestone the next day before turning back. Farther up on the left is a Wetherspoon's pub – the **Standing Order (3)** – a remarkable conversion of a banking hall into a huge saloon. A little farther on the right is the cathedral of All Saints, with its 15th-century tower, the rest being a rare example of Georgian ecclesiastic architecture.

At the end of the block on the right in Queen Street is the ***Dolphin (4)***. This is Derby's oldest surviving pub, said to date from 1530, but most of the present building is 17th-century. The snug is especially pleasant, and the Bass is drinkable.

Continue up Queen Street, past John Smith's clock works on the left. Smith was apprenticed to the great Whitehurst, and the firm specialises in public clocks with examples all over the world. Follow the road round to the left and discover the **Flower Pot (5)**, home of the Headless Beer Company and an ever-changing range of reasonably-priced craft beers always including a mild. It is open all day with good lunches and evening cobs. Walk round into the back bar and see the amazing cellar-as-backfitting. There is frequent live music in the large function room.

Retrace your steps to the Dolphin. Turn left and walk past the Silk Mill Industrial Museum and the statue of Bonny Prince Charlie around the back of the cathedral to the police station and take the road just to the left (Derwent Street). The Council House built in 1941 is on your right. Cross the River Derwent over Exeter Bridge. The Mansfield beers at the ***Royal Standard (6)*** are usually in good shape.

At the corner of Exeter Street, you'll miss a pub if you turn right. Otherwise go through the underpass, turn sharp left and try the **Peacock (7)** in Nottingham Road. This was a roadside inn on the main road to Nottingham. It is open all day Friday and Saturday and serves lunches and early evening meals. The diversion is worthwhile: it's probably the best Marston's Pedigree in the world, and no-one has been known to leave with less than two pints on board.

Go back though the underpass and left into Exeter Street. The terrace cottage on the right was the home of Herbert Spencer who coined the (often misunderstood and usually misattributed) phrase 'survival of the fittest'. The pub next door is the **Exeter Arms (8)** in Exeter Place. On the left as you enter is a delightful hearth and range, enclosed by wooden settles. The beers are from Marston's and the lunch time food is good value. It is open all day.

Returning to the Exeter Street corner, turn right, meet up with the river and walk under the Ring Road bridge to happen upon the **Smithfield (9)** in Meadow Road. It opened in 1869 to serve the corporation's transplanted cattle market and for much of its life was an Offiler's house. Now it is a locally owned free house, offering a rolling range of beers along with the ubiquitous Draught Bass and Marston's Pedigree. It is open all day serving lunches and rolls (which are called cobs round here).

On leaving, turn right and continue down Meadow Road by the side of Northcliffe House. Cross the footbridge on the right over the river, turn left and skirt the Holmes, now called Bass's Rec, after Michael Thomas Bass, son of brewer, local MP and donator of the land to the borough. Cross the Mill Fleam footbridge. The path will take you beneath a fly-over. Turn right before the tunnel and across two pelican crossings stands the **Alexandra (2)**. After that walk you deserve a drink!

DUBLIN

Dublin is full of great pubs. What you will not find here is real ale with the honourable exception of the Porterhouse (number 3 on the crawl) which brews its own. But you will find some excellent stout and lots of style and atmosphere. This crawl takes you to some of the best but in no way does it cover all of them. To cover them all takes an age. It has taken the author most of a lifetime.

If you use the DART (Dublin Area Rapid Transit) alight at Tara Street station and after leaving it cross the road into Poolbeg Street and on the right is **John Mulligan (1)**. It is useful to know that this pub is always known as Mulligan's of Poolbeg Street so as not to confuse it with other pubs called Mulligan's in different locations. They are it might be said lesser luminaries. Soaked in literary history, the pub has been here since 1782 and it has a distinct Joycean character. The attractive wooden front with its interesting windows draws you into an atmosphere of friendly conversation and good service. Much of its early days are remembered with dark polished wood screens, large Victorian mirrors, gas lighting, posters from the old Theatre Royal and a general ambience of a more gentle age. One claim made on its behalf is that it serves the best pint of Guinness in Dublin. The pub stands close to some of he city's newspaper offices and journalists have a sixth sense in sniffing out the best of drink. That many of them over the years use Mulligan's as their watering hole is reason enough to accept the claim. It is one of the best known and best loved pubs in Ireland.

"The seat of this citie is of all sides pleasant, comfortable and wholesome. If you traverse hills, they are not far off. If you be delited with fresh water, the famous river called the Liffie runneth fast by. If you will take the view of the sea, it is at hand."

Richard Stanihurst

Proceed to the Quays and head west past O'Connell Bridge to Price's Lane then right into Fleet Street and the **Palace Bar (2)** and another favourite of newspaper people (the Irish Times is nearby). In more bibulous times reporters were given their assignments in a corner of the bar known as 'the intensive care unit'. The place has been frequented by more serious literary figures as sketches on the wall (of James Joyce, Samuel Beckett and Seamus Heaney) testify. The wood panelled front bar is long and narrow, and served by a counter with a bank of redundant handpumps while the

handsome wood back bar is topped by old casks, copper serving jugs and a wind-up gramophone. Look out for the engraved mirrors advertising Power's 'pure pot still whiskey'. Beers include Guinness and Murphy.

Take another walk along the Quays glancing the handsome Ha'penny Bridge and turn left at Gratton Bridge into Parliament Street and the **Porter House (3)**. This is one of Dublin's newest pubs and within its capacious interior is a ten barrel brewing plant from which a porter, two stouts, three lagers and two Irish ales are produced. It has been created in a derelict building and has three storeys or five levels depending which way you look at it. It is delightfully airy with a central well and is decked out in stripped pine. Look around and choose which part of the pub you want to drink or eat in. The restaurant on the first floor has a fine reputation.

Top: *Stag's Head.* Bottom: *John Mulligan.*

Appropriately, Plain Porter has quickly established itself as one of the favourite drinks at the Porter House. It takes its name from the one-time standard drink of the Dubliners although porter was actually a London import. Flann O'Brien in his comic novel At Swim Two Birds eulogised the style:

When money's tight and is hard to get
And your horse has also ran,
When all you have is heap of debt –
A PINT OF PLAIN IS YOUR ONLY MAN.

Another beer, a strong Irish ale called An Brainblasta, is sold only by the glass. This play on words actually means 'a tasty drop.'

From here walk up the hill turning left into Dame Street and on the right pavement look out for a splendid mosaic for the next stopping off point the **Stags Head (4)** which is one of Dublin's great pubs, known across the world and a favourite of business people, tourists and what Flann O'Brien called 'the plain people of Dublin'. There has been a pub on the site since 1770 but the present one dates from 1895 when it was rebuilt in the high period of Victorian baroque with loads of mahogany and etched glass mirrors.

The mirrors are magnificent soaring in to a lofty roof void and roaring out of them is a wonderful stag's head guarding the marble topped bar from which thousands of pints are poured each week. This is a busy pub. The main room is broken up by attractive screens and large whiskey vats give it further appeal. Stained glass windows also contain the stag, a handsome brute that deserves the display he gets. Food is important here with simple but substantial fare at lunch times and early evenings. At the back is a comfortable snug with leather upholstery and the downstairs bar is the place for music.

Below: *The Long Hall.*

Back track along Dame Lane and turn right into the busy South Great George's Street. Take care in crossing to the **Long Hall (5)** which is an appropriate name for a pub said to have the longest bar in Dublin. It is certainly an notable one made of highly polished wood with an impressive inlaid brass belt and foot rail. Behind it is dispensed a fine pint of stout. A large clock displays what it claims is the 'correct time'. Mirrors, screens with coloured glass and fine panelling abound and a wild assortment of chandeliers light up the rooms. The walls are full of prints showing an assortment of cartoons of politicians and caricatures of Gilbert and Sullivan characters. An archway leads to a large lounge and on it are the names of former owners of the business. G V Hoolihan, a Kerryman, has presided here since 1973 and in the 150 years of its life the Long Hall has had only four owners.

Return along the opposite side of the road to Exchequer Street and the **Old Stand (6)** which stands proudly on a busy corner, black painted with discrete gold lettering and pleasant window dressings. It is a stylish pub with a dignified personality catering for locals rather than internationals. Not that visitors aren't welcome for this is a very friendly pub. Good value roast meat lunches at reasonable prices are in demand here and the pub has a high reputation for steaks. The screened compartments along the wall are good places to dine in. There is also a smaller room at the back.

Move along Exchequer Street which becomes Wicklow Street turning right into elegant Grafton Street and enter Duke Street with **Davy Byrne's (7)** on the right. Many people know the pub by its appearance in James Joyce's Ulysses. Initially the book doesn't tell us much beyond the famous enigmatic line: 'He (Leopold Bloom, the book's hero) entered Davy Byrne's. Moral pub.' The eponymous landlord himself appears and states his opposition to gambling. Maybe that is why his pub is moral. It takes its place as one of Dublin's best pubs with three comfortable rooms catering for differing tastes. It has a reputation for good food and it has always been experimental in its drinks policy. When Dublin toyed with cask beers in the early 1980s it was one of the first pubs to install handpumps. Australian, Chilean and Californian wines now add to the established, original range. And there is a choice of good stouts. This is a good area for trying out other Dublin delights such as Bewley's Coffee Shop, the Gotham Café for posh pizzas, Brown Thomas and Switzer departmental stores and Trinity College and the Book of Kells.

Stroll up Grafton Street to St Stephen's Green and take the north side which leads into Merrion Row and **O'Donoghues (8)** which is the home of traditional Irish music. It is where the Dubliners and many other famous musicians have gathered and played and is probably the most popular pub in Dublin. Miss it and you miss out on a cornerstone of Irish popular culture. It was built in 1789 as a

grocery selling wines and spirits and it was not until 1934 that it became a pub. Its musical credentials date from the early 1960s when the Ronnie Drew Group, later to become The Dubliners, started playing there. They were followed by such names as Seamus Ennis, Dominic Behan, The Fureys and Christy Moore. The pub was largely rebuilt after a disastrous fire in November 1985.

Above: *O'Donoghue's.*

The long narrow front bar has two entrances, only one of which is open at a time depending on how busy the pub is – you must visit the place to understand! The floors are covered in Liscannor flags and drawings of Dublin decorate the walls while high stools play sentry at the bar. The small back snug contains a massive collection of photographs of musicians from all over the world who have played there. The scene is completed by a large covered yard with access to a food bar and the interest of many old enamel trade signs. And whatever reason brings visitors to O'Donoghues it will be the great pint of Guinness that wins your vote.

Merrion Street and its continuation, Westland Row, lead you to Pearse Station the nearest DART station.

DURHAM

Durham is a truly historic and beautiful city and it is now one of the most popular tourist attractions in the north of England. Its magnificent 900 year old cathedral, rivalled possibly only by that of Lincoln for its splendid hill top setting, can be seen for miles around, complemented by the large and imposing castle. There are also many other ancient buildings set at various levels on the hillsides of the city and a number of these are pubs which are well worth a visit in their own right.

Durham is well served on the main east coast railway line with fast trains to Newcastle and Scotland to the north, and York, Leeds, London and a good many other places to the south. The station stands in a well-elevated situation a little away from the centre and the view of castle and cathedral when emerging from here is worth an initial photograph. There is also a centrally-placed bus station situated almost under the huge and impressive railway viaduct.

A good starting point is the **Colpits (1)** on Hawthorn Terrace up a steepish hill out of the town. This frequent *Good Beer Guide* entry sells a brew that is uncommon for the area – Samuel Smith's Old Brewery Bitter, which is by far the cheapest beer to be found in Durham, selling at about two thirds the price of most others. The pub itself, built in 1856 of local stone, is a veritable time warp. The shape is basically triangular to fit in with the road junction.

Grey Towers of Durham, yet well I loved thy mixed and massive piles. Half church of God, Half castle 'gainst the Scot.

Walter Scott

Cut through Alexandra Crescent to the **Old Elm Tree (2)** which is a quiet, peaceful pub set on a steep hill named Crossgate. It dates from 1601 and though partially opened up, there are no really large areas and there is a good assortment of furniture. Beers on sale are handpumped Wards Best Bitter, Samson, Waggle Dance and a guest beer; food is available at lunch times. It was Durham CAMRA Pub of the Year for 1998. Bed and breakfast is available. Note the old-fashioned 'sneck' on the outer door. Also the lovely cobbled road surface and the solid stone-built houses opposite.

Proceed further down Crossgate until a point where it swings sharply left and the **Fighting Cocks (3)** will be

spotted at the nearby junction with Silver Street and South Street. This is a large and impressive pub which has been partly opened up yet manages to maintains its intimate atmosphere. On sale here are Draught Bass, Stones and Worthington Best Bitters.

To reach the fourth port of call, proceed along Silver Street, the first part of which takes you across a bridge over the River Wear before turning sharply left at its nearest point to the castle. This once busy thoroughfare has now lost most of its through traffic and is all the better for being pedestrianised. Turn right into Saddler Street and look out for the **Shakespeare (4)** on the right. This is probably the smallest pub on the tour and it has earned itself a 'star' symbol in the *Good Beer Guide* for its delightfully unspoilt nature. It is a favourite with members of the cathedral choir. The front snug is particularly intimate and friendly, and a dozen or so folk make it seem crowded. The beer list is Courage Directors, Theakston's Best Bitter, McEwan's 80/- and Webster's Yorkshire Bitter, a brew now very rarely found in its former home town of Halifax.

Top: *Old Elm Tree.* Bottom: *Half Moon Inn.*

Rubbing shoulders with the Shakespeare is the **Hogshead (5)**. Whilst this pub may be fairly typical of its standardised format it has much to commend it and does a brisk trade with its large and impressive range of real ales which includes not only the usual Boddington's Bitter, Flowers IPA and Wadworth 6X, but also Fuller's London Pride and other guest beers. Beer prices here are rather high for the area, but the food is of good quality and not over expensive.

Now for a short 'sobering-up' walk. Retrace your steps a little until Elvet Bridge is seen on the right. You will shortly cross the River Wear again, but this time it is flowing in the opposite direction due to the massive curve just beyond the city centre. When you reach the busy cross-roads look for the **Half Moon (6)** at the junction of Old and New Elvet. This is a large split-level pub with an excellent public bar fronting onto the road. The crescent-shaped servery gives the pub its name. There are original windows and many other features of interest. The beer is Draught Bass and a guest beer from the Durham brewery. There is food at lunch times.

Just in passing, the former City pub in Old Elvet is now a Scruffy Murphy which unfortunately does not have real ale. It's a pity, for this has clearly once been a fine old pub with much character.

Walk along Old Elvet for a short distance until a tiny pub is spotted on the left opposite a Roman Catholic church. This is the **Dun Cow (7)** which is built on the 'side passage' system with two small bars, one behind the other, heavy metal tables, and also outside toilets which are now something of a rarity in many areas. The locals here are particularly friendly and even a complete stranger is made to feel immediately welcome. The beers on sale regularly are Boddington's Bitter and Castle Eden (the latter selling especially well) and a guest beer which may be Taylor Landlord.

To reach the final calling point, either return along Old Elvet, turning sharp left into New Elvet, proceeding right along until it becomes Hallgarth Street, or alternatively cut through Court Lane almost opposite the Dun Cow turning left into New Elvet. **The Victoria (8)** is a magnificent pub in all respects and, whilst it is some way from the town centre, it is well worth making the few minutes extra journey. It fully merits its 'star' symbol being completely unspoilt with a distinctly triangular profile with separate rooms, wood floors, etched glass, a street corner door leading straight into the public bar and many other features of note. It is, in fact, everything a traditional pub should be and certainly very much of a dying breed. There is a bank of five relatively modern handpumps dispensing Theakston Best Bitter, Marston's Pedigree, Hodges Original from Crook in County Durham and guest beers. Lunch time food is available as well as overnight accommodation. This is the sort of place to linger, but not too long; you should allow approximately twenty minutes to return to the station.

EDINBURGH

Edinburgh is known as 'the Athens of the North' because of the number of intellectuals who lived there in the eighteenth and nineteenth centuries – Boswell, Carlyle and Scott amongst them. It is the administrative and legal capital of Scotland and the seat of the new Scottish parliament. The contrast between the elegant and well laid out New Town to the north and the mish mash and winding lanes of the Old Town is remarkable but, wherever you are in Edinburgh there are good pubs to be found.

Start at the rear (southern) entrance to Waverley Station in Market Street and directly opposite is Fleshmarket Close. Half way up the stairs is the *Good Beer Guide* listed **Halfway House (1)**. It is tiny, friendly, noisy, often smoky and usually crowded so is well worth a visit. The beer range is constantly changing but there are never less than four on sale. There is some interesting railway memorabilia.

Go down the steps and turn left into Market Street and then turn right to cross over Waverley Bridge. Turn right into Princes Street, cross it and find West Register Street and the **Guildford Arms (2)**. This is a classic Scottish Victorian gin palace with brewery mirrors, a minstrels gallery, screens and a wonderful ceiling. It sells Belhaven 60/-, Caledonian Deuchars and 80/-, Orkney Dark Island and up to six guest beers including at least one from Harviestoun. Food is available on weekday lunch times.

Edinburgh...a lyric, brief, bright, clear and vital as a flash of lightning.

Charlotte Bronte

After leaving the Guildford, take a sharp left along the incongruously named Gabriel's Road (it's a footpath) keeping Register House, the original home of the world's first public land register, on your right. Carry on down West Register Street to St Andrew Square. Turn right and follow the road all the way down the hill where it becomes Dublin Street. If the weather is good there are great views across the River Forth to the sunny kingdom of Fife. At the bottom of the hill take the next left into Cumberland Street and the **Cumberland Bar (3)**. This elegant, functional New Town pub has half-wood panelling, dark green leather seating and a fine collection of brewery mirrors and framed posters. It won a

Top: *Kay's Bar.* Bottom: *The Cambridge*

CAMRA pub refurbishment award. Beers on sale are Caledonian Murray's Summer Ale, Deuchars IPA and 80/- along with up to six guest ales all dispensed through tall fonts by air pressure. There is good food at lunch times.

Turn left out of here following Cumberland Street for its full length into St Vincent Street and the **St Vincent Bar (4).** This welcoming traditional bar has a superb gantry and many interesting wall decorations. It sells Caledonian Deuchars IPA, Marston's Pedigree and three guest beers and does lunches during the week. From here turn right and go up the hill turning right again into Jamaica Street. Go through the mews houses and at the other side is **Kay's Bar (5).** Cosy, comfortable, convivial and consistent was the alliterative description in the *Good Beer Guide.* It sells Belhaven 80/- and beers from the Scottish Courage range along with 50 single malt whiskies and good value lunches.

From Jamaica Street turn left into India Street to Heriot Row. Turn right and then sharp left up Wemyss Place to Queen Street. Turn left along Queen Street and take the first right up Castle Street which affords a marvellous view of Edinburgh Castle. Halfway up the hill you will find Young Street on your right and the **Oxford Bar (6)**, unmissable, one of the few remaining unspoilt turn of the century pubs left in Edinburgh. For many years it was run by the inimitable Willie Ross who refused to serve – in no particular order – lager, women and Englishmen! There is an ode to Willie on the wall as you enter the pub. It sells Belhaven IPA and 80/- and a basic range of food – try the pies.

Thirty yards away on the left is the **Cambridge Bar (7).** This bar dates from 1775 and is built in classic New Town

Top: *Oxford Bar.* Bottom: *Guildford Arms*

style. The wooden floored interior has an eclectic collection of knickknacks. The regular beers are Caledonian Deuchars IPA and 80/-, Harviestoun Schiehallion, Marston's Pedigree and an exciting range of guest beers. Good food is served at lunch times although the pub is closed on Sundays.

Carry on along Young Street and turn left into North Charlotte Street. Pass George Street on your left and turn right along the southern boundary of Charlotte Square. Follow Hope Street round until it becomes Queensferry Street and here you will find **H P Mathers (8)** designed and built at the turn of the century. There are four tall founts dispensing Caledonian Deuchars IPA, Courage Directors, two guest beers and two handpumps for Theakston Best Bitter and a guest. Basic bar snacks are available all day. Admire the many old Scottish brewery mirrors on the walls including a rare one from the Edinburgh United Brewery. It was closed down and the head brewer and managing director were jailed after the Customs and Excise inspectors raided the brewery on Christmas day, 1934, and caught them brewing undeclared beer.

You are now no more than 100 yards from the fleshpots of Princes Street. If you are hungry then it is worth knowing that Edinburgh has more restaurants per head of population than any other city in Britain.

EXETER

Exeter is a Roman town that was once a great port although it has a great Maritime Museum with more than 100 craft in the former docks. The cathedral has a 300 feet-long nave – the longest span of unbroken Gothic rib-vaulting in the world. The crawl starts from St David's Station.

Cross the car park to the **Great Western Hotel (1)** a free house bar in a small independent and former railway hotel. It is comfortable and friendly with excellent beer and good value food. The bar manager is a real ale enthusiast. Real ales include Draught Bass, Fuller's London Pride and five or six beers mostly from independent breweries. Very popular with railway workers and the travelling public. It has overnight accommodation and is listed in the *Good Beer Guide*.

Cross the road to the **Jolly Porter (2)** a basic ale house, long and narrow on several levels. It is very popular especially with students. Well kept beers. Real ales include Courage Best, Courage Directors, John Smith Bitter, a Courage supplied guest beer and a genuine independent guest beer. Good value food. Jazz on Wednesday evenings. There is a beer festival in the autumn lasting two weeks. The pub is in the *Good Beer Guide*.

"The city derives a very great correspondence with Holland, as also directly Portugal, Spain and Italy; shipping off vast quantities of woollen-manufactures..."

Daniel Defoe

Before heading up St David's Hill it is a short way to the bottom entrance of the **Imperial (3)** a vast Wetherspoon pub standing in its own grounds. This has been tastefully converted from a former hotel. It has three bars and conforms to the usual Wetherspoon's policies of no music, a non-smoking area, food all day and reasonably priced beers. And a visit to the orangery is a must – it was designed by Isambard Kingdom Brunel. Regular beers on sale are Draught Bass, Courage Directors, Exmoor Stag and two guest beers. Westons cider is sold in the Orangery bar.

Leave the Imperial by the same way you went in and continue along St David's Hill, over the Iron Bridge to the **City Gate (4)** which has been recently renovated and reopened as a free house. In the main bar there is a very civilised

atmosphere with quiet music, the cellar bar is livelier. Draught Bass is a regular beer with several changing guest offerings often from local microbreweries. Food is available all day and bed and breakfast will be available soon.

Cross the road and walk down the steps to the **Fizgig & Firkin (5)**. It is a large single-bar pub typical of the Firkin chain housed on the ground floor of a former tower brewery – the St Anne's Well Brewery that owned 150 tied houses. Brewing ceased in 1967. The real ales are the usual Firkin range from its own brewery including the ubiquitous Dogbolter and an occasional guest beer. A well set-up pub with food all day, frequent live music and facilities for the disabled.

Walk under the Iron Bridge down Exe Street at the opposite end of which stands the **Mill-on-the-Exe (6)** a flagship pub for the St Austell Brewery. It is large and smart with good views over the river from the terrace. A good range of St Austell beers are sold: XXXX Mild, Tinners Ale, Trelawny's Pride and HSD. It is open all day and food is available most of the time. There are facilities for the disabled.

Above: *St. Anne's Well Brewery, home of the Fizgig & Firkin*

Leave by the front of the Mill-on-the-Exe, turn left and continue along Bonhay Road back to the station.

HISTORIC GREENWICH

As one might expect in such a popular area for tourists there are many pubs in and around Greenwich. The crawl visits the best and some of the most historic pubs in the area and takes in most of the sights although the Millennium Dome is not covered but it can be seen in the distance from the riverside pubs. A good start can be made from Greenwich BR and Docklands Light Railway station at which buses 180 and 199 also stop.

On leaving the station cross Greenwich High Road into Lang Place, then turn right, left and right again for the **Ashburnham Arms (1)** in Ashburnham Grove. This outstanding Shepherd Neame pub is well worth seeking out. On sale are Shepherd Neame Best Bitter, Masterbrew, Spitfire and seasonal beers. It was named London CAMRA Pub of the Year in 1995 and has recently been extended to reflect its popularity. Excellent food is available at lunch times and it was a recent winner of the brewery's Community Food Pub of the Year award. The beer garden is very popular during the summer. A *Good Beer Guide* regular.

Turn left on leaving and walk to the end of the road. Cross Greenwich South Street and follow Royal Hill as the road bends round. After the Prince Albert (Courage beers) you reach the **Richard I (2)** which sells Young's Bitter, Special and seasonal beers. This popular two-bar, bow-windowed pub has previously featured on CAMRA's national inventory of pub interiors. The pub was once owned by the Tolly Cobbold brewery of Ipswich and is still known locally as the Tolly House. It has a large beer garden featuring a barbecue area that is very popular in summer. It comes as a welcome relief from the hectic central pubs.

Continue to the end of Royal Hill and right into Greenwich High Road. A few yards along adjoining the Greenwich Cinema is the **Funnel and Firkin (3)**. This is a recent welcome conversion by the Firkin Brewery of a pub that previously only sold keg beers. It sells Firkin Shipshape, Funnel, Set's Ale, the ubiquitous Dogbolter and seasonal beers supplied by the Flag and Firkin in Watford. It has the standard Firkin decor and innuendoes that will keep some folk amused.

Top: *Cutty Sark.* Bottom: *Trafalgar Tavern.*

Take a turn right and continue along Greenwich High Road towards the centre. When you reach the one-way system cross Nelson Road to enter the 'central island'. Go into the market through the alleyway running alongside Oddbins. At the far end of the market is the **Admiral Hardy (4)** in College Approach. This traditional one-bar pub is situated at the northern end of Greenwich market close to all the tourist attractions. Interesting nautical memorabilia adorns the walls. It sells Shepherd Neame Best Bitter, Masterbrew and guest beers.

From the front door turn left then cross College Approach turning right into Greenwich Church Street. About 25 yards along on the right is the **Gipsy Moth (5)** which sells Adnams Bitter, Tetley Bitter and regular guest beers. It is a large recently refurbished pub situated closer to the Cutty Sark than to Gipsy Moth IV. The pub was formerly known as the Wheatsheaf but was renamed and reopened by Sir Francis Chichester's widow in 1974. It is popular with tourists and local students.

The easiest way to get to the next pub is to head towards the river past the Cutty Sark, the famous tea clipper now in dry dock, following the riverside path in front of the Royal Naval College and you will arrive at the **Trafalgar Tavern (6)** in Park Row. This large multi-roomed pub is a listed building and was the Evening Standard Pub of the Year in 1995. The beer range has improved considerably in recent years following the introduction of guest beers from independent regional breweries and microbreweries. On regular sale are Courage Best and Directors. Good quality food is served in a separate dining area open lunch times and evenings. Live jazz on Monday evenings.

Turn left and then take the first left into Crane Street. Follow the river past the rowing clubs and the power station until you arrive at the **Cutty Sark (7)** in Ballast Quay. This quayside, Georgian pub claims to have the only riverfront seating area in Greenwich. The nautical internal and external decor is interesting. Upstairs there is a large seating area where families are welcome at lunch times. It sells Fuller's London Pride, Harveys Sussex Bitter, Morland Old Speckled Hen and a guest beer.

On leaving here head back along the river until you get to Hoskins Street. Turn left and continue until the end of the road. Cross Trafalgar Road and start to go up Maze Hill taking the first right into Park Vista, which, as the name suggests, runs along Greenwich Park, home to the National Maritime Museum. The Queen's House and Maritime Museum stand near the River Thames and alongside the famous baroque buildings of the Royal Naval College. These buildings are set against rolling parkland that sweeps uphill to the Old Royal Observatory from where all of London unfolds before the eye. The Royal Observatory has long since left London due to light pollution.

On the right towards the end of the road is the **Plume of Feathers (8)**, our last stop. It is believed to be the only pub in Greenwich that actually lies on the Meridian. There has been a pub on the site since 1691. The current beer range – Morland Old Speckled Hen, Ruddles Best, Webster's Yorkshire Bitter and Young's Special – may soon change. Excellent home-cooked food is available throughout the day. The pub has a walled garden and toys available for children.

About five minutes walk away is Maze Hill BR station and buses 177, 180, 286 and 386.

HORSHAM

Horsham is a medium size town at the northern end of West Sussex, easily accessible from London by train – three trains an hour on weekdays, two on Sundays, the journey taking about an hour. Probably the most significant feature of the town for most ale drinkers is the long-established King and Barnes brewery. But that is not the whole story.

Our crawl starts at Horsham station, and involves about two miles of walking in total. So from the station cross the footbridge from the main entrance and ticket office to the exit in Station Close. Immediately opposite the end of this road is our first stop, the **Bedford Hotel (1)**, a large and welcoming street corner pub with two bars. The larger bar has two pool tables and a large screen TV which particularly attracts locals for big sporting events. When things get busy, quiet can be found in the other bar, and time taken to savour a pint of Fuller's London Pride, Morland Old Speckled Hen or, although it is not a tied house, King and Barnes Sussex Bitter.

Leaving the Bedford, we take the longest part of the walk without any refreshment. Turn left along Station Road, third left into Oakhill Road, second right into Elm Grove, fourth left into Bennett's Road, right at the T-junction into Compton's Lane and right again into St. Leonard's Road. After a few yards you will come across the **Forester's Arms (2)** with its fenced front garden. It is one of Shepherd Neame's farthest flung outposts. This small one bar pub has a stone flagged floor, open fire, original exposed beams and hops draped over the bar. It is one of only a few pubs in Horsham where you can play a game of Sussex bar billiards, whilst supping your Master Brew or Bishop's Finger.

Suitably refreshed, leave the Forester's and continue along St. Leonard's Rd to a T-junction. Ignoring the St. Leonard's Arms (no real ales available) turn right along Brighton Road. After a couple of hundred yards, you come to the **Tanner's Arms (3)**, the first King and Barnes tied house on this crawl. This is a small roadside local with the emphasis on beer rather than food. There is a long public bar and a small-

Top: *The Tanners Arms.* Bottom: *The Bedford.*

er lounge cum snug. This pub keeps most of King and Barnes's beers, including their Mild Ale.

On leaving the Tanner's, continue along Brighton Road. After a while you will pass by the ***Queen's Head (4)*** on the right, only worth a stop if you are very thirsty or completing the King and Barnes ale trail. Continue under the railway bridge, across the mini roundabout into East Street and you come to the Tut'n'Shive, a town centre pub which is inexplicably popular with youngsters. Although they have a range of hand pumps, it is not unusual to see no real ales at all in this pub.

On arriving at the Market Square, you can turn left to find Bar Vin, one of an uninspiring chain of wine bars which sells Greenall and Tetley beers, or far better, on the opposite side of the square, the **Bear Inn (5)**, with its conspicuous sign. This compact King and Barnes town centre hostelry has a range of reasonably priced food, but gets very busy in the evenings. Just around the corner can be found the Horsham museum.

Turn left out of Market Square to continue along West Street to Shelley's Fountain, a 'work of art' erected as part of the pedestrianisation of this area of the town centre to commemorate the author, Percy Bysche Shelley, who lived nearby. At this corner is a new Wetherspoon's pub named the ***Lynd Cross (6)***, in premises formerly occupied by a pine shop. From here, continue on past the ***Green Dragon (7)***, a recently refurbished King and Barnes house, to the **King and Barnes Brewery (8)** itself. Tours are available during the week, although booking is advisable, and there is a brewery shop where one can buy King and Barnes ales, bottled beers and souvenirs together with an interesting selection of wines. For those completing the King and Barnes trail there is another pub just beyond the brewery on the right in the Bishopric called the ***King's Arms (9)***.

Top: *Ye Old Stout House.* Bottom: *The Malt Shovel.*

Turning left out of the Brewery, and left again into Albion Way, continue around the bend to the **Malt Shovel (10)** on the corner of Springfield Road. This pub is North Sussex CAMRA Branch's 1999 Pub of the year and is part of the Hogshead chain. On entering the visitor is confronted with six handpumps and, just out of sight around the corner, three beers 'on gravity'. The enthusiastic landlord always gives a warm welcome to CAMRA members, and keeps a continuously varied range of ales, all in excellent condition, as well as a selection of continental bottled beers. A 'month-long 'beer festival' is held each spring.

After enjoying this hostelry, go directly across the dual carriageway Albion Way and down the road opposite to return to the Shelley Fountain. Turn left into the pedestrianised West Street and left again at the junction with South Street to pass by the Crown (an uninspiring, noisy pub) bearing right to arrive at the **Ye Old Stout House (11)**. This is a popular town centre pub, and concentrates on providing the full range of King and Barnes beers in excellent condition. This pub is closed from 4 pm until 7.30 pm each day, and doesn't open at all on Tuesday evenings. A very limited range of snacks is available. It was refurbished a few years ago, losing its small back bar, but it retains an intimate atmosphere. It was deservedly voted Sussex CAMRA Pub of the year, and also won the Peter King Memorial Shield in 1997. From the Stout House, turn right and go up the steps directly ahead, continue over the footbridge by the Sun Alliance building and straight along North Street to return to the station in about 10 minutes walk.

HULL

Kingston upon Hull to give the city its proper name has a great maritime tradition and it still remains one of Britain's major ports. Old docks have been converted into a modern eye-catching marina yet history is never far away. The Old Town with its wandering High Street is the base for our crawl. Pubs and museums combine to add interest to this crawl and it also takes in three ornate, award winning toilet blocks!

From the rail or bus station cross busy Ferensway, pass the Cenotaph and proceed up Paragon Street. You will soon see the City Hall where the Tourist Information Centre can be found on the corner of Queen Victoria Square. Ferens Art Gallery, the Town Docks Museum, and the first of the three toilet blocks are also situated on the square. Continue towards Whitefriargate past the Princes Dock Shopping Centre and turn right into the cobbled Princes Dock Street. A short distance down, the first turning on the left, is Postengate and here is our first pub, **The Mission (1)**, the city's only Old Mill tied house.

Hull, though a sea-port, a place that I shall always look back to with delight.

William Cobbett

Originally a seaman's mission, it reopened in 1995 after extensive internal alterations to a former club layout. The interesting interior includes the Old Chapel, refurbished to its former glory and complete with pulpit and stained-glass windows. This is the largest of the Old Town's pubs and is somewhat like a baronial hall together with its minstrel's gallery. It gets very busy at weekends. The full range of Old Mill beers are available and it offers a wide range of food every day until 3.00 p.m. and until 5.00 p.m. on Friday and Saturday. The pub has a Children's Certificate.

When you come out of the pub's main entrance, turn left down Dagger Lane and continue in a southerly direction to Castle Street, an extremely busy dual carriageway (A63) taking lorries and passengers to the docks and North Sea Ferries. Cross at the pedestrian crossing onto the site of the Hull Marina. Proceed down Humber Dock Street alongside the Marina until you reach the River Humber. On the river front in Nelson Street is the **Minerva Hotel (2)**.

The building dates from 1831 and has a strong nautical feel with displays of maps, charts and prints. It has a central bar serving several different areas including possibly the smallest in the country, a former ladies' loo that now seats four people. Good food is available every lunch time and from 6 p.m. until 9 p.m. Mondays to Thursdays. Accompanied children are welcome in the non-smoking area if taking meals. There are pleasant views across the Humber towards Lincolnshire on a fine day. Unfortunately, if you wish to use the outside drinking area a local area by-law insists on the use of plastic glasses. The pub sells Tetley Bitter, Taylor Landlord and a regular guest beer (two in summer) often from Scottish breweries. Just across the road from the pub is the second of the ornate toilet blocks, catering for both ladies and gentlemen.

Continue along the river front past the former Humber Ferry Terminal and the junction of the Humber and Hull Rivers will be seen. We now follow the River Hull in a northerly direction up Queen Street. Turn right into Humber Street and at the end is the Tidal Surge Barrier that is lowered when high tides threaten. Proceed up High Street under the Myton Bridge and the busy A63. This route is easier than trying to cross at the junction of Queen Street and Castle Street where there is no pedestrian crossing. When you emerge from under the bridge take the signed footpath to the left that will bring you out at the foot of the bridge, then turn right into Market Place past the gold gilded statue of King Billy and the last of the three ornate toilet blocks – this one serves gentlemen only. Continue towards Holy Trinity, the largest parish church in England, which was founded in 1285 and retains much of its medieval brickwork.

Look for a large blue bell hanging above the entrance to an alley on the left hand side of the road. This leads to one of Hull's most unspoilt pubs **Ye Old Blue Bell (3).** It is owned by Samuel Smiths and sells value for money Old Brewery Bitter and traditional food. The pub has three downstairs rooms and a drinking corridor and an upstairs games room. It is closed on Sunday afternoons. The entrance alley actually continues through an outdoor drinking area into Hull's covered market.

Returning up the alley to Market Place, continue left for a few yards before turning left into Silver Street. Not far down and on the right hand side look out for the hanging sign of the next pub, **Ye Olde White Harte (4),** another pub only accessible from an alley. It is probably one of the oldest buildings in the city and was once the home of Hull's military governors. This Grade II listed building is famous for its upstairs 'Plotting Parlour' where in 1642, according to local folk lore, Sir John Hotham decided to bar Charles I from the town, an act which is said to have triggered off the Civil War. It has two downstairs bars on either side of the dark-wood staircase, each of which features sit-in fire places. There are two upstairs dining rooms and an outside drinking area. Beers featured are Courage Directors, McEwan 80/- and Theakston XB and Old Peculier with an occasional guest.

Retrace your steps up Silver Street and cross Market Place straight into Scale Lane. Continuing to the end, the last building on the right, now a tea room, is the oldest domestic building in the city. Turn left, back into the medieval High Street and just round the comer is **Ye Olde Black Boy (5)** now owned by Enterprise Inns. It retains a bar, a wood-panelled front room where the pub's history is displayed, and two upstairs rooms. On-sale are eight constantly changing real ales, real cider and foreign bottled beers, including draught Hoegaarden wheat beer from Belgium.

Continue up High Street and on the right are three of Hull's museums. First is the Hull and East Riding Museum, then the Street Life Museum and finally Wilberforce House is the birthplace of the famous anti-slavery campaigner William Wilberforce. Continue until you reach the junction with Alfred Gelder Street. You may now wish to leave the main route to include another pub on the crawl that is worthy of a visit because it is the only tied house of the present Hull Brewery.

Top: *The Mission.* Bottom: *Ye Olde Black Boy.*

Extra Pub Route: Cross Drypool Bridge to your right and go straight across at the traffic light junction with Great Union Street into Clarence Street. ***The Red Lion (6)*** is only 400 yards from Drypool Bridge and was built for local brewers Moors and Robson in 1939. It has all the style of a thirties pub with a shop front bar in the main room. Hull Brewery Bitter is sold here and an occasional guest beer. You are now at the furthest point from the rail and bus stations and if short of time you may now wish to catch one of the many buses that stop on the same side of the road as the pub. To rejoin the main route of the crawl return to the cross roads and turn right down Great Union Street. At the main road junction with Witham turn left and cross North Bridge to return to the west side of the River Hull with Wincolmlee to your right.

Staying on the Main Route: Cross Alfred Gelder Street and continue along the western bank of the River Hull via Dock Office Row. When you reach the main road you will see North Bridge to the right and Wincolmlee straight ahead.

Whatever your decision you should now head along Wincolmlee where you will find the **Bay Horse Hotel (7)** situated 400 yards down on the corner of Mitchell Street. This small cosy street corner local has a small bar full of Rugby League memorabilia and a spectacular lofty stable lounge. Good value home cooked food includes tea time special offers and Sunday lunches. Most of the range of Bateman's beers from Lincolnshire are on offer.

The rail and bus stations are some twenty minutes away at a steady walk. There are a number of return routes but one of the quickest allows you to take in another decent pub if you wish. Return down Wincolmlee turning right into New

Above: *The Minerva.*

George Street and continue across into Francis Street. Turn left at the cross roads and head down Charles Street and cross the main road (Freetown Way) which splits the street into two. On the corner of John Street is the ***New Clarence (8)***. Built across the road from the original Clarence this is a Tetley Festival Ale House that is a very reasonable conversion from the Co-op store that it was originally. It sells Tetley Dark Mild and Bitter, Marston's Pedigree and a good selection of guest ales and bottled beers from Belgium. Food is available at lunch times and in the early weekday evenings. You're now only ten minutes from both stations and you are advised to use Bond Street and Jameson Street as the quickest route back.

HYDE ROAD, MANCHESTER

This is a linear crawl of about one and half miles starting about two miles from the centre of Manchester through the suburb of Gorton along the A 57 towards Hyde. The road eventually goes to Glossop and over the High Peak to Sheffield. Several buses (numbers 200, 201, 203, 204 and 207) run roughly every ten minutes from Piccadilly Gardens in the city centre along the entire length of the crawl. Alight at the Pottery Lane stop. An hourly train service (two hourly on Sundays) runs from Piccadilly station to Marple calling at Belle Vue station which is part way along the crawl as the maps shows.

Hyde Road is quite historic. It was built by the Manchester, Hyde and Mottram Turnpike Trust through fields between Ardwick and Hyde. Work commenced in 1819 with toll bars at Canal Bridge in Denton and the other at Devonshire Street near Ardwick station. Later a number of side bars were opened including one at the Plough of which more later.

The first and appropriately named stop is the **Travellers Call (1)** on Hyde Road at its junction with Pottery Lane (A 5184). This is a Hyde's pub with a tap room in the good old-fashioned Manchester basic style. It is a robust boozer, which can be noisy particularly on football nights but which is always friendly and has an atmosphere to be cherished. It is open all day. ***The Nags Head*** sells Burtonwood beers and might be worth a call if you feel you have time.

Move along the north side of the road about a quarter of a mile to the **Coach and Horses (2)** which is actually in Belle Vue Street (A6010) at its junction with Hyde Road. A local describes it as the 'quintessential local with the quintessential pint of Robbies'. It is a gem, family run and firmly part of the community. Robinson's cask beers far outsell all other drinks. There is a television in the vault which is popular for sport but otherwise the only sounds are those of conversation. It is not only popular with locals but also with cinemagoers from the Showcase opposite and the nearby Belle Vue speedway track. Open all day at weekends but only from 5.30 pm during the week.

Top: *The vault of The Plough.* Bottom: *The Plough.*

A little further along on the opposite side of the road is Belle Vue railway station and set back from the road staying on the north side is the ***Pineapple (3)*** another Hyde's pub selling the budget priced Billy Westwood's Bitter. There is also a good collection of photographs of the fondly remembered Belle Vue Zoo and Amusement Park. Stay with the north side for the **Suburban (4)** a John Willy Lees street corner pub now on an island site and part of a rebuilt town centre. It has a comfortable lounge and a basic vault with some fine prints of nineteenth century Gorton. There is also a 'Morris Room' used by the local Gorton Morris Men who take an active part in the annual Rushcart procession in mid-September. The pub has a fine collection of cartoons.

Next comes the **Plough (5)**, another gem owned by Robinson's. It is listed as a building of architectural and historic interest which no doubt helped to save it from a threat of demolition for road widening. A local says the vault 'is a symphony in wood'. Note the beautiful tiles.

A little further along is the Lord Nelson which is mentioned merely as a landmark. Just after this pub is a footpath that leads to the otherwise hidden **Vale Cottage (6)** which sells beers from Scottish Courage's extensive list as well as guest ales. This is a country pub and so completely different to the others on the crawl. It has a relaxed atmosphere with high standards and excellent lunches and is well worth the slight detour. There are evening meals until 7.30 pm.

Cross the road and note the Brookfield Unitarian Church which dates from 1871 with its tower housing eight bells. Two partners in a local firm built churches at the same time; the other was the Anglican parish church, and agreed that the first to complete would have the privilege of installing bells. This one won. It replaced the old Dissenting Chapel which dated from 1703.

Close by is the **Waggon and Horses (7)** a Holt's pub with the tradition of fine beers at low prices. It has been sensibly modernised with four distinct areas: a vault, a games area, a main lounge and a 'back room'. It is justifiably popular and apart from live entertainment on Saturday evenings it is yet another temple of conversation and drinking. Open all day.

Our final stop is two hundred yards along Hyde Road to the **Friendship (8)** which is owned by Marston's but which also sells Bateman's Mild. This is a well named pub with sing-along style entertainment at weekends and four separate rooms if you include the lobby. The vault is particularly characterful. It closes in the afternoon during the week.

KENDAL

Kendal, often known as the 'Auld Grey Town', is a picturesque market town in attractive surroundings only a mile or two outside the Lake District National Park. It is built of local stone and has many old yards and alleys often identified by numbers. There are two particularly interesting buildings, the amazingly spacious parish church at the south end of the town and the castle that stands on a mound a little to the east. The view of the Lakeland mountains from the castle is spectacular. Kendal is well served by public transport. It is on a branch line from Oxenholme on the main west coast railway line with some fast trains from Manchester Airport. The Ribble bus company runs a Stage-coach service (No. 555) from Lancaster to Keswick which stops at Kendal.

So an appropriate start would be at either the railway or bus station. Turn right out of the first, left out of the other into Sandes Avenue and at the end on the right in Stricklandgate is the **Sawyers Arms (1)**. This is a pub from the former Hartley's brewery of Ulverston now owned by Robinson of Stockport and it sells Best Bitter and Hartley XB. Hot lunches are served and there are evening meals in summer. There is also bed and breakfast accommodation. This is a characterful three-storey pub with an attractive frontage and some well-preserved, etched Hartley's windows.

Carry on along Stricklandgate towards the town centre turning left into the bustling Market Place. The easily-located **Globe Inn (2)** is Thwaites's only tied house in Kendal and in the last couple of years it has been tastefully modernised. Thwaites Bitter and the stronger Golden Charmer are on sale along with good value food at lunch times.

Proceed further down Stricklandgate to where it becomes Highgate near the handsome Town Hall with its clock tower. Look carefully for a sign stating simply 'Yard 2' on the right. The **White Hart Hotel (3)** is in an exceedingly quaint alley yet the pub itself is very modern. This is another Robinson pub selling Best Bitter and Hartley XB as in the Sawyers Arms. Meals are served at lunch times when families are welcome but there is no food on Sundays. It provides accommodation. Also it has fine Hartley's windows.

It is a bit of a climb to the next pub but well worth it. Go up All Hallows Lane to the **Black Swan (4).** It dates back to 1764 and is one of the few basic and unaltered pubs around in the area. There are two rooms, no juke box or games machines, real fires, a great welcome and loads of atmosphere. Theakston Best Bitter is the only regular beer but there are guest ales in summer. Lunch time food is available on Sundays and everyday in summertime. There is accommodation. Back track a little to the **Cask House (5)**, a back to basics town centre pub with wooden floors. There are usually three regular beers – Boddington's Bitter, Marston's Pedigree and Wadworth 6X – on sale, together with a traditional cider and guest beers in summer. Meals are served up to 7.30 p.m.

Return to Highgate and cross it and take note of Beers in Particular, an off-licence where a great selection of bottled beers is sold including many from abroad. Draught beers, usually from Dent Brewery, can be taken away in containers. Move on to the **Ring O'Bells (6)** which is actually situated within the parish church graveyard and is on consecrated land. This lovely little pub can hardly have changed during the present century. It has tiny rooms, an interesting assortment of miscellaneous chairs and tables and a welcoming coal fire. Don't miss the tiny snug, found between the two bars, with its unusual coffin table. It is on CAMRA's list of historic pub interiors. Beers sold are Lorimer's Best Scotch, Vaux Bitter and Samson, Wards Best Bitter and a guest ale. The pub closes during the afternoon but food is available during both sessions. Bed and breakfast is available.

Cross over and return towards the town centre for the **Brewery Arts Centre (7).** It stands on rising ground and is clearly marked from Highgate. This was the former Whitwell Mark brewery which ceased brewing in 1968. There is plenty going on here so finding the bar may be a problem but do persist. The beers are from the Vaux and

Wards range together with a guest. There are also some splendid catering facilities here with much imagination shown in the choice of menu.

You are now faced with a longish walk – ten to twelve minutes – along Highgate, turning right into Finkle Street. This is the heart of old Kendal and there is much wonderful and ancient property to be seen. The name changes to Stramondgate and just before the broad, normally shallow River Kent is reached, the **Bridge Hotel (8)** is seen straight ahead. This pub has atmosphere as well as consistently good beer although the choice may be restricted to Boddington's Bitter and Marston's Pedigree. The rooms are small, well-maintained and intimate and there is a large and welcoming coal and log fire. Catering is a prominent feature but this is essentially a pub with a public bar and eating facilities rather than a restaurant which also serves drinks. Accommodation is available.

Top: *The Ring O'Bells.* Bottom: *Bridge Hotel.*

Carry on along the same road crossing the river towards the station and turn right into Castle Street. The long, low, stone-built pub the **Castle Inn (9)** is your final stop. This is a most successful pub selling Tetley Bitter, Theakston Best Bitter, several guest ales and a house beer Castle Gate, a medium strength bitter brewed by the Cartmel Brewery which is actually in Kendal. Food here, served at lunch times, is extremely good value and the range and quality is remarkable. Note the framed windows from the former Dutton brewery. There is bed and breakfast accommodation.

Allow yourself a few extra minutes to return to the stations. They are not far away but there is a busy road to cross and there is a final slope up to the railway station.

KINGTON

Kington is a small Herefordshire market town close to the Welsh border. It is famous for magnificent displays of 30 foot high rhododendrons in spring and its autumn sheep sales. It stands on the A44 which runs from Worcester, Bromyard and Leominster through Kington into Wales, close to Llandrindod Wells, and eventually to Aberystwyth.

Start at the **Queens Head (1)** in Bridge Street (A44). The pub has a functional public bar with wooden floor boards where traditional pub games, notably quoits and darts co-exist with gaming machines and a juke box. The beer range consists of Dunn Plowman Brewhouse Bitter, which is brewed on the premises, Hobson's Best Bitter and S.P. Sporting Ales Double Top. Food is served in the lounge bar, at present only on Friday, Saturday and Sunday lunch times. and the exposed beams and comfortable seats and tables provide an attractive setting in which to have lunch. Pizzas are a speciality..

Next door to the Queens Head is ***The Talbot (2)*** an undistinguished one bar pub popular with younger drinkers but only offering a basic Scottish Courage range.

Top: *Ye Olde Tavern.* Bottom: *Queen's Head.*

Turn right from Bridge Street into Victoria Road, walking past some old black and white cottages on the right, and after about five minutes walk you come to a row of Victorian brick built terraced houses at the eastern edge of the town. Among them is **Ye Olde Tavern (3)**. This absolute gem was joint winner of Herefordshire

Above: *The Old Fogey.*

CAMRA's Pub of the Year Award in 1993 (it then went on to win the area award for that year) and runner-up in 1997 (losing by only one vote!).

The only beer sold is Ansells Bitter through a lovely old beer engine, with no swan-necks or sparklers, but this does prevent it from having a bit of a foaming head. There are two bars with settles and benches and they are packed with curios. The pub is on CAMRA's register of pubs with outstanding interiors.

Retrace your steps and instead of turning left back into Bridge Street continue straight on into High Street. On the left nestling amongst the shops is **The Old Fogey (4)**, a warm and welcoming, basic, one bar pub with an unspoilt interior. It serves a variety of beers from independent breweries including Hobsons Best Bitter, Wood Special and Fuller's London Pride. There is a patio drinking area at the back of the pub.

Continuing along the High Street you come to the Market Hall which, unusually for this area, is a red brick structure with an imposing clock tower. Take the right fork, into Church Street, and come to the **Swan Hotel (5)** on the right. This is mainly food oriented with a good restaurant. The lounge bar in which Ansell Bitter is sold includes an original stone fireplace dating from when the pub was built in the seventeenth century. Accommodation is available here.

At this stage you might consider walking a further 100 yards along Church Street to satisfy the curiosity of visiting 'the last pub in England' – the Welsh border is just up the road! ***The Royal Oak (6)***, which is also known as 'the first and last' has a rather plain public bar at the front with a real fire and a comfortable lounge at the back. Beers vary but are usually somewhat mundane and rather expensive offerings.

LANCASTER

The name of Lancashire's first city comes from being a Roman camp (castrum) on the River Lune although it has prehistoric origins. John of Gaunt was the first Duke of Lancaster and ancestor of the royal house. For centuries it was an important port much involved in the slave trade. The castle dominates the city and still houses the law courts and a prison. Start with three pubs on St George's Quay on the south bank of the River Lune at the north end of the city.

The **Wagon and Horses (1)** is a small traditional pub, with a decor of Irish football and rugby shirts, scarves and photos, and is the perfect start to a crawl. There is a choice of three traditional beers from Robinson's including Hartley XB which recognises a former owner. There is a small menu of home-made food served during lunch times and in the evenings. Live music on Saturday evenings and bed and breakfast available all the year round. Great riverside views.

Head back towards the city centre and call in at the **George and Dragon (2)**. This small, pleasant pub has some excellent windows from the former Yates Castle brewery of Ardwick, Manchester. It sells Wards Best Bitter and Thorne Best Bitter and also a guest beer. A little further along is the **Three Mariners (3)** which was formerly known as the Carpenters Arms. Its handsome large facade is covered in ivy and makes a pleasing contrast to the factories that surround it. This is said to be Lancaster's oldest pub dating back to the thirteenth century. Ask to see the cellar – it's upstairs! Mitchell's beers are on sale, including the seasonal specials.

"Lancaster... locked in between the hills on one side high as the clouds, and the sea on the other..."

Daniel Defoe

Carefully cross the busy A6 and behind the bus station is **The Bobbin (4)** which was originally called The Priory. This large, bright, modern pub was completely refurbished in 1997. It serves Mitchell's draught beers including Mitchell's Original Bitter and the renowned Lancaster Bomber. A variety of hot and cold snacks are available all day and there is a pool table in the middle of the bar. There is live music on Thursdays and big band jazz on the first Sunday in the month.

Head south east to the **Friary and Firkin (5)** which was a church before opening as a pub in the spring of 1997. The renovations have not changed the inside of the building a great deal. One can still climb the steps and sit in the upper level with a view of the whole bar. Beers served include Tuck's Tipple and the Firkin brewery favourite Dogbolter. This is not a brew-pub; the beers are from another Firkin pub. One of the main attractions of this large pub/monastery are the giant games such as Jenga and Connect 4, which stand about four feet high, and draughts.

Top: *The Three Mariners.* Bottom: *Water Witch.*

The Penny Bank (6) is in Penny Street which runs parallel to and between the two main roads of Lancaster. It is another pub that has taken its name from the building's original use. It opened in 1996, following its conversion from a Natwest Bank. An array of regular beers including Boddington's, Castle Eden and Marston's Pedigree are served, together with a selection of guest beers which change every week. There is a rather daft practice here called the 'gallon challenge'. Find out about it but do not be tempted to take part.

At the south end of the town is **The Water Witch (7)**, a canal-side pub and one of the most popular pubs in Lancaster, especially during the summer when the beer garden rapidly fills up. There are two floors inside the pub and a long bar offering rapid service. Boddington's and John Smith's are the main beers, along with Witches Water, the house beer. Food is served during lunch hours, with the second floor converting into a restaurant during the evening. Live music at weekends. The annual Lancaster Canal Festival in June draws many boat owners to the tow path garden.

Turn back towards the town centre and on the station approach is **The Merchants (8)**, another claimant to be the oldest pub in Lancaster which has been in business since 1668. This lively pub is next to the prison, and the entire pub is situated in the old sewer system of Lancaster. There are three main drinking areas, long rooms with tables on each side, and a spacious beer garden which makes it ideal for groups. Most of Theakston's beers are served with good food available all day. This pub gets very busy during the weekend.

Move back into Market Street and the precinct for the **John O'Gaunt (9),** a small city centre pub with a splendid original frontage which still retains traditional hours (i.e. it closes between 3 p.m. and 6 p.m.). This is a great pub for jazz with music most evenings and every Sunday lunch-time. Jim (Bullseye) Bowen is often in and makes guest appearances on the trumpet. The atmosphere is lively and there is a good choice of beers: Tetley's Bitter, Draught Burton Ale, Jennings Bitter, Boddington's and guests. Families are made very welcome when taking meals.

LEDBURY

Ledbury is an unspoilt market town in Hereford's hop growing country overlooked by the Malvern Hills. The seventeenth century Market House standing on oak pillars is the town's most outstanding building. Poet Laureate, John Masefield was born here. The pubs reflect the historic nature of the town.

The six pubs in this crawl are all very close together – indeed the furthest away and the most southerly, The Royal Oak in The Southend is only fifteen minutes walk from Ledbury railway station, which is at the far north end of the town and served by direct trains from Hereford, Worcester, Birmingham and London (Paddington). Three of the pubs offer accommodation and make ideal places to stay in to explore this idyllic part of England.

The railway station is as good place as any to start the crawl. Walk up The Homend to the **Horseshoe Inn (1)** which is on the left. Enter this black and white building up a short flight of stairs into a single bar pub. It is owned by the Hereford-based Rustic Pub Company and serves a variety of ales mainly from independent breweries such as Hobsons Best Bitter and Wood Shropshire Lad. Food is served all day. Despite twentieth-century refurbishment and trappings it still retains some character including some exposed beams and cosy alcoves. There is a small outdoor drinking area.

"...fair and half-timbered houses black and white."

John Masefield

Turning left out of the Horseshoe and head south down The Homend into High Street to view the impressive black and white building on oaken stilts. This is the seventeenth-century Market Hall and from here turn left into Church Lane, a narrow cobbled street that has changed little since the middle ages. In this delightful setting is the **Prince of Wales (2)**, a cosy welcoming little gem dating from the sixteenth-century which appears on the lid of many a chocolate box. It serves Banks's and Hanson's beers and Weston's cider during the summer. Food is served at lunch time through the year and there are evening meals in the summer months from Fridays to Sundays. There are two main bar areas mixing comfort and character and there is live folk music on Wednesdays.

Top: *Picturesque Ledbury.* Bottom: *Prince of Wales.*

Retrace your steps back to the High Street and cross over by the public library then head down Bye Street, past the cattle market and fire station and on the right in a narrow back street is the **Brewery Inn (3)**, a red-brick structure owned by Marston's but which also sells Banks's Mild and a traditional cider. The snug which is full of character was not touched during a recent refurbishment and claims to have the smallest bar in Herefordshire. There is also a games room on the first floor. Sandwiches and snacks are served at lunch times but not on Sundays.

Return along Bye Street turning right into the High Street, past the Feathers Hotel which will be visited later, and continue straight on at the cross roads into The Southend to the **Royal Oak Hotel (4)**. This pub shares a base with the Ledbury Brewery which is in the original brewhouse which was closed for 75 years but reopened in 1996. The main bar is food orientated but a smaller downstairs public bar is more for drinkers. Meals are served at lunchtimes and in the evenings. Beers are from the attached brewery and are usually from single varietal hop strains: Ledbury Challenger SB and Northdown Winter are examples and there are also seasonal offerings. Overnight accommodation is available.

Retrace your steps along The Southend and turn left into New Street to the ***Ye Olde Talbot (5)***, another black and white fronted pub which dates back to1596 and was formerly a coaching inn. It sells beers from the Carlsberg Tetley stable, it also has a restaurant and provides overnight accommodation.

Finally, heading back along New Street turn left at the cross roads into High Street to the **Feathers Hotel (6)**, an imposing black and white structure close to the Market Hall.

Draught Bass, Worthington Bitter and Fuller's London Pride are the cask beers on sale here. It has a restaurant and there are bedrooms to let. A beer festival is held here on August bank holiday weekend as part of the Ledbury Carnival with its procession which takes place on the Monday.

Top: *Feathers Hotel.*
Bottom: *Royal Oak.*

LEEDS TO MANCHESTER AND BACK BY RAIL

Here is a crawl that is a bit different. It calls for very little walking – from the train to the bar and from the bar to the train! You can suit yourself and do this crawl the other way round if you wish or even join it part way through. The advantage of starting from Leeds is that you are on the correct platform at the first two stops. There are two routes to Manchester from Leeds so make sure you use the Huddersfield line otherwise if you go via Halifax and Rochdale you will miss out all the interesting bits and privatised railway tea is no better than it was in the days of British Rail. A sound bit of advice is to pick up a copy of the Metro Train timetable at the Gateway Yorkshire tourist information office by the station entrance.

If you start after 11am then make your first stop at **Coopers (1)** which is just inside the concourse of Leeds City station. This is the former refreshment rooms which now operates as a bar with all the facilities that were previously there, coffee, tea, soft drinks, snacks and hot meals. Three cask beers are sold with John Smith's Bitter and Draught Bass as regulars and a guest beer. There are also some interesting bottled beers amongst the dross such as Hoegaarden and Staropramen. All the beers are pricey so if you have the time and are not simply following this pub crawl you would be better off crossing the road to the Scarbrough which is a Festival Ale House giving better value and better choice. However the food at the Coopers is reasonably priced and the large room is comfortable and well appointed with plenty of indications of the coopers' trade.

There are three trains in each hour to the first stop which is Dewsbury. Just be careful not to catch an express to Liverpool (usually at eight minutes past the hour) for these trains do not stop at Dewsbury. Here is the **West Riding Refreshment Rooms (2)** which you can enter directly from the platform. There is a range of Black Sheep beers and

Top: *Coopers.* Bottom: *The West Riding.*

several guests, mainly from local breweries, including one beer from the Linfit brewery. There is a main bar with a dining room to one side and a smaller room to the other with its own hatch. Food is well prepared and reasonably priced and a great favourite is the curry night on Wednesdays. The music, both recorded and live is good and there are frequent festivals. As one might expect there is a fair amount of railway memorabilia and a collection of pictures of Dewsbury pubs in older times. Check your train times although every westbound train from here stops at Huddersfield.

The refreshment room here is the **Head of Steam (3)** one of a group that includes pubs at Euston station in London and Newcastle. It was formerly the ticket office and waiting room of the Lancashire and Yorkshire Railway the junior partner to the London and North Western Railway in the ownership of the impressive classical style Huddersfield railway station. Black Sheep Bitter, a Bass beer, along with two local beers and three guests are on sale together with a variety of bottled beers and there are regular themed beer festivals. Beers at Head of Steam are not cheap but they are interesting and they are kept in excellent condition. The food is also superb and is reasonably priced. There is live music – blues, jazz, folk – Sunday through to Thursday evenings and a jazz brunch on Sunday lunchtimes.

If you take a stopping train to Manchester you could drop off at Marsden where the Burtonwood beers at the **Station Hotel (4)** are usually in excellent form, and at the **Station (5)** at Ashton-under-Lyne for a great choice of beers from independent breweries. However the service through these stations is hourly and takes you to Manchester Victoria station where the **Station Bar (6)** serves rather expensive Draught Bass and Boddington's Bitter but which is

Top: *Station Buffet.* Bottom: *Head of Steam.*

worth visiting to see the amazing decorated glass globe, marble pillars and carved wood which are happy memories of the days of real railways but sadly spoilt these days by garish posters and signs. From Victoria catch the Metrolink tram to Piccadilly, which is where you would have arrived if you had taken a fast train from Huddersfield. Incidentally whichever way you travel do not be tempted to alight at Stalybridge – save this delight for the return journey.

From the Metrolink station take the ground level exit to London Road and opposite is **Munroe's (7)** a tribute to the much loved Marilyn. There are photographs and models of her all over this very comfortable pub which has a split-level lounge and a smaller dining room. Boddington's Bitter and Flowers IPA are on sale at what might be termed mid-Manchester prices. There is a bistro during the lunch hours. From here return to the main line station and take a Leeds train making sure it stops at Stalybridge.

You will be on the correct platform for the **Station Buffet (8)**. Although it is not the only buffet bar of this sort it is the best known. It has remained unchanged since 1885 and there was a forerunner dating from 1845. It has been refurbished recently and extended to now boast two bars with a room linking them. On regular sale are Wadworth's 6X and Flowers IPA along with up to six guest beers and a traditional cider. Bar snacks are available including the famous black peas. Saturday is folk night and there are periodic beer festivals. (For more information see the pub crawl of Stalybridge – No. 44).

You are on the right platform to return to Leeds. It's been a long day so have a nap. Or a cup of tea. And there is always Coopers at the other end.

LEE VALLEY BY BOAT

Good Beer Guide editor Roger Protz once wrote 'there can be no better way to see the rural delights and industrial heritage of Britain than along the country's canals and rivers.' So here is an opportunity. Much of the detail is from The Best Waterside Pubs by Chris Rowland and John Simpson. This out of the ordinary pub crawl along the River Lee starts in suburban London and finishes 25 miles out in rural Hertfordshire. That is, of course, unless you choose to travel in the opposite – southbound – direction. It will take you as long as you like depending on how many stops you make and whether you decide to stay over night. Sadly, only one of the recommended pubs provides bed and breakfast. You could, of course walk the tow path but it is quite a long way between pubs.

The starting point is at the first pub: **The Princess of Wales (1)** at Lee Bridge on Lee Bridge Road, London E5. The nearest railway station is Clapton on the Liverpool Street line to Chingford. There are plenty of buses and car parking is available at the pub. Up until December 1997 this pub was called The Prince of Wales but the name was changed in memory of Diana, Princess of Wales, who was a personal friend of John Young, Chairman of Young's Brewery. As one would expect it sells Young's Bitter, Special and the brewery's seasonal ales. There are three bars all finely panelled and well furnished one of which is a separate restaurant. There is a good selection of food including a seafood stall on the riverside. It is a popular pub with boaters and anglers.

Cast off for the short run by the Walthamstow Marshes to the **Anchor and Hope (2)** in Upper Clapton. This small one-bar pub is approved of by residents and visitors alike, just about anyone who passes along the towpath. Fuller's London Pride and ESB are on sale. It is an East London institution and without doubt it is in the correct type of pub crawl for finding it by road is very difficult.

Go along under Horse Shoe Bridge and past a series of reservoirs stopping if you wish at the ***Narrow Boat (3)*** at Tottenham Hale which may, or may not have real ale on sale.

Top: *The Old Barge.* Bottom: *Anchor and Hope.*

There are three handpumps but they are not always dispensing beer. Better to move on to the **Watersedge (4)** half a mile to the north at Stonebridge Lock. This former cafe has been successfully converted into a small pub with the obvious intention of serving users of the waterways. It sells the full range of Fuller's beers.

It is a long run alongside innumerable reservoirs, sports clubs, housing estates and light industry – all the trappings of suburbia – to Enfield Lock and the **Greyhound (5).** It is on the east bank across the road from the lock. Nearby is the former Royal Ordnance small arms factory where the famous Lee Enfield 303 rifle was manufactured, named after the place it was made and the river that flowed past it. This is a straightforward boozer probably built during the Great War. The pubs at Enfield Lock, like Carlisle, were part of the State Management Scheme, in effect nationalisation but in reality an attempt to keep munitions workers sober to help the war effort. It is a welcoming pub with dart board and lino in the public bar and comfy chairs and carpet in the lounge. In summer there is a pleasant terrace by the water. McMullen's Original AK and Country Best Bitter are the beers on sale and food is available on weekday lunch times.

It is a short trip to the **Old English Gentleman (6)** at Waltham Abbey, a fine old pub and though modest in scale is a delightfully situated architectural gem. The building is L-shaped and has a splendid tiled roof with decorative barge-boarded gable ends. A large vine, growing on trellis work supported by rustic beams, shades the little towpath-level beer garden giving it a continental feel. Inside there are two small low ceilinged roofs, plenty of interest on the walls, high stools at the bar and a good pubby atmosphere. Sandwiches

and rolls are sold at lunch times. This McMullen's pub sells Original AK and Country Best Bitter. It is a good pub to stop at to recognise the changes from urban north London to rural home counties.

Time for a pleasant, leisurely and relaxing run through the fields and meadows of Hertfordshire. At Hoddesdon the River Stort branches off on its journey to Bishop's Stortford. But your journey goes through a series of pretty villages to Ware and the **Victoria (7)** which stands 250 yards north of the town bridge. History abounds here with the building probably dating back to the seventeenth century or maybe even earlier. The name gives us an idea as to how long it has been a public house. The back of the pub in red brick is Georgian and overlooks a spacious terrace and patrons-only moorings. There are two bars with separate entrances – a tap room where darts holds sway and an attractive, interesting saloon with lots of plates and bri-à-brac on the walls. Only McMullen Original AK is sold, with meals at lunch times.

Top: *Old English Gentleman.* Bottom: *Princess of Wales.*

The last stretch winds its pleasant way though willow-lined meadows to the county town of Hertford and the river's navigational limit in the town centre and by the fine old Mill Bridge is the **Old Barge (8)**. There are some excellent views from its terrace, the bridge, a seventeenth-century mansion and the tower of McMullen's brewery. The pub lies side on to the river and the main building has a discreet orange brick Victorian frontage with an attractive doorway flanked by two bay windows. Inside you will find a cheerful atmosphere with open fireplaces, high backed settles, exposed beams and a variety of drinking and dining areas. Food is important here and the pub is a popular lunch time venue particularly in summer. There is a good range of beers including Adnams Bitter, Green King Abbot Ale, Ind Coope Burton Ale, Tetley Bitter, Young's Special Bitter and Benskins Best Bitter, plenty to reflect on after a journey well travelled.

LINCOLN

Both the main bus and railway stations are at the bottom of the town close to the River Witham. It is a steep climb to the historic part of the city but buses run from both places and if a car is used then start from the Westgate car park just below the walls of the castle and opposite the Toy Museum

Head along Eastgate to the most distant of the chosen pubs, the **Morning Star (1)** on Greetwell Gate. There is a cheery welcome here and a choice of Theakston's XB, Draught Bass, Ruddle's Best, Wells Bombardier and also a guest beer. Meals are served at lunchtimes. A display of drawings, paintings and photographs of aircraft, reflect the landlord's career in the Royal Air Force and with British Aerospace. It is a comfortable pub with two interlinked front rooms where the only noise is conversation. The landlord is appropriately named Mister Beers.

Cross the road and the car park to the ***Bull and Chain (2)*** in Langworth Gate which is geared for the food trade. Numerous blackboards outside announce special offers, dishes of the day and the like. Beers are from Tetley's, Bass and Barnsley breweries.

"By this to Lincoln come, upon whose lofty scite Whilst wistly Witham looks with wonderful delight, Enamour'd of the state and beauty of the place..."

Michael Drayton

The stroll past the east front of the Minster through Minster Yard and Pottergate is interesting. Blue plaques on walls reveal the sites of the previous residences of such luminaries as William Byrd (composer and erstwhile organist of the cathedral) and George Boole (mathematician and former Professor in the University of Cork).

The next stop is the **Adam and Eve Tavern (3)**, a 'period' house at the junction of Lindum Hill. A notice on the front door may halt you in your tracks: 'Due to Excessive wind this door is locked. Please use the rear door through the patio'. Behind the car park are some play areas. This pub is the headquarters of the Lincoln Petanque Club and the game is played here in the summer. Courage Directors and Theakston's XB and Best bitters are sold. There is a wide vegetarian selection on the food menu.

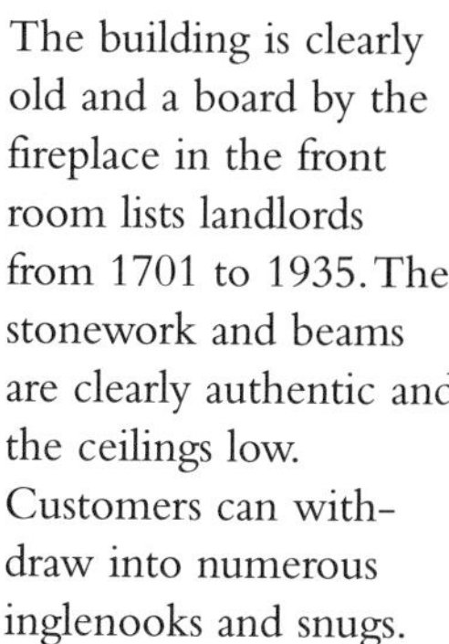

The building is clearly old and a board by the fireplace in the front room lists landlords from 1701 to 1935. The stonework and beams are clearly authentic and the ceilings low. Customers can withdraw into numerous inglenooks and snugs. The decor is interesting and includes posters advertising shows at the Theatre Royal, Lincoln and facsimile front pages of the Daily Worker and the Daily Herald.

Top: *The Adam & Eve Tavern.* Bottom: *The Victoria.*

Amble back up Pottergate to the drinkers Mecca: the **Victoria (4)** in Union Road by the west gate of Lincoln Castle. This is clearly where its all at, as they say. The regular beers listed are mouthwatering enough to keep the average discerning beer buff happy for a lifetime. They include several of Bateman's offerings, Everard's Old Original and Liefmanns Frambozen, The guest beers gild the lily. In addition there is a vast range of British and Belgian bottled beers and a full list of Gale's fruit wines. The menu boards are tempting and the selections reasonably priced and food is served remarkably quickly. The atmosphere is lively, but not intrusive. A kind of reverence pervades the air. The regulars are worshippers and the visitors are pilgrims, the staff are privileged servants – all are believers and everybody knows why they are there, There is nothing pretentious about the place. Two large rooms, solidly furnished, accommodate the congregation.

Tear yourselves away and slip around the corner to the **Strugglers (5)** in Westgate. This is a local. but you will be welcomed and included in the conversation. There is evidence in some of the material decorating the walls that the pub dates back at least to 1838. Draught Bass and Fuller's

London Pride are on the pumps. This is a drinkers pub and whilst the landlord is a chef who prepares excellent food it is available at strictly limited times in deference to his drinkers. For example; Sunday lunch is served from 2 p.m. until 4 p.m. after the lunchtime drinkers have had their fill.

At this point you might try a foray outside the city walls along Union Road towards the Museum of Lincolnshire Life and into Rasen Lane to the ***Lord Tennyson (6)***, a Ward's house which is highly regarded. The food menu is constructed on literary lines inspired by the eponymous Poet Laureate.

And on into Bailgate to the **Duke William (7)** an inn of character, stone built in a terrace of higgledy piggledy houses. Two large, comfortable rooms are connected by a passageway in front of the central bar where Wards and Vaux beers are on offer. At the back is a games room. The daytime trade is largely tourist and professional and in the evenings it becomes a yuppie haven. A limited, rather expensive food menu is available. It has been an inn since 1791 and parts of the building date from the 16th century. Dr Marshall, a former Minster organist, claimed that his best compositions were sketched on beer mats in the Duke William while he supped his barley wine.

Top: *Duke William Hotel.* Bottom: *The Strugglers Inn.*

Westgate car park is nearby but the crawl could be extended to include Lincoln's classiest pub the ***Wig and Mitre (8)*** on Steep Hill. However, be warned, for both the food and the beer in this Sam Smith's house are quite expensive.

LIVERPOOL

Liverpool is one of the world's great maritime cities although trade has declined over recent years. It remains a soccer-mad place with great rivalry between the two teams – Liverpool and Everton. The Merseyside Maritime Museum, the Walker Art Gallery and the two cathedrals are all worth visiting. Beatlemania remains a potent force in this brash, vibrant and exciting city.

Start at **The Dispensary (1)** on the corner of Renshaw Street and Oldham Street which is just a few minutes walk from Lime Street and Central railway stations. The Dispensary was completely refurbished as a street corner local incorporating antique bar fittings by Cain's, the local Liverpool brewery, in early 1998 from a Tetley pub formerly called the Grapes. It is Cain's fifth tied pub in an expanding estate and the first to be called The Dispensary as a new Cain's ale-house concept. In addition to the chemist's bric-a-brac on display, there is a wooden Higson's pin from the brewery sampling room, old brewery adverts and a huge pair of bellows. It sells the full range of Cain's beers plus three guests and serves good value food from 12 noon until 7 p.m.

"I love Liverpool so much that if I caught one of their players in bed with my missus I'd tip-toe downstairs to make him a cup of tea."

Koppite

From here, go up Oldham Street and turn right into Roscoe Street where you will find the **Roscoe Head (2)**, a Tetley pub and one of the very few pubs in the country that has featured in every copy of the CAMRA *Good Beer Guide* since 1974. The Roscoe is a completely unspoilt pub with a front snug, a tiny front bar, rear lounge snug and small main bar. There is hardly enough room on the walls of the rear snug to display all the awards that this pub has won and some are quite prestigious. It is known that the Roscoe has existed as a pub for more than a century after being converted from a house. William Roscoe was a local benefactor. Tetley Mild, and Bitter, Ind Coope Burton Ale, Jennings Bitter and Morland Speckled Hen are on sale and lunches are available in this friendly local.

Turn right out of the Roscoe and then left up Leece Street that continues into Hardman Street then right into Pilgrim Street and second left to Rice Street. A few yards on is **Ye**

Cracke (3), a legendary Liverpool pub and one of its most quirky. It has remained unchanged for several years and still has exterior advertising signs for Bass and Boddington's from an era when both these beers were much sought after. Ye Cracke has sold beers from the Oak brewery since it was a local micro-brewery at Ellesmere Port. It also sells Cain's, Marston's Pedigree, guest beers, real cider and good value lunches. A small front bar, a snug called the 'War Office' and other small rooms join with the cosmopolitan clientele to add to the cosy atmosphere. There is an interesting stained glass window set in the wall of the main bar.

Continue up Rice Street and left into Hope Street and at the junction with Hardman Street is the impressive **Philharmonic Dining Rooms (4)**. The 'Phil' is a world famous pub featured in most books on pub architecture. It was built in between 1898 and 1900 for the Robert Cain brewery. It has an amazing wrought iron gateway and the marble walled gents' toilets are legendary. There is a public bar, a back bar, two side rooms named Brahms and Liszt and upstairs dining rooms all decorated in Victorian Gin Palace garishness with engraved windows, ornate ceilings, mosaic tiled floors and elaborate mahogany carvings. In Brahms there is a stained glass window which, together with decorative tile work on the bar, is a local feature of Victorian Liverpool pubs. Tetley beers are on handpump and lunches are sold.

Above: Roscoe Head.

Now continue along left Hope Street and in front of you is the Catholic Cathedral (or Paddy's Wigwam as it is affectionately called). The Cathedral is open from 8 a.m. until 6 p.m. and is most impressive inside when the sun shines through the stained glass in the spire. Building started in 1933 on an initial grandiose scheme of which only the crypt was completed. Then in 1962 a new design by Frederick Gibberd was adopted and the cathedral was consecrated in 1967. The buttresses are adorned with bronze sculptures by local artist Sean Rice. Also at the end of Hope Street is the ***Everyman Bistro (4a)*** that features in the

CAMRA Good Pub Food Guide for its imaginative menu and good beer.

After the Everyman, turn right onto Oxford Street and then next right onto Mulberry Street and you will find the **Cambridge (5)**. The Cambridge, styled as a 'Forshaw's Ale House', offers the full range of Burtonwood beers plus a guest beer. Being alongside the university campus it is a popular haunt of students in term time. Continue along Mulberry Street and then along Catherine Street, past two old Higson's pubs, the Caledonia and the Blackburne Arms, and just befor you reach the junction with Upper Parliament Street, on the left is Egerton Street and **Peter Kavanagh's (6)**. This Victorian pub's most striking feature is the two semi-circular snugs leading off the bar. It is named after a designer in the Heath-Robinson mould and the tables in the snugs were one of his designs with locking mechanisms for the use on ocean liners. Some of Peter's patents are on display along with a multitude of quirky bric-a-brac with old radios, bicycles and model cars hanging from the ceiling. The range of beers includes Cain's and Tetley and a couple of guests.

Top: *The Dispensary.* Bottom: *Philharmonic conveniences.*

Go right onto Upper Parliament Street towards the massive Liverpool Anglican Cathedral. Designed by Giles Gilbert Scott in Gothic style, building started in 1904 and was only completed in 1978. It was built of local stone from a quarry in Woolton, home to the Quarrymen who went on to become the Beatles. The main stained glass window is one of the largest of the twentieth century at more than 1,600 square feet.

Carry on down Parliament Street, past the Cain's brewery to the left and take the next left, Grafton Street, and at the next junction is the **Cain's Brewery Tap (7).** Built into the corner of the Robert Cain Brewery, this is a true brewery tap. Once a run-down and neglected backwater under

Higson's ownership, it was acquired with the brewery when Whitbread sold it in 1990. It became Cain's first tied pub. Magnificently restored, the former Grapes was re-opened under its new name in 1994, and was soon honoured by an English Heritage/CAMRA award for the best re-furbished pub in Britain in 1995. It has a fine moulded brick and terracotta facade and superb engraved windows illustrating the brewery. Its interior is that of a Victorian street corner local, unspoilt by those modern scourges of intrusive machines and noisy juke-boxes. The splendid bar counter with its scrolled supports was rescued from a nearby pub about to be demolished, whilst the rear bar gantry came from the unlikely source of a dogs' home. It now incorporates a portrait of Robert Cain, the founder of the brewery in 1850. Note the dog's head carved in the woodwork below the portrait.

An interesting collection of breweriana adorns the walls, a reminder of long gone breweries and some not so long forgotten such as Threlfall's, Birkenhead and Higson's, all closed by Whitbread; and Bents, closed by Bass. The Tap sells the full range of Cain's beers plus three guest beers and lunches are available until 2.45 p.m. If you walk down Stanhope Street to the dock road (Sefton Street) about 100 yards, there is a Smartbus stop to the left which will take you back to the city centre.

Below: *The Philharmonic Dining Rooms is on CAMRA's inventory of pub interiors which must be kept. It features in the full-colour book* Heritage Pubs of Britain.

The Smartbus 4 travels past the Roman Catholic cathedral, along Hope Street and Catherine Street and then down to the central bus station, through the famous Albert Dock, and then onto Sefton Street. It covers most of this crawl. The Smartbus 3 goes in the opposite direction. Some of the stops have electronic times of the next bus (hence Smartbus) which are generally every 30 minutes.

LLANDUDNO

The description as 'a jewel among Victorian resorts' is absolutely right. Nothing much has changed here since the nineteenth-century entrepreneurs established the town. The wonderful beach and the elegant Promenade are crowned and protected from the west by the sentinel of the Great Orme, the summit of which is best reached by the Edwardian tramway. It was here in Llandudno that Lewis Carroll told the fantasy stories of Alice in Wonderland to the young Alice Liddell. The pub crawl takes in five very close together pubs at the west end and one a good fifteen minutes stroll away across the town. Start in Church Walks near to the pier at the western end of the Promenade and the first stop is at the **Parade Hotel (1)**. There are two bars and a garden and the pub is typical of the seaside. Beers on sale are Greene King Abbot which is a most unusual beer to find in North Wales, Theakston Best Bitter and a variety of guests. All day opening.

Close by is the **Olde Victoria (2)**, popularly known as the Old Vic. It is a popular, traditional, Victorian house with a homely atmosphere. Victorian photographs of Llandudno adorn the walls. It sells Banks's Mild and Bitter, Camerons Strongarm, Marston's Pedigree and occasional guest beers. Good value home cooked meals at lunch times and in the evenings are available in the bar and the restaurant. There is a garden and there are quiz nights and folk music sessions. Children are made welcome.

Carry along Church Walks turning left into Upper Mostyn Street and a few yards along on the left is the **Fat Cat (3)**. It is in the traditional cafe bar style with wooden floors. Beers on sale are Boddington's Bitter, Theakston XB and guests. Meals are available lunch times and evenings and there is a garden.

Close by is the **London Hotel (4)** with its Dick Whittington sign. A large central bar serves several small lounge areas. One oddity is an old red telephone box. At the back of the pub is an excellent family room which transforms into a piano bar in the evenings. There is a folk club on Saturdays. Burtonwood Dark Mild and Bitter beers are sold and food is served at lunch times and evenings. Bed and breakfast is available.

Cross over the roundabout into Mostyn Street and turn first right into Market Street and on the right is the **Cottage Loaf (5)** sometimes called "the village pub in the heart of the town". It was formerly a bakery and the flagged floors are a reminder of this. Courage Directors is on regular sale but there is a good moving selection of guest beers. A varying menu of food is sold at lunch times. There is live music on Tuesdays and Sundays. Kids welcome up to 8 p.m.

And now for the fit and thirsty. It is a good 15 minutes walk to the next pub but well worth it. Return to Mostyn Street and turn right. Carry on to the right fork of Conway Road (A470). Go past the first roundabout and at the second one the **Links Hotel (6)** is on the right. The name comes from its proximity to two golf courses and the building itself resembles a golf club house. There is plenty of room here in this pleasantly busy and welcoming pub. The beers are from John Willy Lees of Middleton Junction, Manchester, and include GB Mild and Bitter. Good value food is served at both lunch times and evenings and bed and breakfast is available. Kids are well provided for with a conservatory and an outdoor play area. The Links is open all day.

LONDON BRIDGE AND THE BOROUGH

There are scores of pubs in the area and those in this crawl are considered to be the better ones. Six of them are in the 1999 *Good Beer Guide*. Because this is essentially a business and not a residential area you will find that some of the pubs are closed at weekends but there are still plenty open to make the walk an enjoyable one. The best starting point is Borough station on the Northern line which is an easy five minute walk to Borough Road and the first chosen pub. Alternatively you could start from Lambeth North on the Bakerloo line which is a little further away to the west. Buses 35, 40, 133 and P3 stop close by.

"The Knight in the triumph of his heart made several reflections on the greatness of the British Nation; that the Thames was the noblest river in Europe; that London Bridge was a greater piece of work than any of the Seven Wonders of the World; with many other honest prejudices which naturally cleave to the heart of a true Englishman."

Joseph Addison

The Ship (1) is on the north side of Borough Road. This all-day opening pub sells Fuller's Chiswick Bitter, London Pride, ESB and seasonal beers. It is a long, narrow one-bar pub with ship-related memorabilia adorning the walls. An enclosed outdoor drinking area, running alongside the pub, is open during the summer. From the Ship turn left into Borough High Street, take the first right into Trinity Street, then the first left and follow Swan Street to the junction with Great Dover Street. Turn right and take the first left into Nebraska Street. (About five minutes walk.) The next stop is the **Royal Oak (2)** in Tabard Street. This is Harvey's first London-based pub, which opened in August 1997 following a major refurbishment including a welcome return to a two-bar format. As well as full range of Harvey's beers – Mild, Pale Ale, Best Bitter, Armada and seasonal beers the pub serves excellent home-cooked food throughout the day starting with breakfast from 8 a.m. It is normally closed at weekends.

From the Royal Oak, turn left into Tabard Street. At the end of the road, turn left into Long Lane. Cross Borough High Street and follow Marshalsea Road. Take the third right into Ayres Street. The next pub, **The Lord Clyde (3)** is about 25 yards on at the corner of Clennam Street. The outstanding feature of this traditional two-room pub is the splendid external tile work, a relic of its former days as a Truman pub. It was the 1997 Daily Mirror London pub of the year. It opens all day except on Sunday afternoons and sells Courage Best, Webster Yorkshire Bitter, Morland Old Speckled Hen, Young's Bitter and occasional guest beers.

From the Lord Clyde, retrace your footsteps and turn left at the end of Marshalsea Street into Borough High Street. Go into a courtyard towards the top end of the road for the **George Inn (4).** This impressive seventeenth-century coaching inn is currently owned by the National Trust and leased to Whitbread. It is popular with tourists and the local business community and hosts a regular beer festival in the fourth week of each month. The tap room was once used by coachmen waiting for their passengers and the former bedrooms have been converted into a restaurant and dining rooms. Beers on sale include Boddington's Bitter, Flowers Original, Fuller's London Pride, Greene King Abbot, Morland Old Speckled Hen, Wadworth 6X and guests. It is open all day, every day.

From the George, cross Borough High Street at its junction with Southwark Street. Cross Southwark Street and Stoney Street with the **Wheatsheaf (5)** directly ahead. This excellent two bar pub is in the heart of the Borough market conservation area and has recently been granted a Grade II listing. However, the pub is threatened with demolition in Railtrack's Thameslink 2000 plans. The pub is a rare outlet for mild ale in the area so visit it while you still can and join the campaign to preserve it. It sells Courage Best Bitter and guest beers and occasionally real cider.

Three doors along on the corner of Stoney Street and Park Street is the **Market Porter (6)** a large multi-roomed pub opposite the former Bishop's Brewery. It is popular with tourists and the local business community. The beers on sale are Fuller's London Pride, Harvey Sussex Best Bitter and up to five guests. In a time-honoured London tradition the upstairs restaurant is open from Monday to Friday for lunches.

The easiest way to get to the next pub is to cut through Borough Market and turn left towards Southwark Cathedral

directly in front of you. There has been a church on the site for at least a thousand years, but it has not always known good times. In 1212 it was badly damaged by fire and it also went through a period of neglect when owned by King James I. In 1604 four parishioners bought the church from him, and began to restore it. Now in the twentieth century it is in its full splendour being made a cathedral in 1905. There are several interesting features within the church, including a memorial to William Shakespeare and a thirteenth century wooden effigy of a knight. Follow the path around the cathedral and go up the stairs to London Bridge.

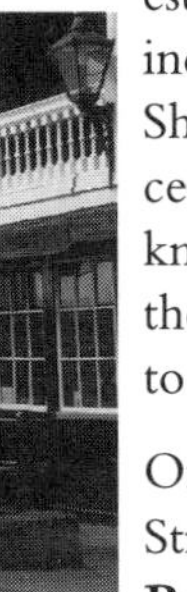

Top: *Wheatsheaf*
Bottom: *George Inn.*

On the left in Borough High Street is the **Barrowboy & Banker (7)** yet another pub that closes at the weekends. Beers sold are Fuller's Chiswick Bitter, London Pride, ESB and seasonal ales. The pub is in former bank premises on the approach to London Bridge, lavishly converted into a Fuller's 'Ale and Pie' house. There is a large bar on the ground-floor level and an upstairs balcony area. Very popular with the local business community. Good food menu in which pies play an obviously prominent part. On leaving the pub, cross the road, turn left then right into Tooley Street. The entrance to Hays Galleria is about 350 yards on the left past the London Dungeon. At the waterfront end overlooking HMS Belfast is **Horniman at Hays (8)**. This large waterfront pub built on the site of Hays Wharf has all day opening during the week but only opens from 11 a.m. until 4 p.m. at the weekends. The pub is named after John Horniman, a Victorian tea-trader who traded from Hays Wharf and also founded the Horniman Free Museum at Forest Hill in London SE23. Food is served in a separate dining area on weekday lunch times. Beers on sale are Adnams Bitter, Fuller's London

Pride, Marston's Pedigree, Morland Old Speckled Hen, Tetley Bitter, Charles Wells Bombardier and guests.

On leaving take the time to view the river. Walk past HMS Belfast and go back through Hays Galleria turning left into Tooley Street. At its junction with Bermondsey Street, is the **Shipwrights Arms (9)** which opens all day, every day. This large former Courage pub was taken over in early1997 and extensively refurbished. It offers a range of three or four good quality beers that are reasonably priced for the area. Take note of the tiled mural by the bar and the fantastic views of Tower Bridge.

Above: The Lord Clyde.

The nearest railway station from here is London Bridge (BR, Northern line and Jubilee line) and buses 47 and P11 go past the door with many others leaving from London Bridge station concourse.

LOUTH

Louth is one of Lincolnshire's most handsome market towns. There are many fine buildings and it is dominated by the elegant parish church of St James which rises to 295 feet above the flat fenlands and can be seen from miles around; it is the highest steeple in England except for Salisbury Cathedral. Tennyson, born nearby at Somersby, was a scholar at Louth Grammar School which he is said to have hated. There is an interesting connection between this pub crawl and the earlier one in Greenwich because the meridian line passes through Louth and is marked by a plaque.

The town also has an abundance of fine pubs and this tour takes in five of them along a linear route through the town, with the parish church at one end and the Riverhead at the other. The pubs date from the seventeenth to the twentieth centuries and provide the most dedicated beer drinkers with a range to suit their palate. The railway has long gone from Louth – the nearest stations are Grimsby, Market Rasen and Skegness – but from all three of these towns, as well as Horncastle and Maplethorpe, there are good bus services to Louth. The bus station is near the centre of town close to the final two pubs on the crawl.

The crawl starts at the **Wheatsheaf (1)** on Westgate, a street containing many fine Georgian buildings, with the pub itself dating from 1625. Words of warning though, watch your head if going in through the front door! This is a beautifully presented and well-appointed pub with both the beer and the food of exceptional quality. The beers are mainly from the Whitbread range with Boddington's Bitter, Flowers Original alongside Draught Bass, Tipsy Toad Ale and a range of guest beers.

Moving on from here, turn left when leaving the building and admire the splendour of the church spire directly in front of you, it is a truly magnificent sight. Cut through the churchyard along the cobbled road and spare the time to visit this splendid work of ecclesiastical architecture. Pass through the gate, turn right and beware of vehicles on roads which are unsuitable for today's levels of traffic. At the corner of

Top: *Woodman.* Bottom: *Woolpack.*

Mercer Row turn left and then left again to enter the Market Place where you will see the **Masons Arms (2)** in front of you. This building was a Samuel Smith's house until the mid-1970s when it fell into a state of disrepair. It was bought by Mike Harrison who restored it to the level in which you find it today. The pub itself is an old coaching inn from the eighteenth century and provides the customer with a level of service and comfort one would expect from a country hotel. The beer range varies, but normally includes Marston's Pedigree, Bateman XXXB and Dark Mild as well as a choice of guest beers, of which Timothy Taylor Landlord seems to be making a permanent place for itself.

Moving on from the Masons, turn left from the front door into the Market Place and take a stroll past some particularly fine buildings including the spectacular Market Hall, now being used as a shop, with its clock tower, superb glass roof and stone flagged floor. On Wednesday market day enjoy the character and banter of a genuine street market. Go into Eastgate and ahead of you is the beautiful façade of the **Olde Whyte Swanne (3)**, the oldest pub in Louth, built in 1612. The front bar of this pub is a little gem and should not be missed, especially in winter when two open fires are guaranteed to keep out the coldest chill. The beers are usually from the Bass range supplemented by a guest beer. This pub is reputed to be haunted, so those of you of a nervous disposition have been warned!

From here take a walk along Eastgate, with the church behind you. Pass the Packhorse on your left and carry on until you reach the **Woodman (4)** on your right. This one-roomed basic town pub is handily placed to break your journey through the town and a well-kept pint from the John Smith's range or one of the guest beers will be your reward. There is an impressive collection of film posters and Gary Larson cartoons. Lunches are served every day except Sundays.

The walk between the final two pubs passes through an area of Louth seldom seen by the tourist and gives you the chance to see more wonderful old buildings. Leaving the Woodman, turn right and walk along Eastgate for about 300 yards until you come to the war memorial. The almshouses behind are well worth a second glance. Turn left at the memorial along Ramsgate and follow this road until you come to the junction with Newbridge Hill where you will see the Wellington which, at the time of writing, only sold keg beer. Follow the road to your right and go up the slight incline which was once an embankment on the Grimsby, Peterborough and London railway line. The new houses on your left are built on the site of old railway premises and you should take a couple of minutes to walk through this estate and admire the old station buildings. This done, proceed over the crest of the hill and walk along Riverhead Road, passing the superbly restored warehouses on your right.

Top: *Wheatsheaf and Parish Church.* Bottom: *Ye Olde Whyte Swanne.*

Go past the swimming pool on your left, and about 100 yards further on you will see the splendid facade of your last port of call, the **Woolpack (5)**. Many folk have put forward differing theories on the past history of this pub, with claims of various uses, but the most recent licensee has discovered that the building has always been a pub since it was built in 1770. It was a CAMRA favourite in the 1980s but suffered a period of decline in the early nineties. But now it has regained its former, well-deserved, status as one of the best pubs in the area. It offers a range of beers from Bateman's brewery at nearby Wainfleet (Mild, XB and XXXB) along with Marston's Pedigree and a guest beer coupled with superb value-for-money food. It is easy to see the attraction of this pub, especially on a hot summer's day when full use of the very pleasant beer garden is possible.

The crawl finishes in an interesting part of Louth and before returning to the town centre you should take the opportunity to have a look round the Riverhead area with a walk along the towpath of the Louth canal, once the busiest in the country, and the River Lud.

MERTON & SOUTH WIMBLEDON

Merton is famous as the home of Lord Nelson. He bought Merton Place and lived here in a curious menage à trois with Lord and Lady Hamilton. He left it to his mistress after his death at Trafalgar but she is reputed to have lost the lot through gambling. Merton Abbey was founded by Gilbert the Norman in 1114 near the River Wandle and it was here where William Morris, the socialist artist, designer and poet, worked in the late nineteenth century. Wimbledon is perhaps best known for the All-England Tennis Club where one of the world's four great championships is held and, of course the Wombles of Wimbledon Common.

Begin the crawl at South Wimbledon Northern Line station. It may be easier to travel to Wimbledon station (BR and District Line) and then catch a bus (57, 93 or 155) to the starting point.

From the station cross the road to **Grove Tavern (1),** a spacious modern pub where there should be one guest ale on sale alongside Draught Burton Ale and Tetley Bitter. There is good home cooked food here. An Irish atmosphere prevails and there is live TV coverage of Gaelic football matches and live Irish folk music on Sundays. It stays open until midnight and until 1 a.m. on Fridays and Saturdays when there may be an entrance charge.

Then follow Morden Road, stopping at the recently renamed **Princess of Wales (2)** where, in the view of some folk, you can drink the best pint of Young's Bitter in the area. It also sells Young's Special and seasonal beers. It started a new lease of life under a new name suggested by one or two locals after concerted campaigning spearheaded by customers, residents and CAMRA had seen off the threat of disposal of the pub (then called the Prince of Wales – one of three so-named in Merton) in favour of a car showroom and repair yard. Of particular note is the outstanding nineteenth-century facade. Food is available both at lunch times and in the evenings. The pub closes between 3 and 5 p.m. from Mondays to Thursdays. It is twinned with the Horse Brass pub in Portland, Oregon.

Top: *Riverside.* Bottom: *Nelson Arms.*

Head back towards South Wimbledon station and turn right past the parish church of St John the Divine into High Path, reaching the **Trafalgar (3)** at the junction of the first road on the left. Ask Tom, the landlord, which beer he recommends – he'll probably have about four on tap which may include Draught Bass, King and Barnes Sussex, Gales HSB, Fuller's London Pride and maybe a couple of guests. Food is available on weekday lunch times but the pub is open all day. The Nelson association is in a ship's wheel which is incorporated in a wooden partition that divides the two bars of this intimate pub.

Then carry on along High Path and turn left into Abbey road, stopping at the **Princess Royal (4)** on the first corner. It sells Courage Best Bitter and Directors and Fuller's London Pride with usually a guest beer such as Wadworth 6X and Morland Old Speckled Hen. This is a gem of an early nineteenth-century street corner pub with two bars and a large secluded patio at the back. Food is available at lunch times. The pub is closed from 3 and 5.30 p.m. from Mondays to Thursdays.

At this point anyone pressed for time can head up Abbey Road to the Nelson Arms (8) and up Norman Road to the Sultan (7), but those enjoying a more leisurely outing should cross Abbey Road and head back towards High Path turning left into Station Road thence on to Merantun Way where a controlled pelican crossing allows access to a path leading over the River Wandle into the Abbey Mills heritage site and through to the **William Morris (5)** in Watermill Way. Breakspear's Bitter, Theakston XB and Wadworth 6X are the regular beers alongside a house beer and two guests, one of them routinely from Young of Wandsworth. This pub opened in 1990 in a restored former silk printing works. There are bars on two floors and families are welcome. Food is available lunch times and evenings in the bars and the restaurant.

Go back across Merantun Way and turn right on to a footpath along the left bank of the River Wandle which leads back to Merton High Street at the pedestrian entrance to the Savacentre. By this route it is less than five minutes walk from the William Morris to the **King's Head (6),** the stately Young's pub next to the bus garage. There are various claims as to how long this former coaching inn has been in business, the earliest date of which is 1496. It has been with the company since 1831 and it was rebuilt with a new fascia a century later. It is wood panelled throughout and there is a family room and a non-smoking lounge. It sells Young's Bitter, Special and Winter Warmer and food is available most of the time.

Top: *Sultan.* Bottom: *Princess of Wales.*

From here follow the north side of Merton High Street westwards, then turn right into Norman Road. On the north east corner of the junction with De Burgh Road is the **Sultan (7)**, the only Hopback Brewery pub in the London postal area. Most of the prize-winning Salisbury brewery beers are available: GFB, Best Bitter, Entire Stout, Summer Lightning and Thunderstorm. Sultan was a racehorse and this pub was rebuilt in 1950 after the original had been destroyed by wartime bombing. A patio adjoins the main bar and the Ted Higgins bar – named after a CAMRA stalwart – is usually quiet. There are barbecues in summer and occasional beer festivals.

To complete the circuit to South Wimbledon station retrace your steps down Norman Road, cross Merton High Street and turn right arriving at the north end of Abbey Road and the **Nelson Arms (8)**, now opened out into a single, clean, spacious

bar selling Fuller's London Pride. Note the magnificent tiled facade from former owners Charrington and the sign. This is a listed building which was once the home of Lady Emma Hamilton.

Head back westward and stop at the **Kilkenny Tavern (9),** now a most welcoming, bright open, genuine Irish pub with regular live music, no unnecessary mock-Irish paraphernalia and decent cask conditioned beer – Courage Best Bitter. The South Wimbledon tube station is barely twenty yards down the road.

Top: *Grove Tavern* Bottom: *Princess of Wales.*

NEWBURY

A poem entitled A Nightmare (probably caused by war whiskey) was supposed to contain the names of all the pubs in the former borough of Newbury. This piece of doggerel listed 75 pubs in its 18 verses and probably dated from World War I. A typical verse went:

THE ATLAS TAP didn't care a rap
that THE BELL on the hill should ring.
THE WEAVERS clothed LORD FALKLAND'S ARMS
and I found THE NEWMARKET INN.

Many of the pubs mentioned were actually outside the old borough, and time hath wrought many changes, so that of the five hostelries mentioned above, only one, The Bell, 'on the hill' still stands – nearly two miles from the town centre. But there are still enough pubs left in the town to make a good pub crawl. Indeed, your tour starts with Newbury's newest one, which opened in August 1997.

Arriving at either the bus or railway station, both of which stand to the south of the town centre, it is a short walk up Cheap Street to the Market Place, where **The Hogshead (1)** stands in the far corner. This was once a local auctioneers' sale room, and the conversion has tried, not always successfully, to retain some of the former character. The entrance is down a long wide corridor, past a room which used to be the auctioneers' office and which, for some bizarre reason, only has an off-sales licence. Consequently it tends to be used as a meeting room.

The main body of the pub lies at right angles to the entrance, stretching along the side of the Kennet and Avon Canal, so that one can sit on a raised area by the windows and survey the water. The pub is actually larger than the old auction rooms, as the open yard at the far end was incorporated into the building, making a slightly separated section with an attractive balcony also overlooking the canal. The old wooden joists and tie bars in the high roof have been retained, together with various artefacts, but the effect is rather spoiled by the bright metal trunking which runs the length of the interior. The walls are of bare brick, covered

Top: *The Coopers Arms.* Bottom: *The Hogshead.*

with old posters and documents connected to the former business and to the canal.

The long bar which runs along the wall opposite the windows dispenses about a dozen beers; up to eight on handpumps and four guests on an eye-level stillage at the back. Regulars include Morland Old Speckled Hen, Fuller's London Pride, Wadworth 6X, and Whitbread Abroad Cooper as well as such continental delights as Hoegaarden Wit and Belle-Vue Kriek on draught. There is a good selection of bottled beers including Chimay and Duvel, and real draught cider – normally Biddenden. The Hogshead does tasty, good value food. An even better pub for canalside access is The **Lock, Stock and Barrel (2).** Turn right out of The Hogshead's entrance, past the two continental café bars and the old Town Hall, and right again over the ancient bridge into the partly-pedestrianised Northbrook Street. Immediately on your left is an alleyway leading down to The LSB, as it is known locally. This is a Fuller's pub which opened in 1994, replacing a rather smart, Bass-owned café – a conversion which, strangely enough, caused an outcry among local coffee-drinkers! The narrow frontage in the alleyway, which also gives access to the canal towpath, belies the size of the L-shaped building. The longer arm of the L fronts a branch of the River Kennet and customers can sit either on the roof garden or on the patio which runs the length of the pub to watch the narrow boats negotiating Newbury Lock, with a view of the splendid 16th century St Nicolas Church behind. To the right is a long, half-timbered building which was once part of the Bridge Brewery and the pub's main entrance stands on the site of an old cottage which was the brewery tap.

Being Fuller's first pub in West Berkshire, The LSB quickly became the brewery's flagship managed house, dispensing all Fuller's beers (regulars and seasonals) and good pub food. Except when occupied on a Friday evening with the circuit drinkers, the pub is roomy and welcoming with a free-standing pulpit for vertical drinkers, free daily papers and a no smoking section. Definitely a pub for all seasons.

The quickest way to the next port of call is past the old brewery buildings and out of the LSB's back gate into Northcroft Lane. Turn left past the Salvation Army hall and take the second turning on the right into West Street. At the top end on the corner is **The Lion (3)**. This is another L-shaped pub which in the '70s was the town's only free house and was owned by a catering company whose policy was good beer and good food. Following the untimely death of the owner the pub stood empty for some while but a spirited campaign by the West Berkshire branch of CAMRA prevented it from being demolished for office building. Unfortunately, the neglect and the vibrations caused by pile driving for other new office buildings nearby meant that the new owners, Wadworth of Devizes, had to demolish it anyway. To their eternal credit they rebuilt the pub in almost the same style even down to the entrance steps on the corner. The re-building has produced more internal space from the same ground area. The long, right-angled bar with ornate decorations in Victorian gin-palace style has recently been turned into an island by opening out the area at the back. As well as plenty of conventional tables, there is an open, wooden-floored area for those who prefer to stand. Perhaps the architectural purists will be pained by the enormous pelmets above the semicircular windows, but the beer drinker will appreciate the Wadworth's beers. All the range is available according to season, plus a regular guest beer – Badger Tanglefoot – alongside the usual pub food which includes good toasted sandwiches.

Top: *Lock, Stock and Barrel.* Bottom: *The Lion.*

On leaving The Lion, turn right along the other arm of West Street back to Northbrook Street. Turn left, and a few yards along on the left is **The Monument (4)**. This former Halls of Oxford house was renamed The Tap and Spile after its purchase by that chain in 1995, but many local people resented the change and were very happy when new owners Century Inns restored the original name in early 1999. It is the only pub of that name outside of London marking the fact that the people of Newbury sent aid to the capital after the Great Fire of 1666. The Monument is a long, narrow, building, with the bar on the right and three separate drinking areas to the left separated by partitions with coloured glass panels. The renovation of this 300-year-old, grade II listed building by the new owners was carefully monitored by the local planners, so most of the interior beam work is preserved. There are many old photographs of defunct local breweries. It sells a changing range of ales including the ubiquitous but excellent Tap and Spile Premium. The Monument is now the proud possessor of the original sign after it was rescued by a customer from a heap of rubbish behind the pub following the 1995 renovation.

Our final pub is almost back at the start of the tour, but worth the walk. Turn right out of The Monument and go all the way along Northbrook Street, then over the canal bridge and down Bartholmew Street. Just beyond the bridge on the left is Wychwood's *Hobgoblin* which is worth a visit if you have time. However, almost at the far end of Bart Street on the right, is **The Coopers Arms (5)**. This splendid little street-corner town local is owned by Arkell's of Swindon, who bought it from Courage in 1992. The former owners had neglected the pub badly and it possessed a seedy reputation. To their credit Arkell's eschewed wholesale renovation and the right-angled bar, which runs around the two outer walls of the pub, and the little snug at the back, were retained virtually unchanged and the former games room on the right of the entrance was converted into a pleasant dining-room complete with dark panelling and a baronial-style stone fireplace. Much-needed new toilets completed the transformation, and The Coopers is fit for any company. The locals still have their bar selling Arkell's 3B and Kingsdown together with Noel Ale in the winter. The dining room in which is served good pub food at lunch times doubles as a lounge-cum-function room in the evenings. No better place could be found to complete your pub-crawl around Newbury with the bus station less than a minute's walk away, while the railway station is just beyond that.

NEWCASTLE

The city began life as a fort on Hadrian's wall. It grew into one of the world's great shipbuilding centres and remains a proud regional capital, lively, independent and as sure of itself as it was when the 'new' castle was built on the site of the Roman fort. In the 1970s it was referred to as a 'beer desert'. But now, as you shall see, things are very different.

Start in St. Andrews Street just off Percy Street beside St. Andrews Church which is notable for its crooked tower caused by a gun being fired from it during the Jacobite rebellions. This part of town once housed Newcastle gaol and this heritage is reflected in the name of the nearby Gallowgate bus station and in the buildings, some of which still bear traces of the old prison cells. St. Andrews Street itself was once the site of the prison gardens. Ralph Gardiner, a South Shields brewer was locked up here for breaking the Newcastle monopoly on brewing beer. He is quoted as saying he was "constrained to drink the gaoler's beer, not fit for human bodies".

Newcastle is a spacious, extended, infinitely populous place; 'tis seated upon the River Tyne, which is here a noble, large and deep river and ships…may come safely up to the very town.

Daniel Defoe

The **Newcastle Arms (1)** is a Tetley Festival Ale House and serves a variety of guest beers as well as Tetley Bitter and Ind Coope Burton Ale. It was refurbished in the mid 1990s when the interior was largely replaced. Food is served at lunch times.

Turn left out of the Newcastle Arms and Newcastle's Chinatown, Stowell Street, lies in front of you. Behind Rosie's Bar (formerly the Northumberland Arms and the Darn Crook) is the city wall. Taking this route will take you behind the Chinese restaurants and past Morden Tower, an unlikely venue for poetry reading, but one which has attracted poets from around the globe, refreshed by pints of ale carried by hand along the alley from Rosie's. At the end of the alley turn left, keeping the wall on your left, and cross Bath Lane on to Westgate Road. This follows the course of Hadrian's Wall, although little of this structure is visible in the city itself.

The Bodega (2) is just beyond the Tyne Theatre and Opera House. A former Tyneside and Northumberland

Top: *Crown Posada.* Bottom: *Ship Inn.*

CAMRA Pub of the Year. The pub was previously the Black Bull and was derelict for many years but is an excellent refurbishment and a credit to its owners, the locally based Sir John Fitzgerald pub chain which owns many of Newcastle's finest pubs. This chain kept cask-conditioned beer flowing in the city in the dark days of the 70s and early 80s. The Bodega serves Theakston Best Bitter, Mordue No 9 (otherwise known as Geordie Pride) and Workie Ticket, Butterknowle Conciliation and a number of guest beers. Food is available at lunch times. Note the two original stained glass ceiling domes. Gets very busy when Newcastle United are at home.

Follow Westgate Road down past the Assembly Rooms, the monuments to Joseph Cowen and George Stephenson, and the Literary and Philosophical Society and the road will bring you out opposite the High Level Bridge, built by Robert Stephenson, and the Castle, built by Henry II. The **Bridge Hotel (3)** is another Fitzgerald pub which has undergone recent renovation. Theakston XB, Boddington's Bitter, Black Sheep Bitter complement the guest beers. Again food is available at lunch times. From the back of the pub you can obtain a splendid view of the river with its three most picturesque bridges: the High Level Bridge with its two decks for trains and road traffic, the Swing Bridge and the most recent, Tyne Bridge built in 1936.

Walk back to the Castle, go through the Black Gate and follow the path past the railway arches to Dog Leap Stairs. At the bottom of Dog Leap Stairs is The Side and Newcastle's

most famous pub, the **Crown Posada (4)**. It was once owned by a sea captain who installed his Portuguese mistress as landlady. It is notable for its stained glass windows. This is another quality Fitzgerald pub with no television set, no juke box or similar distractions, a place where conversation holds sway. Jennings Cumberland Ale, Theakston Best Bitter, Mordue Workie Ticket, Butterknowle Conciliation, Draught Bass and a guest beer are available to fortify you for the fifteen-minute walk along the Quayside to the next pub.

The Quayside is undergoing dramatic redevelopment on both sides of the river with the Baltic Flour Mills earmarked as an art gallery for the new millennium. A Sunday market ('Paddy's Market") still thrives on the Newcastle side of the river and the offices of the various shipping companies which once operated from the Quayside are still clearly visible. On the left in Lombard Street is a maritime museum. All Saints Cathedral is an architectural oddity which lies further away from the river up Dog Bank.

Above: Bridge Hotel.

The Tyne Inn (5), formerly the Ship Tavern, lies under Glasshouse Bridge beside the junction of the Ouseburn and the Tyne just south of the Byker area of Newcastle in Malin Street. Three Mordue beers, Boddington's Bitter and Draught Bass are available in this single-roomed free house which also serves good value home cooked food. There is an all-weather garden sheltered by the bridge.

The Free Trade (6) is accessible either by steps leading up from the Tyne Inn or by using the path. This traditional pub is another Mordue outlet (Geordie Pride, Workie Ticket, Radgie Gadgie), this time combined with Theakston's beers (Best Bitter and XB). A magnificent view of the river from the unusual tiered garden is a reward for the climb up from the Quayside.

Head inland from the Free Trade and pass the Ouseburn industrial estate, home to the Hadrian Brewery now owned by the Four Rivers Brewing Company. **The Fighting Cocks (7)** is the brewery tap. Four Rivers Moondance and Hadrian Gladiator are on sale here as well as a draught cider. It was the Tyneside and Northumberland CAMRA Pub of the Year for 1998. This is another pub with a magnificent view. And the juke box is free!

After leaving the Fighting Cocks follow St Lawrence Street and skirt around the Byker Wall housing estate and the **Cumberland Arms (8)** lies just beyond a fringe of trees. In an area where pubs are refurbished on a regular basis as a matter of course it is a delight to enter this unspoilt gem. Local beers such as Mordue and Hadrian are usually on sale along with popular favourites such as Fuller's London Pride. The pub is also a thriving local music venue.

Leave the Cumberland and go down the steps past the city farm to the **Ship Inn (9).** This is another largely unspoilt pub and it has Castle Eden Ale and Boddington's Bitter on sale. A climb back up the bank will bring you to either Manors or Byker Metro station. The area is also well served by buses.

NOTTINGHAM

A city that proudly proclaims itself 'Queen of the Midlands' is famous for its historic lace-making industry and its Goose Fair; but perhaps even more well known for such firms as Boots, Raleigh and Players. There is much to see here and the ancient castle which towers over the city played a major part in the legends of Robin Hood. The city was once a major brewing centre and while closures have left it with only one large plant there are several new micro breweries. And there is a wide choice of pubs as you shall see.

Across the road from Nottingham Midland railway station, to the left, is the **Queen's Hotel (1)** in Arkwright Street. Although this is a Greenall's house (a firm not noted for its inspirational pubs) it is well worth a visit as one of the few remaining in the city with a separate lounge and real public bar with dartboard. It sells Boddington's Bitter, Worthington Bitter and Draught Bass and has two ever changing guest beers from independent brewers. There is also accommodation.

A short step away is the **Vat and Fiddle (2)** in Queensbridge Road, selling Everard Tiger, Castle Rock Hemlock and Elsie Mo, Archers Golden, Hook Norton Best Bitter, four guest beers and traditional cider. It is a simple one-room pub with separate drinking areas which serves good food at lunch times and in the early evenings. The pub is owned by the Tynemill local pub chain. With tongue firmly in cheek the name was inspired by the close proximity of the Inland Revenue and Crown Court buildings. The Castle Rock brewery can be seen next door.

Walk along Traffic Street and up Wilford Road. Cross the canal at the picturesque Castle Lock, then right at the main road and first left into Castle Road. On the left is the Brewhouse Yard Museum and the world famous **Olde Trip to Jerusalem (3)**. It was built partly in the sandstone caves in the Castle Rock and first opened in 1189. It claims to be England's oldest pub but there are other challengers. It has recently been gently restored and although most Nottinghamians approve what has been done purists have

criticised some aspects of the work. Judge for yourself. Beers include Hardy and Hanson's Best Mild, Best Bitter, Classic and seasonal beers and Marston's Pedigree. The pub has a quiet room, and an outside area and a variety of pub games.

Follow the road past Nottingham Castle on the left. On the right is the Nottingham Lace Centre, formerly Severn's Restaurant. This historic building was moved brick by brick from the ancient Broadmarsh area, sadly destroyed to make way for the ugly, concrete Arndale Centre. A visit to the Broadmarsh Caves, which are accessible from inside the centre, is well worthwhile. Moving up Saint James Road takes one past Standard Hill on the left where Charles I raised his standard in 1642. Follow the map round to Nottingham Playhouse where the **Limelight Bar (4)** will be found on Wellington Circus.

Above: Salutation Inn.

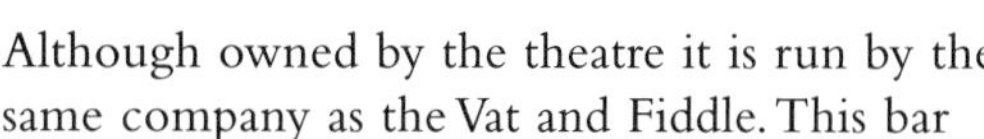

Although owned by the theatre it is run by the same company as the Vat and Fiddle. This bar offers Adnams Bitter, Bateman Mild and XB, Courage Directors, Marston's Pedigree, Theakston XB and up to six guest beers together with real cider. There a delightful outside drinking area, excellent food in the restaurant and occasional live music. Other facilities include a quiet room, and a no smoking area.

Head now for Upper Parliament Street and turn left after passing the Theatre Royal into Sherwood Street. Two pubs adjoin each other across the road but you should head for **Langry's (5)** a Hogshead Ale House owned by Whitbread. Despite a cheap pine interior job the pub has atmosphere and reliable beer including Boddington's Bitter, Castle Eden Ale, Chester's Mild, Flowers IPA,

Whitbread Trophy, up to five guests often from micros and including a mild, and real cider.

Return to the main road and cross into Market Street which leads into Angel Row and the Old Market Place for the fifteenth-century **Bell Inn (6)**. A popular meeting point, the Bell has several rooms and the largest, windowless room at the rear is a regular live jazz venue. There is also a quiet room and outside area. It sells Draught Bass, Black Sheep Special, Jennings Dark Mild and Bitter, Mansfield Bitter, Ruddles County, guest beers and real cider. Meals are available.

Top: *Langtry's.* Bottom: *Bell Inn.*

Architecture aficionados may wish to break off to walk around the Market Square to view the Council House and the fine Watson Fothergill building on the corner of King Street before returning to Saint James Street. Pass the ***Old Malt Cross*** (worth calling in if time permits) until you reach Maid Marion Way, once dubbed "the ugliest street in Europe".

Walk downhill to the **Salutation Inn (7)**. Today this is another Hogshead Ale House, but the Salutation dates back to 1240. There is a large, noisy front bar, but some quiet, atmospheric small rooms at the rear. Boddington's Bitter, Castle Eden Ale, Whitbread Abroad Cooper and four guest beers are sold and meals are served at lunchtimes. Upstairs are pool tables and Sky Sports television. Tours around the historic caves and cellars which date from 900 AD are available on Mondays to Fridays at 3 p.m., 5 p.m. and 7 p.m..

On the way back to the station you may wish to visit the Canal Museum or have a last beer in the ***Fellows, Morton and Clayton (8)*** in Canal Street as you pass.

Connoisseurs of micro breweries may wish to visit the Bunkers Hill Inn in Hockley near to the Ice Stadium. It is too far off the route to be included in the standard crawl but is well worth searching out. It has an ever changing selection of eight beers, almost always from micros and reckoned to be the best selection in town. It is open all day except on Sundays and serves good value food.

OTLEY

This splendid little market town is actually part of the metropolitan borough of Leeds but in reality it is a firmly established independent place. It nestles in the Wharf valley under the shadow of the Chevin, an impressive hill that gives wonderful views across into the lower Dales and the Harrogate area. Thomas Chippendale was born here and a handsome statue of England's greatest cabinet maker stands in Manor Square in the town centre. There is also an interesting monument in the parish churchyard dedicated to labourers who died whilst building a nearby railway tunnel.

There are twenty pubs in Otley, mainly quite old, and everyone of them sells traditional ale. It makes for a good choice for a pub crawl but if you are not satisfied at the end of it you can try out most of the rest for only two are outside the town centre. There are good bus services from Leeds, Bradford and Ilkley and the bus station is as good a place as any to start from.

Turn right into Crossgate and at the top turn left into Bondgate for the **Rose and Crown (1).** This one bar pub dates back to 1731 when it was called the Kings Arms, the name changing on the coronation of Queen Victoria. It sells Boddington's Bitter, Tetley Bitter, Castle Eden Ale and a guest beer. Food is available at both lunch times and in the evenings in the bar and the adjoining restaurant and there are barbecues in summer.

Turn left out of here and you will very soon reach the **Junction (2)** a popular free house that is a regular entry in the *Good Beer Guide*. There is one large bar with tiled floors and some exposed stonework. On sale are a group of regular local beers – Black Sheep Best Bitter, Tetley Bitter, Taylor Best Bitter and Landlord and Theakston Old Peculier – and guest beers. Lunches are served. It has a lively atmosphere and attracts a youngish crowd although oldies are most welcome.

From the Junction turn left and left again into Charles Street and then right to Walkergate for the **Manor House (3)**. This terraced pub lies comfortably between shops. It is tradi-

Top: *Black Bull.* Bottom: *Bay Horse.*

tional in every way, unspoilt and welcoming, selling Thwaites beers. Food is on sale on weekday lunch times.

Turn right out of the pub crossing the road and opposite, where Walkergate joins Boroughgate, is the **White Swan (4).** It dates back to the eighteenth century but apart from the entrance arch most of the pub was rebuilt in the early years of this century. However the original stables and the ostler's house remain. The regulars of this thriving pub who are a lively lot have been responsible for buying many guide dogs for the blind. The White Swan sells Draught Bass, Stones Best Bitter, Black Sheep Best Bitter and a guest beer. There is a sun trap of a yard at the back.

Take a right turn along Boroughgate, passing the bus station on your left. There is no reflection of Otley's most famous son, Thomas Chippendale, amongst the names of its pubs although there was once a Carpenters Arms where the bus station now stands. It stood opposite the house where he was born. It was later named the Wharfedale but was demolished in 1934. Carry on to the **Bay Horse (5)**, a gem of a nineteenth-century pub that is completely unspoilt; it retains its tiny tap room with serving hatch, alcoves in the lounge, a gracefully curving bar, some splendid stained glass and a collection of photographs of old Otley. It has a magnificent garden at the back to complement the outside toilets. Beers are Tetley Bitter and two guest beers, one of which will be from a local independent brewery. Basic snacks including 'possibly the best beef sandwich in the world' are available for most of the day.

From here go straight across the Market Place to the **Black Bull (6)**. This is a magnificent little-altered tavern which retains an atmosphere reminiscent of medieval times. It may be the oldest pub in Otley but there are other claimants. It is long and low, white-rendered and with a proud sign which, like many others in the immediate area, reflects the rural and agrarian location of the town. The main door to the Black Bull, if not original, is medieval, solid and impressive, whilst inside is a stone fireplace probably dating from its origins along with a beautifully preserved bread oven with its original arched brickwork still intact. In its yard are stables, a water pump and a stone staircase. Much of the present Black Bull is eighteenth-century but there is ample evidence that some parts date from even earlier when it was two buildings. In 1648 a party of Cromwell's Ironsides is said to have called here for refreshment and drunk the tavern dry. Such tales are often apocryphal but somehow this one seems quite plausible. Today it sells Tetley Bitter, Theakston Best Bitter and a varying range of guest beers. Good value meals are available during lunch times.

Go left through the Market Palace and next door was the New Inn, a splendid Victorian pub with excellent stained glass bay windows advertising its one-time owner William Whitaker of Bradford. It closed in 1990 and is now insensitively redecorated in the garish colours of a cut price drug store. The windows, sadly, have gone and the only memory is an area behind named New Inn Yard. Turn left by the cross into Kirkgate and across is the **Red Lion (7)** a small well kept pub with three drinking areas served by one bar. There are occasional 'happy hours' for pensioners. Beers usually sold are Courage Directors and John Smith Bitter and Magnet. Food is served at lunch times and in the evenings and vegetarians are well catered for.

Next door is the **Whitakers Arms (8)**, the name reflecting its one-time ownership by a long gone brewery from Bradford. Unlike its former stablemate, the New Inn, the Whitakers, once known as the Dramshop, remains with its stone flagged floors. It is open plan albeit in a traditional style. It sells Tetley Bitter and guest ales. There is a garden at the back and a separate restaurant and food is available both at lunch times and in the evenings. The parish church, with its fine memorial, is 100 yards further on.

OXFORD

The starting point for this crawl is Oxford Bus Station in Gloucester Green. The Tourist Information Office is also situated here. Leave by the main vehicular access road and turn left into George Street. After 150 yards turn right into New Inn Hall Street and then take the first left into St Michael Street. One hundred yards ahead on the right is the **Three Goats Heads (1)**, the only Samuel Smith establishment in Oxford. It has recently been refurbished and there are two bars on different levels with lots of polished wood and tiles. It serves good food and, of course, Old Brewery Bitter on draught.

On leaving, continue along St Michaels Street until you reach Cornmarket. As you look across Cornmarket to your left you will see the church of St Michael at the Northgate. The tower of this church is of Saxon origin, dating back over 800 years, and can be climbed (for a small fee) for an alternative view of the city. Turn left into Cornmarket Street and continue straight ahead into Magdalen Street (pronounced 'Maudlin' by the locals!). At the end of Magdalen Street, if you look left into Beaumont Street you will see on your right the Ashmolean Museum which houses the University's collection of antiquities (entry is free). Looking across Magdalen Street you will see the Martyrs Memorial erected in the 1840s in memory of Bishops Latimer, Ridley and Cranmer who were burned at the stake in 1555 for following the protestant faith during the reign of Mary Tudor, a Roman Catholic. Cross the road to this monument and turn right after walking past it. After 25 yards, turn left into Broad Street. About twenty yards along Broad Street there is a cross inlaid in the road which marks the spot where the three martyrs were actually burned at the stake.

The clever men at Oxford
Know all that there is to be knowed.
But they none of them know one half as much
As intelligent Mr Toad.
Kenneth Grahame

On the opposite side of the road is the Oxford Story where you can ride a mechanised desk through time to learn more about Oxfords history. Continue along Broad Street passing some of the colleges which make up the University. On your left is Balliol founded in 1263 and initially reserved for poor scholars (Harold Macmillan, Edward Heath & Dennis Healey were students here). Next comes Trinity College, founded in

Top: *The Crown.* Bottom: *The Kings Arms.*

1555 on the site of a previous religious institution closed down by Henry VIII.

You then come to Blackwell's, Oxfords famous bookshop. Sandwiched between the entrances to the shop you will find the **The White Horse (2)**, a quite small sixteenth-century pub. Due to its popularity and size it can get a little crowded. Beers available include Ind Coope Burton Ale, Tetley Bitter, Benskins BB, Wadworth 6X and a guest. Food is available lunch times and evenings.

On leaving the White Horse, opposite is the Museum of the History of Science, which was the original Ashmolean Museum. It houses a collection of early scientific instruments (including Einstein's blackboard!). Next to the museum is the Sheldonian Theatre, recognisable by the many stone heads on the wall around it. This was built by Christopher Wren in 1664-68. As well as musical recitals, it is still used for its intended purpose – university occasions such as degree ceremonies.

Continue along Broad Street and cross the road to enter **The Kings Arms (3)**. It is a large, popular, lively pub which has many separate drinking areas – the Don's bar at the rear is worth visiting. A full range of good food is also on offer and there is a tea room – for the non appreciators of alcohol – which opens at 10.30 am on Sundays. For those in need of alcoholic refreshment the choice is good, including a range of Young's beers, Wadworth 6X, and a good selection of bottled beers. There is no music – live or recorded.

From here turn left into Holywell Street and walk about 50 yards until you reach Bath Place, a very narrow alley which leads off to the right (if you reach New College you've missed it). Walk down Bath Place towards the Bath Place Hotel but immediately before its gates, turn left into an even narrower passage (trust me, there is a pub down here!). At the end of the passage you will find the **Turf Tavern (4)**. It is tucked out of the way but it's certainly worth a visit. This thirteenth century rambling sort of pub has low beamed ceilings and three garden and courtyard areas which are pleasant to sit in, even during cold weather due to the practice of having braziers to provide warmth. It has literary connections with a place in Hardy's Jude the Obscure. The pub serves good food, both snacks and full meals. This is definitely one not to miss in terms of the vast selection of beers brewed by small independent breweries. There is an ever changing choice with Adnams Broadside, Archers Golden, Flowers Original, Morland Old Speckled Hen, Whitbread Abroad Cooper as regulars and up to five guest beers. You can never be sure what might be available. As well as the beers, mulled wine is sold in winter.

On departure leave by the second passageway at the end of which you will emerge into New College Lane, almost directly beneath the Bridge of Sighs. This is a nineteenth century copy of the Venetian original which links the two parts of Hertford College. Turn right and walk towards the metal railings on the far side of Catte Street. From these railings, directly ahead you will see the side of the Sheldonian Theatre. The building on the left is the Bodleian Library. It has a collection of more than five and a half million books and is one of only six libraries in the world entitled to a copy of each new book published in the UK – including this one!

From the railings, turn left and walk down Catte Street, past the front of the Bodleian and into Radcliffe Square where the Radcliffe Camera dominates the area. This was built between 1337-49 as a reading room for the Bodleian Library and is still used for this purpose. Camera is a medieval term for a room. Walk past it towards St Mary's Church. It was here that the martyrs Cranmer, Ridley and Latimer were tried for heresy prior to being executed in Broad Street. The church has a high tower which is accessible (for a fee) and provides another good vantage point to view the city. The church also contains a good coffee shop where drinks and light meals can be obtained.

Once past the church, turn right into High Street and walk past Brasenose College which was founded in 1509. It is allegedly named after the original college door knocker which had a 'Brazen Nose' and now hangs behind the high table in the dining hall of the college. Just before the junction with Turl Street you will pass Lincoln College Library and All Saints Church, which from 1896 until 1975 was the city church. At this point, cross High Street and walk down Alfred Street, at the end of which you will find **The Bear (5)**. It is a very small seventeenth-century pub built on the site of the original thirteenth-century Bear Inn. It is famous for its collection of 6000 bits of ties which adorn most walls and some ceilings. There is a shared courtyard area at the rear of the pub. There is a limited choice of beers – Tetley Bitter, Ind Coope Burton Ale and Morland Old Speckled Hen. A visit is a must for the experience, a pint and a bowl of chips!

On leaving The Bear, turn right into Blue Boar Street and then take the first passage on your right. Half way along this passage you will find the ***Wheatsheaf (6)***. Call in if you feel you need an extra stop!

Continue up the passage to rejoin High Street. Turn left and walk to the end and in front of you is Carfax Tower, the remains of the fourteenth-century church of St Martin and a third opportunity to gain a higher perspective of the city!

Turn right into Cornmarket Street, walk for about 25 yards, then turn left into the passageway immediately before McDonalds, where you will find **The Crown (7)**.

The Crown is the only Bass pub in Oxford. The original inn on this site was several hundred years old but the building

Top: *Three Goats Heads.* Bottom: *The Bear.*

has been modernised, although it still retains some character. There is a courtyard area for the outdoor drinkers and good food is served.

From the Crown, walk back into Cornmarket street and turn right. Walk to the junction, turn right into Queen Street and walk its full length, past the shops and the memorial in Bonn Square. At the end of Queen Street, continue straight ahead into New Road. On your left you will pass what was Oxford Prison, a typical Victorian building, and the Castle Mound. At the end of New Road, turn left into Tidmarsh Lane and follow it round into St Thomas Street. Walk for 25 yards and you will come to **The Brewery Gate (8)**, immediately adjacent to what until recently was Morrells Brewery. As you would expect, the full range of Morrells products are on offer although these days they are brewed by the Thomas Hardy brewery in Dorchester.

From the Brewery Gate, retrace your steps back along St Thomas Street and Tidmarsh Lane. Cross New Road and walk along Worcester Street, turning right into George Street where you will find Gloucester Green Bus Station on your left hand side.

PRESTON

Preston was one of the important centres of the cotton industry – a cradle of the industrial revolution. The Harris Museum and Art Gallery contains exhibits that tell the history of the cotton trade. It is the administrative capital of Lancashire. Every twenty years the famous Preston Guild is held – an event dating from the twelfth century when the town received its charter.

The best place to start this crawl is Preston bus station by catching any bus going along Fylde Road. Ask for the **Hogshead (1)** which is your first stop. It opened as recently as June 1995, being converted from a former doctor's home and surgery which had been derelict for several years. It was known as 'Moss Cottage' and this name has been retained on outside signs. A large, imposing building set back from the road – inside there is one large room decorated in the typical Hogshead style, although it does feature a glass wall for customers to view the barrels in the cellar. Regular beers are Boddington's Bitter and Whitbread Abroad Cooper, but, more importantly, there are up to twelve, usually interesting, guest beers. Food is served all day up to 7 p.m. The pub was voted CAMRA's West Lancashire branch's first ever Pub of the Season in Autumn 1996, and in 1998 was awarded the George Lee Memorial Trophy, which recognises outstanding achievement in promoting traditional beers. A very popular pub, especially with students as it is close to the university campus. Nearby in Pedder Street is St Walburges church, Preston's most prominent feature and the third highest church spire in Britain. It was designed by Hansom of Hansom cab fame.

Head back towards the town centre and across the large double roundabout to the **Lamb and Packet (2)** in Friargate. This prominent white building at the edge of the town centre is a comfortable, one-roomed pub smaller than its external appearance suggests. The regular beers are Thwaites Bitter and either Chairman's Premium Ale or one of Thwaites monthly and seasonal beers. It is a pub that has long been famed for its food and attracts a good lunch time trade from office workers and students. The name derives from a connection between the lamb on the town's coat of arms and the packet boats that used the Lancaster Canal.

Carry along Friargate turning right into Heatley Street where on the left is the **New Britannia (3)** a smallish pub with just one room although there is a separated games area. Note the Britannia windows. It is a young persons' pub, very popular with students and bikers and gets very busy at weekends. The same family has been in charge for many years and the pub has been a regular entry in the *Good Beer Guide*. This is a Whitbread pub selling Boddington's Bitter, Flowers Original, Castle Eden Ale, Goose Eye Bronte Bitter, Marston's Pedigree and two or three guest beers. Real cider is also served. Some twenty years ago this was the first Whitbread pub in Preston to re-introduce real ale. It has remained popular with local CAMRA members ever since and was the winner of the George Lee Memorial Trophy for 1999. There was once an Old Britannia on nearby Friargate which has long since been demolished.

Top: *Lamb and Packet.* Bottom: *Old Black Bull.*

Return to Friargate, turn right and the **Olde Dog and Partridge (4)** appears shortly on the right. This is another one room pub, but with a small separated area for dining and meetings. This pub, too, can become very busy. It was well-known as a bikers' pub and most impressive machines were often to be seen parked on the pavement outside. Until 1993 this pub sold only keg beers but is now another pub popular with CAMRA members. Regular beers are Worthington Best Bitter, Highgate Dark Mild (mild is rare in the town centre) and two guest beers. The pub is known for its good value lunch time food. The tag 'Olde' was recently restored to the pub's name after many year's absence. The pub was the winner of the local CAMRA branch's Autumn 1997 Pub of the Season award, chosen on the theme 'the best pub in which to introduce students to real ale'.

Top: *New Britannia Inn.* Bottom: *Black Horse Hotel.*

A little further down Friargate is the **Old Black Bull (5)**. This very busy but homely pub is prominently sited at the junction of Friargate and Ringway, which is the main road through the centre of Preston. It is a distinctive building with a mock-Tudor frontage and tiling round the entrance. A year or so ago it was extended to take over the shop premises next door. Once a Boddington's Bitter stronghold, it has taken full advantage of the guest beer ruling in the 1990s and now sells up to eight guest beers and draught cider as well. There is a lounge, a snug and a public bar. It is a long-standing *Good Beer Guide* entry and it won the George Lee Memorial Trophy (see Hogshead above) two years running in the early 1990s; the only pub to achieve this in the last twenty years.

Across Friargate from the Old Black Bull is the **Greyfriar (6)**. This Wetherspoon's pub is a very large pub even by Wetherspoon standards. It has been converted from a building which was once a carpet showroom among other things. It is a very busy pub especially at weekends. It is one of the few town centre pubs which currently serves a mild – Thwaites Best Mild is on the handpumps along with Courage Directors, Morland Old Speckled Hen, Theakston Best Bitter and guest beers. It has all the familiar features of Wetherspoon's pubs including cheap beers, regular beer festivals, no-smoking areas and no music.

Cross the Ringway and remain on Friargate until you reach the final stop at the **Black Horse (7)**. This is generally accepted as Preston's most highly rated pub from an architectural point of view. It is a well-preserved street corner house among the shops in a pedestrian precinct. Its features include a tiled bar, mosaic floors, wood panelling and mirrors. It received an English Heritage/CAMRA award in 1998 for the Best Refurbishment. It is certainly old fashioned for a town centre pub and there are a couple of rooms separated from the main bar. A good range of Robinson's beers is sold: Best Bitter, Bitter, Frederics, Old Tom and Hartley's XB. The pub has had a regular entry in the *Good Beer Guide* over the last 25 years. It is popular with students and tends to attract a Bohemian clientele. There is no real ale in the upstairs room. The bus station is no more than five minutes walk from here. Have another?

ST ALBANS

Where better to booze than in St Albans, home of the Campaign for Real Ale? With its mediaeval Abbey and Cathedral dominating Verulamium Park – site of Roman Britain's third largest town – the city rewards the walker with a rich brew of architecture and beers. St Albans was one of the first places in England where coaching inns sprang up to provide a resting place for weary pilgrims. At the start of the 19th century they could shelter some 300 travellers and stable 700 horses. Several of them still stand today including a contender for 'the oldest pub in Britain' – and the inevitable claim of ghosts from Roman centurions to love-crossed barmaids. When Austin penned his rhyming list there were more than 80 pubs and five breweries in St Albans.

If you arrive by train, take the bus from St Albans City station to the city centre, and get off at the top of Victoria Street – opposite the Philanthropist and Firkin, as it happens. Walk up to the traffic lights, cross over, and go round the front of the handsome Old Town Hall (Tourist Information on ground floor), and continue left into Market Place, forking right down an ancient alley called French Row where King John of France was said to enjoy a happy imprisonment after failing to raise three million crowns ransom. Pause by the Clock Tower, built in the first half of the first century, then turn right towards our first watering hole.

I'll mention the name of each pub in town,

North Western, the Marlborough, the Anchor, the Crown,

The Maltster, the Postboy, the Trumpet and then,

The White Hart, Two Brewers, and the Famous Peahen

William Austin

The Tudor Tavern (1) at the corner of Verulamium Road and George Street is one of the oldest buildings in St Albans. This rambling white washed inn with upper storey jutting out over the pavement and typical mediaeval black beams was originally a guest house for the abbey. Part of it dates back to 1400 and the impressive crown post roof still survives and there is an original window. Earlier this century it was an antiques emporium, but in 1963 became the Tudor Tavern and had a spell as a sort of steak, sherry and keg beer house. Today it features four or five real ales on handpump including Boddington's Bitter, Marston's Pedigree, Flowers Original plus, on rotation, Greene King Abbot Ale, IPA or Wadworth 6X. There is quite a large dining area where you can still get a steak or choose from a predictable menu. It occupies a huge corner site and there is a wide paved area where tables are set out. The pub is open all day.

Now for a bit of culture. Turn right out of the Tudor Tavern, go down George Street passing some fascinating antique and craft shops until you come to the first cross roads, with public loos on the corner. Cross to the other side of George Street and turn left down Abbey Mill Lane passing the soaring cathedral on your left (well worth a visit), through the historic abbey gateway. The road passes the Bishop's Palace and finishes at **Ye Olde Fighting Cocks (2)**. This unusual octagonal shaped hostelry with its high free-standing chimney, once a mediaeval pigeon house, is listed in the Guinness Book of Records as the oldest inhabited licensed house in England, and clocked up 1,200 years in 1993. Once known as the Old Roundhouse, it actually had a purpose built cock pit installed in the seventeenth century which is now preserved as a sunken bar. The cruel sport continued on the premises until 1849 when it was outlawed by the government. It has a plaque on the wall outside dispensing nuggets of history including the unsubstantiated tale that Oliver Cromwell once spent a night there. What is true is that the pub has secret passages which once linked it to the Abbey to help fleeing monks in more troubled times. At least nine real ales are served at any one time with Tetley Bitter and Marston's Pedigree always available plus a changing range of guests such as Oakhill Black Magic Stout and Exmoor Gold. Hot food is available lunch times and evenings.

The River Ver runs past the pub and we're going to follow it for a while. Cross the bridge and turn right into Verulamium Park, then carry on with the river on your right and the lake on your left. If you glance across the lake you will see the remains of the Roman walls and possibly see two pairs of herons who have taken to nesting on the small island. If you have any bread the swans and geese will be delighted. At the end of the lake ignore the hump back bridge to your left and carry straight on out of the park into a little community known as St Michael's Village.

Cross the road and turn left to the **Rose and Crown (3)**, another ancient hostelry. This timber framed building dates back to the sixteenth century and has been called the Rose and Crown since 1639. The two bar interior has huge open fireplaces, beams, and cask ales including Adnams, Tetley Bitter, Wadworth 6X and guest beers. With a pleasant trellised garden to the side and rear, and a fair range of food, this friendly pub which does much to help local charities is sited at the entrance to the Roman City of Verulamium.

Turn left out of the door and, re-passing the park entrance, continue over the Ver bridge, pausing to look at beautifully restored Kingsbury Watermill built in the sixteenth century, its massive waterwheel once more slicing through the mill race. On the sharp bend, cross into Fishpool Street (a pub on each corner) and enjoy a stroll along the most picturesque residential street in St Albans, a hotch potch of architectural styles cheek by jowl as the pavement rises crazily above the level of the road, a throwback to its coach route past.

Top: *The cathedral.* Bottom: *Ye Olde Fighting Cocks.*

Carry on until, on your left, you come to the **Lower Red Lion (4)**, St Albans's only genuine freehouse where a historic interior is married to a thoroughly up-to-the-minute approach to sourcing ale. The enthusiasts who run it can be relied upon to bring in the newest beers from the newest micro-breweries as well as a wonderful and ever-changing selection of cask ales from regional brewers up and down the country. The house beer Roaring Success comes from the small Tring Brewery in Hertfordshire's Chiltern Hills, while regulars include Adnams and Fuller's London Pride. The Lower Red is a favourite watering hole of CAMRA members and a previous local branch Pub of the Year; it also hosts two annual beer festivals in a marquee in the garden. Good value snacks and light meals are sold at lunch times, and bed and breakfast is available. The old coaching arch leads through to car parking space and garden at this two bar inn which dates back to the seventeenth century.

Top: *Lower Red Lion.* Bottom: *Farriers Arms.*

Turn left out of the front door up the hill, first left into Welclose Street and at the end right into Lower Dagnall Street. Just up the hill on your left you will see a pub whose fame has spread well beyond St Albans. **The Farriers Arms (5),** a perfect example of a back street boozer, is set at the end of a Victorian terrace and bears a blue plaque on the wall outside proclaiming it the place where the first branch meeting of CAMRA was held on 20th November, 1972. The Farriers is a tenancy of the county's main brewery, McMullen's, and serves superbly kept pints of AK, Country, Gladstone and a seasonal or guest beer. An unadorned public bar is home to pub games including darts and crib, and the HQ of two football teams; whilst one step up is the carpeted saloon containing interesting memorabilia and a large water-colour of a pint and a ploughman's by artist Gail Lilley, wife of former St Albans MP Peter Lilley who painted it as a leaving gift when they moved out of their home on the opposite corner. Lunch time food includes filled rolls, sausages and chips and the like. From here continue straight up the steep hill

to the city centre, and you will find yourself back at the Old Town Hall. If you've got the energy you can turn your back on historic hostelries and visit a very welcome newcomer – a brew pub. Simply walk round the town hall and continue downhill along the main street to a major crossroads with another McMullen's house, the ***Peahen (5a)***, on the corner.

Turn left here into London Road and a three minute walk will bring you, on the right hand side, to the **Farmer's Boy (6)**. This modest one-bar pub suffered a spell as a wine and ale cafe but was rescued by spirited brewer Viv Davies who had formerly operated a brew pub ten miles away in Harpenden. He now has a micro-brewery at the back of the premises where he produces his house beers Verulam Special, Farmer's Joy and a particularly quaffable IPA – as well as dreaming up something out of the ordinary for St Albans annual beer festival run by South Herts CAMRA. It also sells Adnams Bitter and occasional guest beers and provides reasonable lunch time food including good home-made pies. With a real log fire the Farmer's Boy is an oasis almost halfway between the city centre and the railway station.

Anyone walking back to the station from here can carry on down London Road and turn left into Alma Road where, for many years, CAMRA had its HQ in a rambling Victorian house halfway along on the right. You will find the city station at the other end of Alma Road by crossing the rail bridge to your right.

SALFORD

If you want Coronation Street and the Rovers Return then cross the border into Manchester. If you want a crawl of good pubs selling very reasonably priced ale then stick to the Salford side. The best way to start this crawl is to take a train from one of the Manchester stations: Oxford Road, Piccadilly or Victoria and book through to Salford Crescent. Salford Central might sound attractive but it lands you in the middle of the crawl and is only open during commuter hours. Turn left outside the station and walk along the Crescent (the A6) towards Manchester. If your taste is for art then you are in luck for on your immediate left is the Museum and Art Gallery in which you will find a fine collection of the works of local artist L S Lowry. Spend an hour here if you can but other pleasures await.

Opposite a bow of the River Irwell where Manchester racecourse used to be is **The Crescent (1)**, a popular rambling three-roomed freehouse that opens all day during the week and serves food until 8pm. University folk like this pub and the fact that it has been in the *Good Beer Guide* for more than a decade is clearly understandable. The beer range varies but there are never less than six cask beers, including a house beer from the Titantic brewery. Carry on along the Crescent until its junction with Oldfield Road and half-right spot ***The Jollies (2)*** just behind the statue of the soldier. It sells John Willy Lees beers.

Below: The Kings Arms Ale House.

A hundred yards further on and opposite the Roman Catholic cathedral is **Ye Olde Nelson (3)**. It is an old-fashioned pub with lots of etched glass, brass and mirrors and is described in the *Good Beer Guide* as 'a Victorian gem'. There are several rooms and there is an unusual sliding door to the large front vault. This is a good and quite rare outlet for Chester's Mild, a beer that was once brewed just along the road at the former Threlfall's brewery and known by the sobriquet of 'Chester's Fighting Mild'. It also sells three bitters from Boddington's, Lees and

Whitbread. Overnight accommodation is available and families are welcome.

Continue along Chapel Street turning right into New Bailey Street and ten yards along is Gore Street and **The Egerton Arms (4)**. This is a free house with a separate vault and a comfortable lounge selling a good selection of beers: Holt's Mild and Bitter, Lees Bitter and Marston's Bitter. The lunch time food is excellent and consequently it can get rather full. Coronation Street fans will enjoy the plaque outside the gents' toilet.

Below: *Eagle Inn.*

On leaving, cross the A6 at the traffic lights and go up Bloom Street. ***The Salford Arms*** sells Gray's Bitter (brewed by Mansfield) at a very cheap price. But your real destination is fifty yards further on, **The Kings Arms Ale House (5)**. This is a listed building and the interior is completely unspoiled. The bar caters for a large main room and a snug is served by a small counter. Beers from Bridgewater Ales are on regular sale and there is a house beer – Festival Bitter – and four guest ales along with a traditional cider and a range of Belgian beers. This classic pub is often used for filming and was seen in the television series Cracker and the film Resurrection Man.

The next call is not easy to find but the visit is essential for no pub crawl of Salford would be complete without visiting a Holt's tied house. So try this. Turn left from the Kings Arms up to the Inner Ring Road. Turn right and follow the road towards Manchester and when you reach the Renault showrooms look to your right and there, set back about fifty yards, is **The Eagle Inn (6)**. It is known locally as the

'Lampoil'. This is a classic Holt's back street alehouse, completely unspoiled with several rooms and a drinking corridor and typical Holt's prices. There is a Manchester dartboard in the tap room and a small library in the parlour and more atmosphere than you could shake a stick at.

Complete the crawl by walking back to the Inner Ring Road, turn right and after taking in the aroma of Boddington's brewery find yourself at the back entrance to Victoria station from where you can catch a tram to Piccadilly station.

Top: *Ye Olde Nelson.*
Bottom: *The Crescent.*

SEVERN VALLEY RAILWAY

For some good reason steam railways and real ale seem to go together. So the opportunity to travel on the country's busiest steam line, to sample real ale not only at both terminal stations but at some of the stops between, make this pub crawl something different. There are snags of course. The railway timetable must be kept to and if the beer at a particular pub is so good that one is not enough and a train is missed then the next intended stop may have to be missed out. At best there are ten trains each day but on most days there are only six so you have to be careful. And you also need to fit in your journey with the opening times of the pubs. The best advice is to obtain a timetable by either writing to The Severn Valley Railway, The Railway Station, Bewdley, Worcestershire, DY12 1BG or telephoning 01299 403816. This also contains lots of detail about concessionary tickets, special weekends and restaurant car services There is also a talking timetable on 01299 401001. Reaching the railway is best travelling by British Rail (or whatever it's called these days) to Kidderminster which has direct lines to Worcester, Hereford and Birmingham. The two stations are a few yards apart.

The Severn Valley station at Kidderminster opens early for breakfasts in the cafe. There is also a museum with lots of railway artefacts to which admission is free. In front of the museum is a miniature railway on which children can take a ride. ***The King and Castle*** is part of the station buildings and is an authentic recreation of a 1930s station bar and buffet. There is one bar where a wide range of beers is served with regulars Batham Best Bitter, Marston's Pedigree, Ansells Mild and a selection from Hobsons, Enville and other local breweries. Meals are served at lunch times and in the evenings from Thursday through to Sunday. The bar closes in the afternoons except at weekends. There is full wheelchair access and children are allowed in until 9 p.m.

Choose your train. Some folk choose merely to travel from one end of the line to the other and sample the beers at the two excellent pubs at the termini. The line runs through the beautiful and unspoilt countryside of the Severn Valley and provides several stops, some close to excellent pubs with others a short scenic walk away. The picturesque town of Bewdley which is the first stop just a quarter of an hour from Kidderminster has three excellent pubs close to the railway station which form a mini-crawl. Leave by Station Drive turning right into Stourport Street and then left into Load Street and on the right is **The George Hotel (1)** a town centre hotel with a small, popular bar entered from a side passage and a lounge at the front. It sells Ind Coope Burton Ale, Tetley Bitter and a regularly changing guest beer. Retrace your steps and turn left into Severnside North and backing on to the river with a view of Telford's bridge is the **Cock and Magpie (2)** which is a Banks's house in the traditional style with two rooms. It sells Banks's Mild and Bitter. Summer drinking often spills out on to the front of the pub. Go back towards the station but at Westbourne Street turn left and go under the railway into Kidderminster Road and on the immediate right is the **Great Western (3)** which sells Banks's Bitter and Mild, Hanson's Mild, Cameron Strongarm along with guests such as Morrells Varsity and Marston's Pedigree. There is a bowl of nuts (real metal ones!) on the bar and there is a record of how high people have stacked them. A blackboard outside has some amusing messages, such as when the River Severn flooded and covered the road it read: "Warning – big puddle ahead".

Top: *The King and Castle on Kidderminster platform.* Bottom: *Pedestrian Ferry, Hampton Loade.*

Follow your nose for the way back to the station. If you can tear yourself away from Bewdley then catch the next train north and alight at Arley which was the star in the recent BBC television comedy series 'Oh Doctor Beeching'. Miss out the pub by the river (The

Harbour) and walk up the hill (about one mile) to Pound Green for the **New Inn**. This one-bar pub with several drinking areas serves Banks's Mild, Draught Bass and guest ales. Live music is spontaneous and piano and accordion players are made most welcome. It is open lunch times at weekends and early evening and meals are served at all sessions. Families are welcome and outdoor drinking is encouraged in good weather. If you are too tired to climb the hill then cross the footbridge to the tea rooms at the post office. It makes a change.

Walk back down the hill to catch the next train to the stop at Hampton Loade. Go down to the river and cross it by the wonderful pedestrian ferry. Then walk about half a mile to the **Lion Inn** a splendid country pub with characterful bars. It sells Hook Norton Old Hooky, Boddington's Bitter and guest beers usually from local breweries. The pub closes in the afternoons but good home-cooked food is served at all sessions. There is a large garden to which families are welcome. Go back across the ferry to catch the next north-bound train to Bridgnorth and the **Railwayman's Arms** which is on the platform. It is in the former station waiting room In addition to selling Batham Best Bitter there are three regularly changing guest beers from small independent and often local breweries, a traditional cider, and a good range of malt whiskies. Hot snacks are usually available. The bar is full of an amazing collection of railway memorabilia. If you have time there is a crawl around Bridgnorth in this book (No. 5). Otherwise your return train awaits.

Below: Lion Inn, Hampton Loade.

Another good connection between the terminal stations is the CAMRA Beer Festival held each year on the last weekend of September. It is held in tents on the platforms with beers from the north at Bridgnorth and those from the south at Kidderminster. Entry is free and there are around thirty beers to sample.

SHEFFIELD

Sheffield, the steel city, is also the welcoming city and like many other large cities in Britain is taking advantage of the changing tastes for leisure by attracting visitors from all over the world. It is a great sporting and cultural centre and its modern transport system allows effortless ease of movement particularly between its pubs. Try this for a crawl with a difference then: it's by tram. Most of the way that is. It starts from Sheffield's main railway station from where you take a Supertram heading north-west to either Middlewood or Malin Bridge. If you have plenty of time go all the way to the Bamforth Street stop and your first pub is close by. If time is limited then alight at the Shalesmoor stop and start at the third pub. A Day Rider ticket is available on the trams which provides unlimited travel and is highly recommended for this crawl.

Two minutes down the hill from the Bamforth Road tram stop is the **New Barrack Tavern (1)** in Penistone Road. It is a free house that attracts locals and CAMRA members. There are three large rooms and a beer garden. It is usually quiet but there is live music on some evenings. Food is served at lunch times and early evenings. There are eight real ales including Stones Bitter, Barnsley Bitter and IPA, John Smith Magnet and guest beers, some of which come from the local Abbeydale Brewery, as well as a traditional cider.

Take the tram to Infirmary Road and a short walk will bring you to the **Gardeners Arms (2)** opposite the now closed Stones brewery. This is a genuine free house offering a range of beers from Timothy Taylor of Keighley along with several guests on either handpull or gravity and including a brewery of the month choice. The pub features regular live music sessions and art exhibitions and has one of the few bar billiard tables left in the city.

Back on the tram for the Shalesmoor stop and the **Cask and Cutler (3)** in Henry Street. It is a free house popular with locals and CAMRA members, including many from outside Sheffield. It was Sheffield CAMRA's Pub of the Year in 1995. There are two rooms, one of which is non smoking.

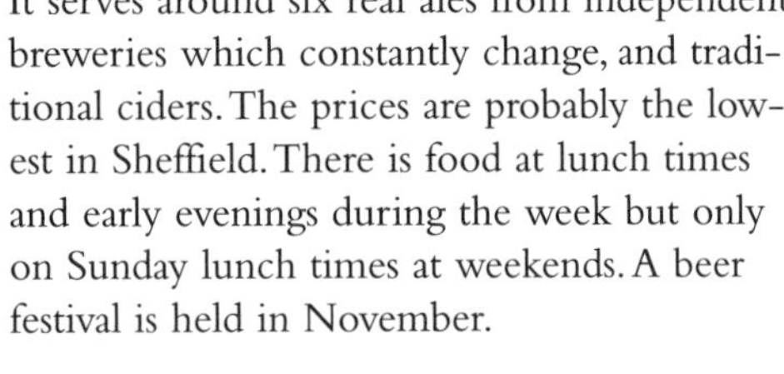

It serves around six real ales from independent breweries which constantly change, and traditional ciders. The prices are probably the lowest in Sheffield. There is food at lunch times and early evenings during the week but only on Sunday lunch times at weekends. A beer festival is held in November.

There is a short walk to the **Fat Cat (4)** which is in Alma Street. This is another free house, frequented by students and anyone else who has had the good sense to hunt it out. It is near to the Kelham Island Industrial Museum. This was the local CAMRA's Pub of the Year in 1996. There are two rooms downstairs, plus a beer garden, and a function room upstairs. It serves good reasonably priced food with many veggie options. There are ten real ales on sale, two of which are from the attached Kelham Island brewery, and a traditional cider. There is a beer festival in August.

Top: *Foundry & Firkin.* Bottom: *New Barrack Tavern.*

From Shalesmoor take the tram to West Street for the next three pubs. Walk back a few yards to the **Foundry and Firkin (5)** which is part of Allied Domecq's Firkin Chain. It is very popular with students and suits at lunch times and busy at weekends. This is a bare boards ale house with assorted games machines and live music some evenings. Beers are brewed on the premises, including some seasonal brews. Food is available up to 7 p.m. There is live music on Sundays.

Opposite the West Street tram stop is the **Hallamshire Hotel (6)**, the first of Tetley's Festival Inns and Taverns. Behind the impressive tiled Gilmour's frontage lies an equally impressive refurbishment. Tetley Bitter, Taylor Landlord and Marston's Pedigree are sold along with two or three guest ales. This popular town centre pub can get very busy at weekends.

Across West street in Division Street is the **Frog and Parrot (7)** a Whitbread brew pub that attracts town centre trade and is popular with students. It has a large split level room. The brewery has recently been refurbished and tours are available. Seven real ales are sold along with a traditional cider. It occasionally produces Roger and Out with a strength of 12.5% abv in both draught and bottle conditioned form. Food is available at lunch times.

You can either walk or ride to the **Hogshead (8)** in Orchard Square. Leave the tram at the City Hall stop. This is a Whitbread Ale House attracting town trade and is busy in the evenings. It is a small, split level pub with bare boards and a cafe at the back. Beers include Boddington's Bitter, Marston's Pedigree, Whitbread Abroad Cooper and three or four changing guest beers along with traditional ciders. Food is served at lunch times and breakfast is available from 9.30 a.m.

Again you have the choice of a walk or a ride to the next pub and either way you will go close to Sheffield Cathedral which has fifteenth-century origins but was largely rebuilt sixty years ago. In Yorkshire terms 'it's nowt special'. By tram alight at Castle Square for the **Bankers Draft (9)** in Market Place. This is a Wetherspoon's pub with a catholic popularity. It is large as you might expect with the conversion of a bank. There are bars on two floors and non smoking areas on both levels. Beers are reasonably priced and include Taylor Landlord, Courage Directors, Tetley Bitter, Theakston Best Bitter and three changing guest ales. Food is served all day until 10 p.m. There is no jukebox or canned music and there is provision for the disabled. Sadly, after all this good news, the toilets are a long walk away with stairs to negotiate. Take the tram again to return to the railway station.

A glance at the map will show you that there is a good deal of flexibility in this crawl. It could, for example, include the first four pubs and the last. Or you can work out one for yourself. It depends on how much time you have – and your capacity!

SHIELDS

Nestling on the banks at the mouth of the River Tyne are the twin towns of South and North Shields with the passenger ferry linking the two. South Shields is at the heart of the Catherine Cookson tourist area and boasts excellent beaches, an amusement park, the Arbeia Roman fort, camping facilities, the Lea's national conservation area and the oldest preserved lifeboat. During October the town also plays host to 40,000 competitors finishing the Great North Run. North Shields is the smaller of the two and is a fishing town based around the fish quay. There is a popular water adventure pool, an annual arts festival and it is the car ferry terminal for Scandinavia and Germany. Both towns are well served by the local Metro train and bus services.

Start in South Shields at the Chichester Metro station. Out of town visitors may wish to make use of the Day Rover ticket for travel on all buses, the Metro and the ferry, it costs £3.50 and can be bought from tourist information centres and major Metro stations. Turn left you are at the first stop the **Chichester Arms (1)**. This large town house has a large bar and comfortable lounge and serves good value, home cooked meals until 2 p.m. The ales on offer are Tetley Bitter, Ind Coope Burton Ale and two guest beers.

Head back and through the Metro station and turn right into Beaufront Terrace and follow the road round and down Laygate. Continue past the roundabout and though the small shopping area. At the junction of Laygate and Commercial Road you will find the *Good Beer Guide* listed **Dolly Peel (2)** on the left. This two-roomed pub is named after a legendary fishwife cum smuggler who had many run ins with the local press gangs. It sells Taylor Landlord, Courage Directors, Black Sheep Special, a house beer from Durham Brewery and two guest ales, with snacks and sandwiches. Of interest is the three-lanterned street light that forms a stand in the main bar.

Head down Commercial Road passing the new courts and police station on the right to come to **Riverside Public House (3)** at the top of the Mill Dam conservation area.

This thriving freehouse has had a chequered past but now proclaims 'Beers from around the UK' as a slogan on the smartly uniformed staff. Permanently on sale are Taylor Landlord. Courage Directors, Theakston Best Bitter and these are complimented by three guest ales. Also available is real cider and snacks and sandwiches Nearby in Coronation Street and worth a visit if time permits is the ***Steamboat (4)***, a nautical pub steeped in tradition that sells Vaux beers.

Head towards the Market Place where you will see the old Town Hall sitting squarely in the middle. Take the first left at the roundabout into Ferry Street and on the left you will find the **Alum Ale House (5)**. This is one of the oldest buildings in South Shields with records dating back to 1763. Up to 1936 it was the William Wood's brewery tap but then was used as offices in the local lead mining industry. The Alum was reborn in 1993 and features an open plan bar area with a downstairs function room cum cellar jazz club. Beers on offer are Cameron's Strongarm, Banks's Bitter and Marston's Pedigree along with three guest ales. Food is simple – snacks, sandwiches and soup.

Turn right out of the Alum, heading to the river and the new ferry landing and the passenger ferry to the Royal Quays (for the shops and water amusement park) and to North Shields. Ferries from South Shields leave at quarter past and quarter to the hour through the day but do not run on Sunday evenings. The journey takes about seven minutes and excellent views of the industrial banks of the Tyne can be seen. North Shields is also easily accessible by public transport from Newcastle by Metro or bus.

Alighting at the ferry landing, turn right along New Quay and you will find the **Port Hole (6)**. This nautically themed pub offers good value food at both the bar and in the small restaurant. It sells Theakston Best Bitter, Courage Directors and a national guest beer that is usually either Marston's Pedigree or Fuller's London Pride.

Go left along Clive Street then up the steps to the **Magnesia Bank (7)** in Camden Street. This CAMRA award-winning pub overlooks the Tyne. It was once a bank and then a club and the building lay derelict until 1990 when it was refurbished to its present excellent state. It is now renowned for a wide selection of beers served in over-sized glasses and also has a reputation for fine food. Local brewers are always well represented in the pub; Durham Magus, Mordue Workie Ticket and Maggie Mayhem, and Castle Eden Nimmos XXXX are staples and are accompanied by a variety of guest beers. An open plan interior provides a number of separate areas for eating and drinking in comfort. The pub has a diary of monthly events including live music in the bar and in the upstairs Bank Suite. There is a montage of photographs of the Lindisfarne folk group as well as old theatrical fliers on the walls of the pub.

The trail heads westward past the ***Garrick's Head (8)*** an excellent refurbishment of what used to be a garish disco bar. Beers include Draught Bass, Morland Old Speckled Hen, Courage Directors, John Smith Bitter and a guest. Another excellent refurbishment just off our trail is the ***Colonel Linskill (9)*** in Charlotte Street which sells Taylor Landlord and up to six guest ales. The trail now goes north, across Tynemouth Road to the **Tap and Spile (10)**. This was formerly the Victoria before opening as the region's second Tap and Spile in the late 1980s. This two room pub always seeks to provide a range of locally brewed beers and a combination of session beers and higher gravity ales and cider. It is rated as one of the

Top: *Chichester Arms.* Bottom: *Ferry across the Tyne.*

best in the Tap and Spile range. The beer range varies but often includes a choice from Hambleton and Durham. It serves food at lunch times.

Follow Tynemouth Road towards Tynemouth and continue down the hill to the **Tynemouth Lodge (11)** a freehouse that was built in 1770. The pub is actually in Tynemouth although the road sign would have you believe you were still in North Shields. Belhaven 80/-, Draught Bass and occasional guest beers are on the beer menu in this two-roomed comfortable hostelry, which can get busy on weekend evenings.

The adjoining buildings are under the same ownership as the Tynemouth Lodge and have their own blue plaque explaining that the living quarters of the pub were once a kitchen providing sustenance for the House of Correction next door. Beyond the pub is the Governor's Tree where another blue plaque outlines the history of this site which dates back to the time when the Pow Burn was a navigable river and ran along the course of what is now Tynemouth Road.

Above: The Dolly Peel.

To get to Tynemouth station go past the architecturally impressive Master Mariners Asylum built in the mid-nineteenth century as North Shields and Tynemouth began their rise to industrial prominence as port and resort for the Tyneside conurbation. Keep on along Tynemouth Road and bear left for the station. Newcastle is about twenty minutes by Metro through North Shields or half an hour using the coast route and through Gosforth.

STALYBRIDGE

Stalybridge was one of the most important cotton towns of the Greater Manchester area and also in the heart of the Chartist movement. Frederich Engels, the political theorist and friend of Karl Marx, often visited the town and described it as '...disgustingly filthy town...in a beautiful setting'.

Unique is a word that cannot be qualified and this crawl is unique. The 'Stalybridge Eight' starts at the pub in the United Kingdom with the shortest name and finishes at the one with the longest. And both these pubs are recognised in the Guinness Book of Records. Beat that! And you can record your crawl by buying a passport at the first pub and having it stamped at each pub on the way round.

The Q (1) which is close to Stalybridge railway station started life as a mill manager's residence in 1785. It has had various lives and the contents from its period as a bespoke shoemaker's shop are in a local museum. Marston's Bitter and Pedigree are on regular sale here along with at least three guest beers. Sandwiches and bar snacks are available and a traditional Sunday lunch is served. There is jazz on Monday evenings. Be sure to visit the upstairs cocktail bar and conservatory.

Move across to platform 1 of the station to the **Station Buffet (2)**. Although it is not the only buffet bar of this sort and can make no claim to uniqueness, it is the best known and best loved of the genre. It has remained unchanged since 1885 and there was a forerunner dating from 1845. Records show that in the 1870s a local man was given seven days hard labour for pinching a glass worth sixpence from the bar. Attempts by the rail authorities to demolish the property a few years ago met with fierce opposition from many folk, not least the local CAMRA branch. A high quality refurbishment followed which, ironically, received an award for the best heritage work on a railway building and a plaque records this. It has also been extended and now boasts two bars. And now it has won the Best Refurbishment category in the English Heritage/CAMRA pub design awards. On regular sale are Boddington's Bitter,

Wadworth 6X and Flowers IPA along with up to six guest beers, a traditional cider and bottled beers from Belgium. Bar snacks are available, including the famous black peas. Saturday is folk night and big crowds from far and wide assemble. There are periodic beer festivals.

Retrace your steps passing the Q Inn to the next door **Rose and Crown (3)** which was built in 1845. In 1892 it was bought by Shaw's of Dukinfield, a brewery that was taken over by John Smith's of Tadcaster in 1941. This is a friendly pub which has been tastefully restored to respect its history. At one time this and the many other pubs in Market Street – there were more than forty of them – served the workers in the town's cotton mills. Now it has a loyal band of locals who enjoy its atmosphere; it is a hub of community life. Vaux Mild, Bitter and Samson are sold here with regular guest beers and seasonal specials.

Top: *White House.* Bottom: *The Old Thirteenth Cheshire Astley Volunteer Rifleman Corps Inn.*

Turn right and move along Market street to the **Old Fleece (4)**. It was built as a coaching inn in 1803 and called the Golden Lion. The present name dates from 1842. In 1860 Sam Hurst, the 'Stalybridge Infant', lived here. He was a champion prize fighter with an awesome reputation which lasted until, following a good night out, he fell down the backyard steps and never recovered his championship form. John Smith's and Boddington's bitters are sold in this busy town centre pub and there is a wide range of bar snacks. The pub is open all day during the week.

Walk a few yards along Market Street, turning right into Water Street for the **White House (5)**. The fine old building started life as a woollen clothiers in 1729 and a century later became a wine and spirits merchant. Ten years on it became a pub known as Heap's Vaults named after the owner and has remained in the same business for more than a century and a half. This enterprising house is friendly and popular and has something for everybody. Choose to drink in either the front parlour, the main lounge or the bar and games room. There are Marston's Bitter and Pedigree and Thwaites Bitter on regular sale with up to five guest beers along with the choice of fifty foreign bottled beers, fifty malt whiskies and snacks and sandwiches served all day. There is a folk club on Thursday evenings. To add to your pleasure the pub has a friendly ghost! Water Street leads into Caroline Street and here on the right is the **Wellington Inn (6)**. This is a popular town centre pub catering for a regular trade and it dates from 1856 when it opened as an ale house. Not much has changed; it retains two rooms – a lounge and a tap room – and beer is all important. Boddington's Bitter is on sale and sandwiches are available at lunch times. The pub is open all day except Sundays when it shuts down during the afternoon.

Go to the High Street, turn left and along to Kenworthy Street on the right to find the **Pineapple (7)**. The pub opened in 1837, the year of Queen Victoria's coronation. The owner was John Kenworthy who probably built the street and named it after himself – a common practice in those days. This stone built pub has three comfortable rooms and sells beers from Robinson's – always the Best Bitter and maybe the Hatters Mild. There are sandwiches and bar snacks and a traditional Sunday lunch. The pub is open all day on Fridays and Saturdays.

Turn left on leaving the pub then first right, first left and follow the road round until you reach Astley Street and on the right is **The Old Thirteenth Cheshire Astley Volunteer Rifleman Corps Inn (8)**. It is a bit of a mouthful and a bit of a walk but well worth it in the end. It is officially recognised by the Guinness Book of Records as the pub with the longest name in Britain, with 55 letters. This delightful Victorian terraced inn with great views over the town first opened as a beer house in 1855 close to the drill hall for the volunteer militia, the forerunner of the Territorial Army. The militia's job was somewhat different to the TA for they were required to put down civil uprisings and were often used in Stalybridge during the Chartist riots. There are many photographic memories of the area in former times and much militaria. John Smith's Bitter and a couple of guest beers may be on sale but the beer range is flexible. The pub opens from 3 p.m. (sometimes earlier) until 11 p.m. except Sundays when it closes during the afternoon. This is a friendly and welcoming pub and a good choice to end the crawl on and then take a gentle stroll back to the railway station. Perhaps there may be time for another pint.

At the time of writing this book, Stalybridge was going through a pub boom with a number of new pubs opening. Much of this activity is associated with the completion of the restoration of the Huddersfield Narrow Canal and the anticipated tourist trade. Two of the new pubs are on the route of this crawl. Between the Rose and Crown (3) and the Old Fleece (4) is the ***Pavilion*** which is described as being decked out in 'traditional Victorian' style. And between the White House (5) and the Wellington (6) a former plumbers' merchant's premises have become the ***Bridge Inn*** and is in the same ownership as Q and the White House.

STOCKPORT

Although historically it is part of Cheshire Stockport is one of Manchester's major satellites. Essentially it is an industrial town which has suffered extensive redevelopment but it retains some areas of surprising character and historic interest, especially around the market place. Stockport is the home of Robinson's, one of the largest remaining family brewers, whose brewery stands on a cramped site right in the town centre. It also boasts one of the finest selections of unspoilt pubs in the country, with five entries on CAMRA's National Inventory of pub interiors within a mile of the town centre, three of which are visited on this crawl.

The town is dominated by the gigantic viaduct which dates from 1840 and claims to be the largest brick structure in the world. It carries the main Manchester to London railway line across the steep-sided valley of the River Mersey. Right under the viaduct on Heaton Lane is your first pub, the **Crown (1)**, which once enjoyed the splendid description in the *Good Beer Guide*: 'Awesome view of the viaduct from the outside gents'. Inevitably, the wind of change has overtaken this, and the toilets are now inside – whether this constitutes progress is up to you to decide. The former multi-roomed character of the pub has been eroded by being opened out a little, but it retains a distinct vault and three drinking areas opening off the main bar which would qualify as separate rooms were it not for the absence of doors. When owned by Boddington's it was converted to an alehouse format and since then it has offered the widest choice of real ales in Stockport, with up to ten available at any one time, particularly featuring local micros such as Phoenix and Whim. However choice has not been achieved at the expense of quality and the Crown features regularly in the *Good Beer Guide*. It can be quiet at lunch times, but becomes very busy and lively in the evenings, especially towards the end of the week.

From the Crown turn left up Heaton Lane, then cross the A6 in Mersey Square by Debenham's and continue straight on down Princes Street to reach the **Swan With Two**

Necks (2) ▮, on your left about half-way along. This is a small pub in a terrace of shops, a rare survivor in the kind of location where pubs are increasingly being turned over to retail use. It has an unspoilt 1920s interior making extensive use of light oak panelling, with the superb top-lit snug behind the bar being the best feature. Robinson's Hatters Mild and Best Bitter are available on handpump. In contrast to the Crown, the Swan can be very busy at lunch times but is often quieter in the evenings, when it closes early on Mondays and Tuesdays. Follow Princes Street along to the end where you could put your nose around the door of the ***Tiviot (3)***, another Robinson's pub which has been altered rather more than the Swan, but still retains an atmosphere reminiscent of pubs thirty or forty years ago, and is popular with older regulars, particularly at lunch times. Otherwise, turn right to pass through a small paved square at the end of the Merseyway shopping precinct. Carry straight on along Bridge Street, then follow the road round to the right along Great Underbank. On the right along here is Underbank Hall, a 16th century half-timbered mansion which now forms part of the Natwest Bank.

At the small roundabout by the White Lion, turn left up Little Underbank, and the ▮**Queen's Head (4)** ▮ is on your right just before the bridge which carries St Petersgate across the street. This is another small, single-fronted pub which is also known as Turner's Vaults which goes back a long way. Into the late 1980s it retained an interior which had changed in few respects for 150 years. It was then in such poor repair that the new owners, Sam Smith's, had to effectively gut it and rebuild it as new, but the end result is so convincing that you would never guess it was not original. It was the deserved winner in 1991 of a CAMRA award for pub conservation. There are three rooms – a convivial front bar with a counter adorned by a wonderful set of spirit taps, a small, cosy, wood-panelled 'news room', and a slightly larger and smarter rear lounge. The only real ale available is Sam Smiths' Old Brewery Bitter, but you can also sample their extensive range of distinctive bottled beers. On the opposite side of the street, just past the bridge, Stockport town centre has recently gained its first Holt's outlet: **Winters (5)**. This former jeweller's shop had a chequered career as a wine bar before passing to Holt's in 1998. They have done an excellent job of refurbishing it, with a down-to-earth vault on the ground floor and a more comfortable lounge upstairs, from where the workings of the superbly restored ornamental clock can be viewed. Holt's Mild, Bitter and the new premium beer DBA are available at Holt's' usual bargain prices.

Return to the Queen's Head, and then take the steep flight of steps immediately opposite the pub which leads up to the level of St Petersgate and the Market Place. Dominated by the impressive iron-and-glass Victorian Market Hall, Stockport's Market Place is also home to five pubs, four of which between them are the centre of the live music scene in the town. All have their merits, but pick of the bunch is undoubtedly the **Baker's Vaults (6)**, on the left, an impressive free-standing pub built in the 1840s in the Italianate style. The interior is basically one large room, but it is divided by the central bar counter into distinct vault and lounge sides. On first entering, you could be forgiven for thinking that no real ale is available, as the bar sprouts nothing but Continental-style T-bars, but, rest assured, the Robinson's Hatters Mild and Best Bitter are definitely real, dispensed through free-flow electric pumps. A wide selection of high-quality home-made food is available at lunch times, when the pub is very popular with shoppers. Most evenings it gets extremely busy when its character changes into that of a buzzing live music venue, mainly featuring R'n'B and jazz.

Coming out of the Baker's Vaults, go straight ahead along the left-hand side of the Market Hall until you reach the Parish Church. Then turn left down Millgate and the **Arden Arms (7)** is on your left just by the mini-roundabout. This is a redbrick corner pub dating back to the 1830s. It retains a feature of early Victorian pubs which is exceptionally rare and may now even be unique namely a delightful, intimate snug at the rear of the bar which is part of the public drinking space, but can be reached only by walking through the serving area. The bar itself, partially encased by windowed panels, is another fine traditional element. There's also a lobby with an original tiled floor, a lounge on the apex of the building, and another lounge which has been created by extending the former vault. Robinson's Hatters Mild, Old Stockport and Best Bitter are dispensed from handpumps set against the back wall of the bar. Despite its outstanding architectural features the Arden Arms is a busy, down-to-earth local.

Turn left outside the Arden Arms, pass under the bridge linking the Asda superstore to its car park and then turn right at the traffic lights along Great Portwood Street. Your final call, the **Railway (8)**, is about two hundred yards along on the left, opposite a row of modern superstores. This pub went through various tacky incarnations as 'Cheekies' and 'Byrons' and seemed destined for closure until it was rescued in 1996 by Dave Porter, owner of the eponymous microbrewery based in Haslingden. It has now reverted to its original name – which relates to the old Cheshire Lines Railway which once ran through this part of the town – and has been transformed back into a proper pub. It is a fairly plain and unassuming single bar, but it is clean, pleasant, comfortable and welcoming and offers good home-made food at lunch times. The chief attraction though is the beer as it sells the full range of Porter's excellent, distinctive beers – Mild, Bitter, Rossendale Ale, Porter, the dangerously drinkable Sunshine, a house beer called Railway Sleeper together with various one-off brews and real cider too. The prices are very reasonable. Not surprisingly, the Railway has rapidly established itself as a favourite amongst Stockport drinkers and can have a lively atmosphere in the evenings. It is open all day apart from Sundays and Bank Holidays when it closes in the afternoon.

Public Transport: The Crown is five minutes walk from Stockport bus station and less than ten minutes from the railway station. The very frequent 192 bus service from Manchester along the A6 bypasses the bus station, but stops only a couple of hundred yards away. The Railway is about fifteen to twenty minutes walk from both the bus and rail stations, and for the extremely lazy, is served by numerous buses from Stockport in the direction of Brinnington and Bredbury, such as the 330.

The Queen's Head is the starting point for the annual Hillgate Crawl which has takes place on the last Friday before Christmas, and must be one of the longest-running fixtures in the CAMRA calendar. Often attracting more than fifty people, this takes in the fifteen or so extremely varied pubs – some superb, some average – up the three-quarters of a mile of Hillgate, finishing at the Blossoms which is a largely unspoilt multi-roomed Robinson's pub which is well worth a visit.

SWINDON

Swindon is a town of two centres. Near the railway station is New Swindon, dating from the 1840s onwards and inextricably tied up with the fortunes of the Great Western railway works. At the top of the hill is Old Swindon, formerly a small market town with its success based on its limestone quarries. The coming of the canal in the 1790s boosted the output of stone and brought a spell of prosperity to the town. An unfortunate side-effect was that all the old pubs got rebuilt and there is nothing in this part of town that one could now call quaint or old-fashioned.

After the repeal of the Beerhouse Act in 1869 the magistrates were very strict and few new pubs opened. In fact, Swindon, with three times its population, had a similar number of pubs to Salisbury. Consequently, brewers have over the years concentrated their money into the comparatively few pubs in the town so, sadly, no original interiors remain. Nevertheless there are some pubs of character, although their existence is probably more due to accident than design!

Commencing at the railway station turn right and walk towards the Railway Village which was built to accommodate the first employees of the works. Adjoining the sadly derelict Mechanics' Institute in Emlyn Square is the **Glue Pot (1)**, Archers only tied house in Swindon. It originated as a grocers and beer shop in the 1850s and was later known as the London Stout Tavern. It is a cheerful one-bar pub with a mainly local clientele and keeps the full range of Archers beers and a guest beer. Meals are served at lunch times. Possibly because this is a listed building the keg dispensers are hidden under the bar!

Just to the west of the Mechanics' Institute is the **Bakers Arms (2)**, another former beer shop. This was also a bakery and remains of the oven may be found in the cosy little back bar along with a fine large scale model of a GWR locomotive. Once again this is a locals' pub and serves good pints of Arkell's 2B and 3B, the other local brewer's beer. Live music at weekends. Yet another listed building.

Top: *The Duke of Wellington.* Bottom: *Kings Arms Hotel.*

The Cricketers (3) nearby, was the only purpose-built pub in the Railway Village and serves Ushers beers. It is very popular with the gay community. And another listed building!

It's now a bit of a trek to the next pubs, which are situated half way between the Old and New towns. Best to follow the map than be confused by intricate directions! **The Duke of Wellington (4)**, in Eastcott Hill, has interesting origins. The noble Duke was the originator of the Beerhouse Act of 1830. Under this Act any householder could sell beer without recourse to the magistrates. By 1869 the temperance movement was rampant and the Act was to be repealed. On learning this, John Arkell bought two newly constructed houses, knocked them into one and opened them as a Beer house just in time to avoid the new legislation. As a tribute to a national hero, and as a dig at the temperance movement he named the pub in the Duke's honour! It is a small locals' pub with a bar and a tiny snug. This is the only Arkell pub that serves beer (2B and 3B) by gravity direct from the cask.

The ***George (5)***, next door to the Duke of Wellington is interesting for being the oldest surviving pub building in Swindon, dating from the middle of the eighteenth century, but it was not a pub until after 1830 – prior to that it was a farm. It sells Courage Best Bitter, Marston's Pedigree and Wadworth 6X.

It is but a short walk (turn right, right and right again) to the **Beehive (6)** in Prospect Hill, one of only two Morrells pubs in Swindon. Possibly the town's most characterful (and character-full) pub, it comprises

a series of small rooms. Situated on a steep hill with every room on a different level. Beers are Morrell's Varsity Bitter and a guest beer. The pub itself is the haunt of students of all ages – 18 to 70 – bikers and boozers. Sunday lunch times feature rock bands – Charlie Watts even played here once.

Wander down Union Street into Albert Street for the **Rising Sun (7)**, which is just behind the newspaper offices. This is a small stone-built back street local dating from the 1840s, when it was known as the Heart in Hand. However, to all Swindonians it's the Roaring Donkey, apparently named after the beast that a landlord kept in the back yard many years ago. There's a busy public bar with a pool table and a tiny flagstone floored lounge. It enjoys a mainly local trade and offers the full Usher beer range along with Courage Best Bitter and real draught cider. It is open all day.

Just around the corner in Wood Street is the **Kings Arms (8)** a busy, single-bar hotel that sells Arkell's 2B, 3B and Kingsdown and serves meals lunch times and evenings. It is a listed building. The original building dates from 1835 when it was also a bakery. Overnight accommodation is available and bearing this in mind it is worth mentioning that, time permitting there are some excellent village pubs near Swindon. Well worth a visit are the Carters Rest and Check Inn in Wroughton and the Plough, Harrow and Black Horse in Wanborough.

Top: *Bakers Arms.*
Bottom: *Glue Pot.*

TAFF VALE

Visitors to Wales tend to head for the mountains or the coast. This pub crawl near Cardiff captures the spirit of South Wales. It takes you through the narrow pass where the hills of the old mining valleys reach down to the edge of the capital city on the coastal plain.

On one side the tight entrance of the Taff Valley is guarded by the romantic towers of Castell Coch (the Red Castle); on the other rises up the Garth, celebrated in the film The Englishman Who Went Up A Hill And Came Down A Mountain.

It is an area steeped in industrial history yet with startling scenery – and it boasts some good pubs. This lengthy crawl takes in six. Those seeking a less strenuous challenge, could omit the first two in Tongwynlais. Those wanting only a short stroll, can just wander down the road between the last three.

To reach the start take the Valleys Line from Cardiff Central station. Trains for Treherbert, Merthyr Tydfil and Aberdare all pass this way. Those wishing to enjoy a pleasant half-hour riverside stroll to the first pub, should get off at Radyr station. Otherwise continue to the next stop at Taffs Well and walk back to Tongwynlais.

If you start at Radyr, cross over the river by the footbridge alongside the station and turn left along the Taff Trail. After passing a wide weir and going under the M4 motorway to reach an iron footbridge (giving good views of Castell Coch), turn away from the river up a tarmac road. At the top turn right and then left under the A470 dual carriageway. At the end of the street turn left into the centre of Tongwynlais and the first two pubs.

By the turning to Castell Coch stands the historic **Lewis Arms (1)**. As you approach you can see the castle peering over the roof. This palatial Brain's pub serves the full range of traditional beers from the Cardiff brewery from 11 a.m. during the week, though Brain's Dark is only on handpump in the wood-panelled public bar on the left. This bar also boasts a rarity for the area – bar billiards. The main lounge offers good food and the raised part on the right once rang with

the words of the preacher Christmas Evans in 1827, before the gospel and the glass parted company.

Suitably refreshed, you should wander up the hill and visit Castell Coch. The building of this fairytale castle in the trees was started in 1875 by the eccentric architect William Burges for the wealthy Lord Bute on the ruins of a 13th century fortification. Inside its round towers, their fantasy medieval world soars even higher, with extravagantly painted vaulted ceilings. It must be seen to be believed.

Top: *The Anchor.* Bottom: *Old Ton Inn.*

Back down the hill in the real world, drop into the **Old Ton Inn (2)** on the opposite side of the Merthyr Road from the Lewis Arms. This Whitbread house offers a small range of handpulled beers including Wadworth 6X and Marston's Pedigree. There is a comfortable lounge on the left and a popular bar with a pool table on the right. It also has a beer garden and a skittle alley.

Pull back on your walking boots for a half-hour trek across the valley. Continue on the Merthyr Road to the main roundabout above the A470 next to a sheer rock face. Go left across the River Taff, with the old stone bridge on your left, and turn right at the next roundabout towards Pentyrch. Busy roads now dominate this narrow pass but note the tall pillars of a former railway viaduct. Pass a few turnings to the right and, just before the road goes sharply uphill, turn right to Gwaelod-y-Garth,

Follow the narrow road beneath the hill until you reach the **Gwaelod-y-Garth Inn (3)** on the left. It's tempting just to sit outside on the benches and enjoy the fine views back across the valley, but it's worth venturing inside to see a remarkable wooden price list to the left of the bar. It advertises Fernvale ale at 1s 1d a pint along with Watney's at 1s 8d, plus Webbs bottled beers. All have now vanished, but you can still buy Hancock HB and the odd guest beer for a slightly higher price. There are also old water jugs hanging from the beams and a pool table in the saloon to the right.

Retrace your steps slightly down the road and then go down a public footpath marked to the left. Steep steps lead to a footbridge across the river. Cross and follow the path straight forward past a school to the old road running through Taffs Well.

Immediately on your right is the striking black and white **Taffs Well Inn (4).** This comfortable house offers hand-pumped Tetley Bitter and Draught Bass. A beer garden behind overlooks a park. Among the park's attractions is the healing well after which the village and pub are named. Like the next two pubs, the Taffs Well has a good food menu.

A short stroll up the road to the left and over the railway line leads to **Fagin's Ale and Chop House (5)**. Despite being tucked into a small row of terraced houses, this gem of a free house in the hamlet of Glan-y-Llyn offers one of the widest ranges of real ales in the Cardiff area, some served from casks on stillage behind the bar. There are usually ten to twelve to choose from including Brain's SA, Caledonian Deuchars, 80/- and IPA and Courage Directors. There are occasional beer festivals. Food is served in the evenings from Tuesdays to Saturdays. Note also the stone-flagged floor and odd sayings in 'Wenglish' chalked on the beams.

If you can drag yourself away, walk back past the Taffs Well Inn and along the Cardiff Road to the **Anchor Inn (6)** on the left, close to Taffs Well station. While you wait for the train back to Cardiff, you can enjoy a final pint of Brain's Bitter, Wadworth 6X or Marston's Pedigree. Those who have booked could also try the rare delights of the restaurant which offers Mongolian cuisine.

WALSALL

The football team's nickname – the Saddlers – recalls an era when the town was the heart of the saddle making industry. Today it is much more diversfied in its industries. St Matthew's church is the oldest building in the town with an early thirteenth-century crypt. Jerome K Jerome, author of Three Men in a Boat, was born here and he was a man who knew his pubs and enjoyed a drink.

This crawl can be covered easily on foot, starting at the railway station in Station Street. Leave the station, turn right along Station Street then right again into Park Street. Continue along Park Street onto The Bridge, turning left onto St Paul's Street and at its junction with Bridge Street turn into Darwall Street. Here you will find the **Imperial (1),** a Weatherspoon pub in a converted cinema. Beware of Dinosaur attack!, Confused? Then see for yourself. It is a very impressive renovation with no expense spared. Usual Wetherspoon range of beers – Courage Directors and Theakston Best Bitter and several guests. There is a no music policy and a non-smoking area.

On leaving, turn right along Darwall Street, taking first right into Leicester Street. Continue along to the end, turn left into Lichfield Street, crossing the road to turn right into (narrow) Intown Row. Keep right past car park to junction with Lower Rushall Street, to find the **Victoria (2)**, a two room pub more reminiscent of a 1980s style wine bar although it dates back to 1848 and was originally called the Albert and Victoria and more recently Katz. It sells ABC Bitter, Greene King Abbot, Marston's Pedigree and up to three guest beers. This is a very popular pub which serves good value food. The nickname Katz was coined by Irish navvies whose slang name for Queen Victoria was 'The Cat'. Also of note is the former tower brewery at the back which now forms the living quarters of the pub.

From the Victoria, turn left down Intown Row and carry on to bottom of hill onto Lichfield Street, cross into Hatherton Road, turning right into Lower Forster Street. Here you will find the **Fountain (3)** which is another current *Good*

Top: *Littleton Arms.* Bottom: *The Katz as was – now The Victoria.*

Beer Guide entry serving Draught Bass, Highgate Mild and a guest beer. It is a classic two room pub with a bright saloon bar, a homely small lounge and a loggia. Very snug, must not be missed as this sort of pub seems to fall foul of pub planners who seem to think taking walls out and open planning are the 'in thing'.

Turn right from the Fountain along Lower Forster Street and at the junction of Littleton Street turn left and walk towards the traffic lights, taking the third right into Wisemore, passing the Leather Museum on right. The museum is situated in an old leather works and well worth a visit if you pass during the day. Continue along Wisemore into Garden Street then turn left at the end into Portland Street and right along Stafford Street. First right into John Street will take you to the **Tap and Spile (4)**, the 1997 CAMRA local branch Pub of the Year and a regular *Good Beer Guide* entry. It is known locally as the 'Pretty Bricks" because of the ceramic tiles on the frontage. The Tap and Spile is a two room pub with bright front bar featuring lots of wood and glass. There are eight regularly changing beers including Highgate Dark and excellent home cooked food with frequent theme nights in food – Mexican, Indian etc. This is a genuine pub where the decor matches the period and one not to be missed.

Leave the Tap and Spile and return to Stafford Street, turn left and continue along passing the Law Courts on the right. Turn right into Court Way and left into Green Lane for the **Oak (5)**. It is a regular *Good Beer Guide* entry and more than a century old. This one roomed

Above: The Fountain.

pub has an unusual island bar. Courage Best Bitter and four or five guest beers which change frequently are sold along with good value food. A vibrant pub in the evenings and busy with office workers and factory workers at lunch times. A friendly local with a warm welcome to all.

Turn left along Green Lane then right at end into Townend Bank and Wolverhampton Street, to be faced by the next pub **Wharf (6)**. This brand new pub built and owned by Highgate Brewery only opened in December 1997. It features acres of glass facing onto the canal wharf. With a totally wooden interior you could almost be in Sweden! Highgate's decision to build a brand new pub without any period parody caused some gasps when it was unveiled. It is not to everyone's taste architecturally but it was named the best new pub in Britain in the English Heritage/CAMRA awards. A full range of Highgate beers is available along with good food including breakfasts (available from 8 am). Live music and comedy nights are held regularly.

Leave the Wharf and continue back along Wolverhampton Street, past Woolworths and back into Park Street. Worth a look at is the ***Red Lion*** on the right. To get the best view, stand on the other side of the pedestrian area and look up to see the stone lion guarding the pub. An ongoing fight of twenty years by CAMRA and some keen local councillors eventually persuaded the town planners to build the new shops around the pub. Pass the Red Lion, turn right into Station Street and back to the railway station.

WHARFEDALE RAMBLE

This pleasant circular ramble through Upper Wharfedale links four charming pubs and can be either five miles or seven miles long. It is essentially a summer walk particularly if you use the bus services up the valley for out of season they are, to say the least, irregular. In addition to the pubs it takes in a delightful riverside walk, much of it on the Dales Way, lots of interesting wild life and some spectacular views. OS map 98 (Wensleydale and Wharfedale) or Touring map 6 (Yorkshire Dales) are helpful. Information on bus services can be obtained from Keighley and District Transport telephone number 01535 603284 or Pride of the Dales on 01756 753123. School bus services also take other passengers but do not run out of term times. It is best to plan the route carefully bearing in mind the opening hours of the pubs.

The best starting point is in Starbotton at the **Fox and Hounds (1)** a welcoming village inn with low beams, flagged floors and open fires. It serves above the average good value pub food including vegetarian choices. It also provides bed and breakfast. Handpumped beers include Taylor Landlord, Theakston Best Bitter and Old Peculier and Black Sheep Best with guest beers during the summer months. In summer it closes during the afternoons and on Monday evenings. In winter it is best to check its availability by phoning 0175 676 269. The pub has a sizeable car park but one needs to seek the approval of the landlord to use it whilst walking out from there.

Turn left on the main road towards Kettlewell – 300 yards along on your right is a footpath sign to Buckden. Go down a disused cart track and cross the River Wharfe by a footbridge then turn right and follow the river bank for 500 yards. The path then leaves the river and goes through meadows and alongside Firth Woods. In spring and summer there are many varieties of birds along this stretch and walkers have been rewarded by sightings of buzzards and more common birds such as curlews, mallards, shovellers and dippers. At Birks Wood the path rejoins the river and it is a flat easy walk to the bridge at Buckden. At this point you have a choice of routes, turning left and using the road or crossing

the road and continuing to follow the footpath by the river. Both routes lead to Hubberholme.

Here is the next pub **The George (2),** which nestles at the foot of the hills by the bridge. This 18th century white-washed pub comes as a welcome haven after the first hour's walk. In its early days it was a farmhouse and later the vicarage for St Michael's church across the bridge. Pub, church and bridge form Yorkshire's smallest conservation area. The pub still retains its stone-flagged floors, open fires, and mullion windows. There are five letting bedrooms. The blackboard menu has English, Thai and vegetarian dishes, home-made pies and soups and the beers include Black Sheep Special, Theakston Black Bull and Younger's Scotch Bitter. The pub closes in the afternoons. (Telephone number 0175 676 223)

Top: *Fox & Hounds.* Bottom: *The George Inn.*

Take time to visit the beautiful Norman church and in there view the memorial to Yorkshire's most famous author, J B Priestley, who claimed the George as his favourite pub. The church has the only rood loft in the former West Riding and the stalls were built by 'Mousey' Thompson of Kilburn.

Now go along the road on the north side of the river and just before a road junction take the footpath and the stiff climb up Cray Gill with views of the waterfalls on the left. You soon arrive in Cray at the **White Lion (3)** a seventeenth-century inn, the highest in Wharfedale. It was previously used by packhorse traders and drovers taking their cattle to markets in the midlands and London. Walkers are welcome here but you are expected to take off any muddy boots before entering. There is an open fire and stone flagged floors and the walls are covered with old farming imple-

ments. The interesting old game of Ring the Bull is played here. The beers are Moorhouse Premier and Pendle Witch, Tetley Bitter and occasional guests. There are some sophisticated dishes on the menu and lots of good plain food including casseroles and large Yorkshire puddings with various fillings. The pub is open all day in summer but closes during the afternoon in winter. Bed and breakfast is available with some bargain breaks in the winter. (Telephone: 0175 676 262)

From the White Lion cross the road and the stream by the stepping stones and follow the footpath signs for Buckden. There is a short sharp climb to join the ridge path which turns right along a well defined track which drops through Rakes Wood and ends up in Buckden car park. From the ridge the views over Upper Wharfedale are magnificent.

Above: The Buck Inn.

Cross the car park to **The Buck (4)** a splendid stone-faced country inn which faces the sloping village green. It was here at Christmas in 1945 that Denis and Edna (now Lord and Lady) Healey spent their honeymoon in the loft of an adjoining barn. Today there is plenty of room at the inn. There is a restaurant and bar, open fires and comfortable seating. On sale are a full range of Theakston's ales and occasional guest beers. There is a bar food menu and a full restaurant service including morning coffee and afternoon tea. The bar is open all day. The phone number is 0175 676 227.

If you have travelled by bus from the Skipton direction it is possible to end the ramble here and return south, or you can continue a further two miles along the main road back to Starbotton. The flexibility of this crawl is entirely with the walker. Read it as you wish, but enjoy it.

YORK

York is the most civilised of places and has a lot going for it in history, architecture and culture. And it has some great pubs. This crawl takes in seven of them with a brief glance at three others. It crosses the river twice, skirts the great Minster, goes through the famous walls, visits two very interesting churches and concludes with a stroll through a delightful park. So let's go.

We start at **The Maltings (1)** in Tanners Moat which is close to both the railway station and the bus terminus in Rogier Street. It was originally named the Railway Tavern and was probably built to serve the newly opened station. Later it was called the Lendal Bridge.

It is a small higgledy-piggledy sort of pub, just one main room with a side snug, but is blessed with loads of character and characters. Someone with a sense of humour has been at work here; the walls are lined with old doors and wood panels and there are metal advertising signs aplenty. Sean Collinge runs the place with some style and his selection of beers cannot be faulted. Black Sheep is a regular along with one of the Rooster selection and often one from the nearby York brewery. Others generally come from local micros of which there are many in Yorkshire, along with the excellent Budweiser Budwar and Leffe Blond on draught. Food, substantial and well-priced, is available at lunchtimes every day of the week. York CAMRA chose it as its Pub of the Year in 1996.

The antiquity of York...showed itself so visably at a distance that we could not but observe it before we came quite up to the city..."

Daniel Defoe

Walk to the right across Lendal Bridge and view the Guildhall and some of the other splendid buildings on the opposite side of the river. The first one across the bridge is the former York Club which is now an Italian restaurant and such is the concern that York council pays to conservation that its present purpose is hardly noticeable.

Turn right into Lendal and on the right, next to the Mansion House and in cellars under the main Post Office, is the **Lendal Cellars (2)**. It is a Whitbread Hogshead Alehouse with a wide variety of beers including some from Bateman's, Marston's Head Brewer's Choice and local independents as well as Whitbread beers. It is spacious with newspapers to read and a good menu but can get full of young people in the evenings and consequently rather noisy.

Follow your nose down Stonegate towards York Minster and on the right is the **Punch Bowl (3)** recognised by its impressive frontage of carved bargeboards which date from 1675 and a Hammond's Tower Brewery plaque. There are three rooms in this Bass pub with a good choice of beers from the company's portfolio including guests. The food is good with an accent on midday catering for visitors.

Further along Stonegate the next stop is easily recognised by the rare gallows sign spanning the street. **The Olde Starre Inn (4)** is tucked away down an alley on the left. It is one of York's oldest inns, with parts dating back to the 14th century, and most haunted with at least four different spectres including screams from soldiers in the Civil War being amputated without the benefit of anaesthetic when the pub was used as a hospital. The bar is in a basic lounge although there are two comfortable snugs. A former owner, Brett Brothers, is advertised in a splendid glazed bar screen. There is also a dining area and a courtyard. A selection of Theakston's beers are on sale and food is available, with a wide choice at lunch times.

After leaving Stonegate turn left and take the time to visit the oddly placed little church on your right. The Minster can wait and in any case it takes a day at least to survey comprehensively. This is St Michael-le-Belfrey which has its origins in the eleventh century and was originally a chapel of ease for the Minster but now exists in its own right as a parish church. It has a beautiful reredos, a handsome gallery and some wonderful fourteenth-century stained glass.

Next stop is the **York Arms (5)** on High Petergate, a next door but one neighbour of the Minster. It is in the usual neat and tidy style of Sam Smith's and there are two entrances with that on the right leading to a tiny snug accessed by a sliding door in which locals hold sway. It leads on to a larger, comfortable lounge. The left door opens to a

Top: *Minster Inn.* Bottom: *York Arms.*

large airy room with lots of interest including a wonderful photograph of the Minster taken by Barry Grayson, a former and very popular landlord. There are some great tales of hauntings in this pub – ask the locals. Old Brewery Bitter is, naturally, the only draught beer but Sam's produce a fine range of bottled beers that are worth trying. Food is available at most times and there are also rooms to let.

Carry on in the same direction and go under the famous walls at Bootham Bar crossing the busy junction at Gillygate into Bootham, to the splendidly unspoilt **Bootham Tavern (6)**. This pub is uncompromising in its purpose and has remained unchanged for many years. The tap room is airy, basic and friendly with an old embossed sign for Tetley beers and a hoist once used for lifting casks in and out of the cellar. The smallish lounge is darker, a tad more comfortable and is where visitors who make it this far out of the city walls will drink. Tetley Bitter, always in excellent form, is the only draught beer on sale and food is pretty simple. But the pub is a must.

Cross the road again and take care for it's very busy here with folk thinking they will be able to park in the city centre. They won't. A word of advice here for anyone driving to York is to use the excellent Park and Ride system which offers three large free car parks on the outskirts of the city and a cheap bus service into the centre.

On the corner of Marygate is a semicircular projection, St Mary's Tower, which was once the repository of the records of Yorkshire monasteries and is part of the walls of St Mary's Abbey. It was mined during the civil war and bang! went the records. The rebuilding was on a smaller scale. Just around the corner is a splendid view of the Minster framed incongruously by a bowling green.

Marygate contains many handsome Georgian and Victorian buildings, not least of which is the **Minster Inn (7)**, a little bit out of the period for it was built in 1903 for the Tadcaster Tower Brewery. It has a simple layout with a corridor bar which also serves the tap room and two enclosed rooms, a smoke room and what was originally intended as a coffee room. This delightful former Bass pub now belongs to one of the burgeoning pub groups and has Draught Bass and John Smith's Bitter as regulars along with two guests, often not very inspired choices such as Morland Old Speckled Hen and Theakston Best Bitter. Food is pretty simple, just sandwiches, but rather good ones. Its eponymous neighbour is often used as an excuse for a Sunday lunchtime drink: 'Just off to the Minster dear, won't be long'.

Time now, appropriately, for a little more spiritual refreshment. Cross Marygate and head towards the river and call in at St Olave's church. Its origins are eleventh century but most of it is an eighteenth-century rebuild. Amongst much of interest is a rest for a wooden leg in the third pew from the front. On leaving the church enter St Mary's gardens through the Abbey gatehouse. On the left are the ruins of the abbey and next to this the Yorkshire Museum. The path leads you back into Museum Street. Cross the bridge and you are back where you started so why not try another pint in The Maltings. A good idea. Cheers!

CAMRA BOOKS

The CAMRA Books range of guides helps you search out the best in beer (and cider) and brew it at home too!

Buying in the UK

All our books are available through bookshops in the UK. If you can't find a book, simply order it from your bookshop using the ISBN number, title and author details given below. CAMRA members should refer to their regular monthly newspaper What's Brewing for the latest details and member special offers. CAMRA books are also available by mail-order (postage free) from: CAMRA Books, 230 Hatfield Road, St Albans, Herts, AL1 4LW. Cheques made payable to CAMRA Ltd. Telephone your credit card order on 01727 867201.

Buying outside the UK

CAMRA books are also sold in many book and beer outlets in the USA and other English-speaking countries. If you have trouble locating a particular book, use the details below to order by mail or fax (+44 1727 867670).

Carriage of £3.00 per book (Europe) and £6.00 per book (US, Australia, New Zealand and other overseas) is charged.

UK Booksellers

Call CAMRA Books for distribution details and book list. CAMRA Books are listed on all major CD-ROM book lists and on our Internet site: http://www.camra.org.uk

Overseas Booksellers

Call or fax CAMRA Books for details of local distributors. Distributors are required for some English language territories. Rights enquiries (for non-English language editions) should be addressed to the managing editor.

CAMRA Guides

Painstakingly researched and checked, these guides are the leaders in their field, bringing you to the door of pubs which serve real ale and more...

Room at the Inn 2nd edition

by Jill Adam

324 pages Price: £8.99

This second edition of the hugely popular Room at the Inn is your guide to quality overnight accommodation with a decent selection of real ale for good measure. The guide has been completely resurveyed and researched from scratch by the grass roots experts of the Campaign for Real Ale.

The guide's extensive maps – of England, Wales, Scotland, Isle of Man and Channel Islands – will route you to the nearest inn or ale house waiting to offer you generous hospitality, a comfortable bed, a decent breakfast and a well-kept pint of beer.

Each entry in the guide gives local directions, contact details, opening times, type and extent of accommodation, list of beers, meal types and times, and an easy to understand price guide so you can plan your budget. There are also snippets about local attractions and the sometimes centuries-old tales associated with your resting place.

Use the following code to order this book from your bookshop: ISBN 1-85249-150-7

Heritage Pubs of Great Britain

by Mark Bolton and James Belsey

144 pages hard back Price: £16.99

It is still possible to enjoy real ale in sight of great craftsmanship and skill. What finer legacy for today's drinkers? Feast your eyes and toast the architects and builders from times past. This full colour collectible is a photographic record of some of the finest pub interiors in Britain. Many of the pubs included have been chosen from CAMRA's national inventory of pub interiors which should be saved at all costs. As a collector's item. As such it is presented on heavy, gloss-art paper in a sleeved hard back format. Delve deep into the history of the British pub through the interiors which must never be lost, each one unique, stunning to the eye, and yet a place to gather for ordinary citizens. The pub interiors have been photographed by architectural specialist Mark Bolton and described in words by pub expert James Belsey.

Use the following code to order this book from your bookshop: ISBN 1-85249-146-9

Pubs for Families

by David Perrott

308 pages Price: £8.99

Traditional pubs with CAMRA-approved ale and a warm welcome for the kids! Nothing could be better. But where to find such a hospitable hostel on home patch, let alone when out and about or on holiday? This guide is the adult answer to your eating and drinking requirements, with facilities for your children too! Invaluable national coverage with easy to use symbols so that you know what facilities are available and regional maps so you'll know how to get there. Get the best of both worlds.

Use the following code to order this book from your bookshop: ISBN 1-85249-141-8

Good Pub Food 5th edition

by Susan Nowak

380 pages Price: £9.99

The pubs in these pages serve food as original and exciting as anything available in far more expensive restaurants. And, as well as the exotic and unusual, you will find landlords and landladies serving simple, nourishing pub fare such as a genuine ploughman's lunch or a steak and kidney pudding. You'll discover cooking from a new wave of young chefs who would prefer to run a pub than a restaurant. Many pubs are producing the traditional dishes of their regions, building smokeries, keeping cattle and goats, growing vegetables and herbs, creating vibrant, modern cuisine from fresh ingredients. Recipes from some of them are dotted about this guide so you can try them at home.

Award-winning food and beer writer Susan Nowak, who has travelled the country to complete this fifth edition of the guide, says that 'eating out' started in British inns and taverns and this guide is a contribution to an appreciation of all that is best in British food…and real cask conditioned ale.

Use the following code to order this book from your bookshop: ISBN 1-85249-151-5

Good Beer Guides

These are comprehensive guides researched by professional beer writers and CAMRA enthusiasts. Use these guides to find the best beer on your travels or to plan your itinerary for the finest drinking. Travel and accommodation information, plus maps, help you on your way and there's plenty to read about the history of brewing, the beer styles and the local cuisine to back up the entries for bars and beverages.

Good Beer Guide to Belgium, Holland and Luxembourg

by Tim Webb

286 pages Price: £9.99

Discover the stunning range and variety of beers available in the Low Countries, our even nearer neighbours via Le Tunnel. There are such revered styles as Trappist Ales, fruit beers, wheat beers and the lambic and gueuze specialities made by the centuries-old method of spontaneous fermentation.

Channel-hopping Tim Webb's latest edition – the third – of the guide offers even more bars in which an incredible array of beers can be enjoyed. If you are going on holiday to this region then you'll find details of travel, accommodation, food, beer museums, brewery visits and festivals, as well as guides to the cafés, beer shops and warehouses you can visit. There are maps, tasting notes, beer style guide and a beers index to complete the most comprehensive companion to drinking with your Belgian and Dutch hosts.

Use the following code to order this book from your bookshop: ISBN 1-85249-139-6

Good Beer Guide to Northern France

by Arthur Taylor

256 pages Price: £7.99

Discover the excitement of the bars and cafes, the tranquillity of the village breweries which hold the secrets of generations of traditional brewing. Join the many festivals and cultural events such as the beer-refreshed second-hand market in Lille and the presentation of the Christmas ales. Find out where the best beer meets the best mussels and chips.

Cuisine a la bière and more! Arthur Taylor is a leading authority on French beer and a member of Les Amis de la Bière, who have co-operated in the research for this book. Use the following code to order this book from your bookshop: ISBN 1-85249-140-X

Good Bottled Beer Guide

by Jeff Evans

256 pages Price: £8.99

When early nights and unfriendly traffic conspire to keep you at home, there's no risk these days of missing out on drinking a fine real ale. Britain's off-licences and supermarkets now stock bottle-conditioned ales – real ale in a bottle. The book describes the ingredients and history behind Britain's traditional bottled beer, and conjures up the tastes and smells.

Bottle-conditioned beers, such as Marston's Oyster Stout and Hopback Summer Lightning, contain yeast and continue to mature in the bottle for a fuller, fresher taste, just as real ales mature in the cask at the pub. Discover the seasonal Christmas ales, Millennium Ale, porters and stouts. Find out who brews the supermarket own-brands and check the many varieties of hops and malts in the pale ales, milds and barley wines.

Use the following code to order this book from your bookshop: ISBN 1-85249-157-4

Good Beer Guide

edited by Roger Protz

500 pages approx Price: £10.99

Produced annually in October

Fancy a pint? Let CAMRA's Good Beer Guide lead the way. Revised each year to include around 5,000 great pubs serving excellent ale – country pubs, town pubs and pubs by the sea.

The guide includes information about meals, accommodation, family rooms, no-smoking areas and much more.

Fully and freshly researched by members of the Campaign for Real Ale, real enthusiasts who use the pubs week in, week out. No payment is ever taken for inclusion. The guide has location maps for each county and you can read full details of all Britain's breweries (big and small) and the ales they produce, including tasting notes.

CAMRA's Good Beer Guide is still Britain's best value pub guide – a must for anyone who loves beer and pubs.

Cellarmanship

by Ivor Clissold

144 pages Price: £6.99

This book explains every aspect of running a good cellar and serving a great pint of real ale which does both pub and brewer proud. It's a must have book for all professionals in the drinks trade, for all those studying at college to join it, and for all those who need to tap a cask of real ale for a party.

The CAMRA Guide to Cellarmanship is the only manual dealing with the care of all cask beers. It draws together information previously only known within certain breweries, and adds valuable experience from hundreds of cellar and technical staff.

Farmers, hop growers, maltsters, brewers and drayers all play their part to produce and deliver our great British drink but too often it falls at the last fence: indifferent cellar and bar management – especially in the face of an unknown guest beer – can turn a treat into a tragedy.

Use the following code to order this book from your bookshop: ISBN 1-85249-126-4

Brew Your Own

Learn the basics of brewing real ales at home from the experts. And then move on to more ambitious recipes which imitate well-loved ales from the UK and Europe.

Brew your own Real Ale at Home

by Graham Wheeler and Roger Protz

194 pages Price: £8.99

This book is a treasure chest for all real ale fans and home brew enthusiasts. It contains recipes which allow you to replicate some famous cask-conditioned beers at home or to customise brews to your own particular taste. The authors have examined the ingredients and brewing styles of well-known ales and have gleaned important information from brewers, with and without their co-operation. Computer-aided guesswork and an expert palate have filled in the gaps where the brewers would reveal no more.

As well as the recipes, the brewing process is explained along with the equipment required, all of which allows you to brew beer using wholly natural ingredients. Detailed recipes and instructions are given along with tasting notes for each ale. Conversion details are given so that the measurements can be used world-wide.

Use the following code to order this book from your bookshop: ISBN 1-85249-138-8

Brew Classic European Beers at Home

by Graham Wheeler and Roger Protz

196 pages Price: £8.99

Keen home brewers can now recreate some of the world's classic beers. In your own home you can brew superb pale ales, milds, porters, stouts, Pilsners, Alt, Kolsch, Trappist, wheat beers, sour beers, even the astonishing fruit lambics of Belgium… and many more.

Graham Wheeler and his computer have teamed up with Roger Protz and his unrivalled knowledge of brewing and beer styles. Use the detailed recipes and information about ingredients to imitate the cream of international beers. Discover the role played by ingredients, yeasts and brewing equipment and procedure in these well-known drinks. Measurements are given in UK, US and European units, emphasising the truly international scope of the beer styles within.

Use the following code to order this book from your bookshop: ISBN 1-85249-117-5

Home Brewing

by Graham Wheeler

240 pages Price: £8.99

Recently redesigned to make it even easier to use, this is the classic first book for all home-brewers. While being truly comprehensive, Home Brewing also manages to be a practical guide which can be followed step by step as you try your first brews. Plenty of recipes for beginners and hints and tips from the world's most revered home brewer.

Use the following code to order this book from your bookshop: ISBN 1-85249-137-X

OTHER BOOKS

CAMRA QUIZ BOOK

by Jeff Evans

128 pages Price: £3.99

Fun and games for beer fans, and their relations. Use this book to quiz your mates on real ale and CAMRA history. Great for fund-raising quiz events and for catching up on the campaign.

Use the following code to order this book from your bookshop: ISBN 1-85249-127-2

KEGBUSTER CARTOON BOOK

by Bill Tidy

72 pages, including colour cartoons Price: £4.99

A classic, hilarious, collection of cartoons from well-known funny man and cartoonist extraordinaire Bill Tidy. The perfect gift for the beer lover in your life!

Use the following code to order this book from your bookshop: ISBN 1-1-85249-134-5

BREWERY BREAKS

by Ted Bruning

64 pages Price: £3.99

A handy pocket guide to brewery visitor centres and museums. Keep this in the car on your travels and you'll never be far from the living history of brewing. An ideal reference for CAMRA members, and others, wishing to organise a trip to one of Britain's best known breweries or a tasting at a local microbrewery.

Use the following code to order this book from your bookshop: ISBN 1-1-85249-132-9

JOIN CAMRA

If you like good beer and good pubs you could be helping to fight to preserve, protect and promote them. CAMRA was set up in the early seventies to fight against the mass destruction of a part of Britain's heritage.

The giant brewers are still pushing through takeovers, mergers and closures of their smaller regional rivals. They are still trying to impose national brands of beer and lager on their customers whether they like it or not, and they are still closing down town and village pubs or converting them into grotesque 'theme' pubs.

CAMRA wants to see genuine free competition in the brewing industry, fair prices, and, above all, a top quality product brewed by local breweries in accordance with local tastes, and served in pubs that maintain the best features of a tradition that goes back centuries.

As a CAMRA member you will be able to enjoy generous discounts on CAMRA products and receive the highly rated monthly newspaper What's Brewing. You will be given the CAMRA members' handbook and be able to join in local social events and brewery trips.

To join, complete the form below and, if you wish, arrange for direct debit payments by filling in the form overleaf and returning it to CAMRA. To pay by credit card, contact the membership secretary on (01727) 867201.

I/We wish to join the Campaign for Real Ale and agree to abide by the Rules.

Name(s) ... ...

... ...

Address ... ...

... ...Postcode ... ...

Signature ... ...Date ... ...

I/We enclose the remittance for (please tick):

Single:	£14	Joint	£17	(at same address)
OAP Single	£8	OAP Joint	£11	(at same address)
Unemployed/Disabled	£8			
Under 26	£8	date of birth:		

For Life and Overseas rates please contact CAMRA HQ
(tel: 01727 867201

Send you remittance (payable to CAMRA) to:
The Membership Secretary, CAMRA, 230 Hatfield Road, St Albans, Herts., AL1 4LW

Instruction to your Bank or Building Society to pay by Direct Debit

Please fill in the whole form using a ball point pen and send it to:

Campaign for Real Ale Ltd,
230 Hatfield Road,
St. Albans,
Herts
AL1 4LW

Name of Account Holder(s)

Bank/Building Society account number

Branch Sort Code

Name and full postal address of your Bank or Building Society

To The Manager Bank/Building Society

Address

Postcode

Originator's Identification Number

9	2	6	1	2	9

Reference Number

FOR CAMRA OFFICIAL USE ONLY

This is not part of the instruction to your Bank or Building Society

Membership Number

Name

Postcode

Instructions to your Bank or Building Society

Please pay CAMRA Direct Debits from the account detailed on this instruction subject to the safeguards assured by the Direct Debit Guarantee. I understand that this instruction may remain with CAMRA and, if so, will be passed electronically to my Bank/Building Society

Signature(s)

Date

Banks and Building Societies may not accept Direct Debit instructions for some types of account

This guarantee should be detached and retained by the Payer.

The Direct Debit Guarantee

- This Guarantee is offered by all Banks and Building Societies that take part in the Direct Debit Scheme. The efficiency and security of the Scheme is monited and protected by your own Bank or Building Society.
- If the amounts to be paid or the payment dates change CAMRA will notify you 10 working days in advance of your account being debited or as otherwise agreed.
- If an error is made by CAMRA or your Bank or Building Society, you are guaranteed a full and immediate refund from your branch of the amount paid.
- You can cancel a Direct Debit at any time by writing to your Bank or Building Society. Please also send a copy of your letter to us.

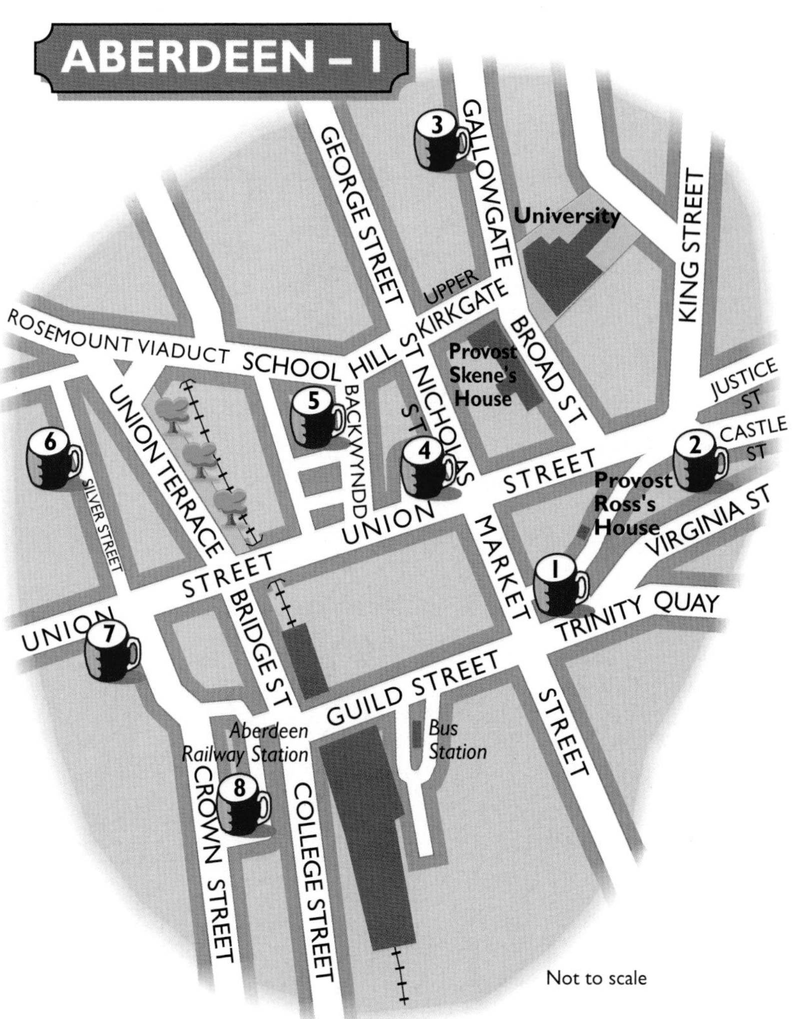
ABERDEEN – 1
GEORGE STREET
GALLOWGATE
University
KING STREET
UPPER
KIRKGATE
ROSEMOUNT VIADUCT
SCHOOL HILL
ST NICHOLAS ST
Provost Skene's House
BROAD ST
JUSTICE ST
CASTLE ST
BACKWYNDD
UNION TERRACE
SILVER STREET
UNION STREET
MARKET STREET
Provost Ross's House
VIRGINIA ST
TRINITY QUAY
UNION
STREET
BRIDGE ST
GUILD STREET
Bus Station
Aberdeen Railway Station
CROWN STREET
COLLEGE STREET
STREET
Not to scale

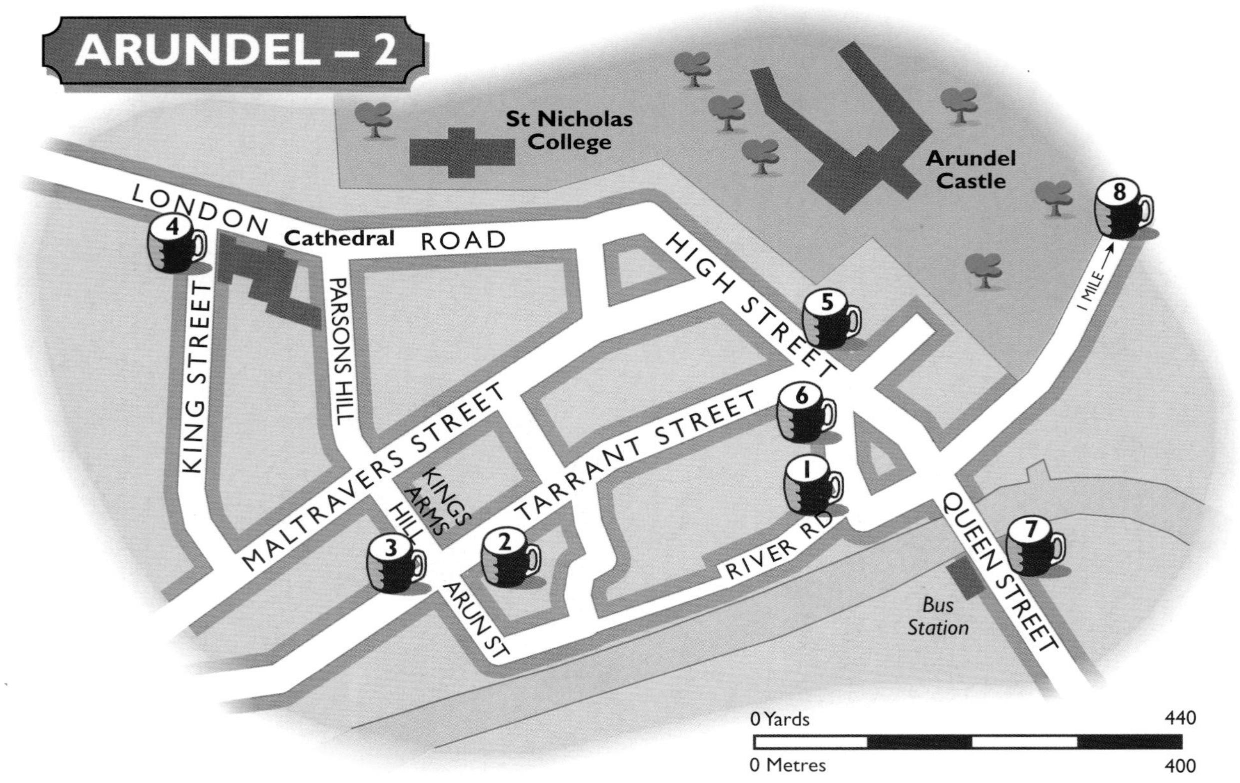
ARUNDEL – 2
St Nicholas College
Arundel Castle
LONDON
Cathedral
ROAD
HIGH STREET
KING STREET
PARSONS HILL
MALTRAVERS STREET
KINGS ARMS HILL
TARRANT STREET
ARUN ST
RIVER RD
QUEEN STREET
Bus Station
1 MILE
1
2
3
4
5
6
7
8
0 Yards
440
0 Metres
400

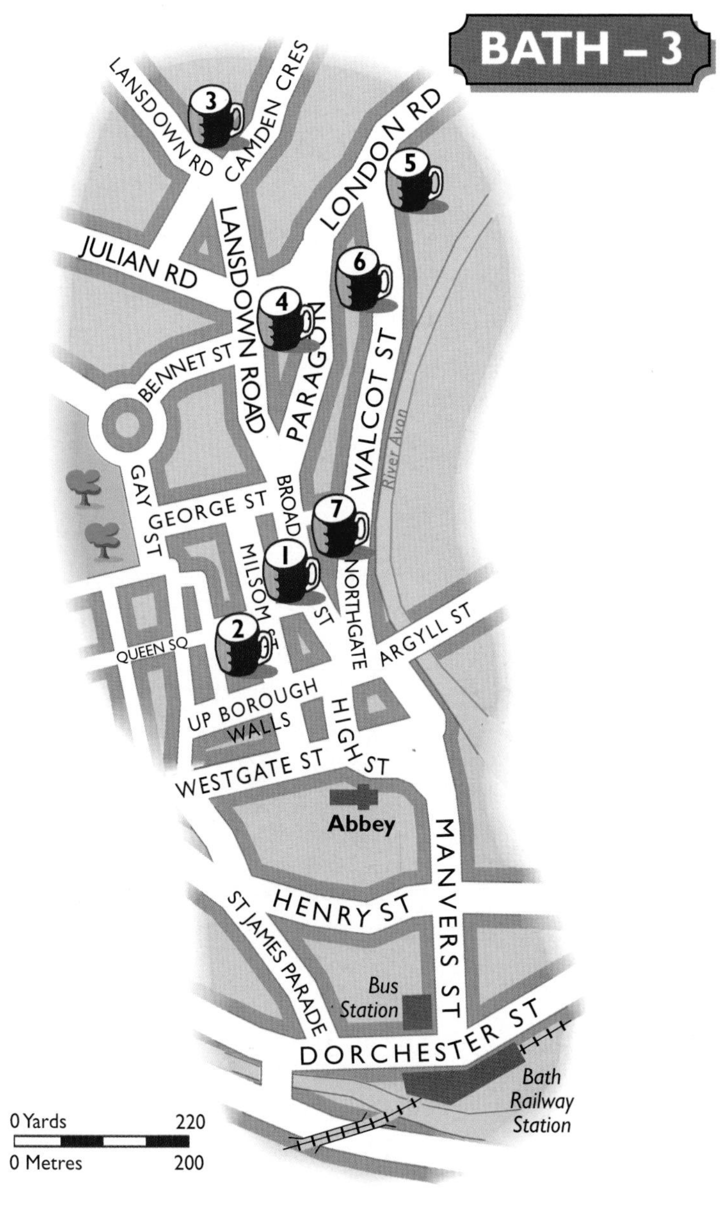
BATH – 3
LANSDOWN RD
CAMDEN CRES
LONDON RD
JULIAN RD
LANSDOWN ROAD
BENNET ST
PARAGON
WALCOT ST
River Avon
GAY ST
GEORGE ST
BROAD ST
MILSOM ST
NORTHGATE
ARGYLL ST
QUEEN SQ
UP BOROUGH WALLS
HIGH ST
WESTGATE ST
Abbey
MANVERS ST
HENRY ST
ST JAMES PARADE
Bus Station
DORCHESTER ST
Bath Railway Station
0 Yards 220
0 Metres 200
1
2
3
4
5
6
7

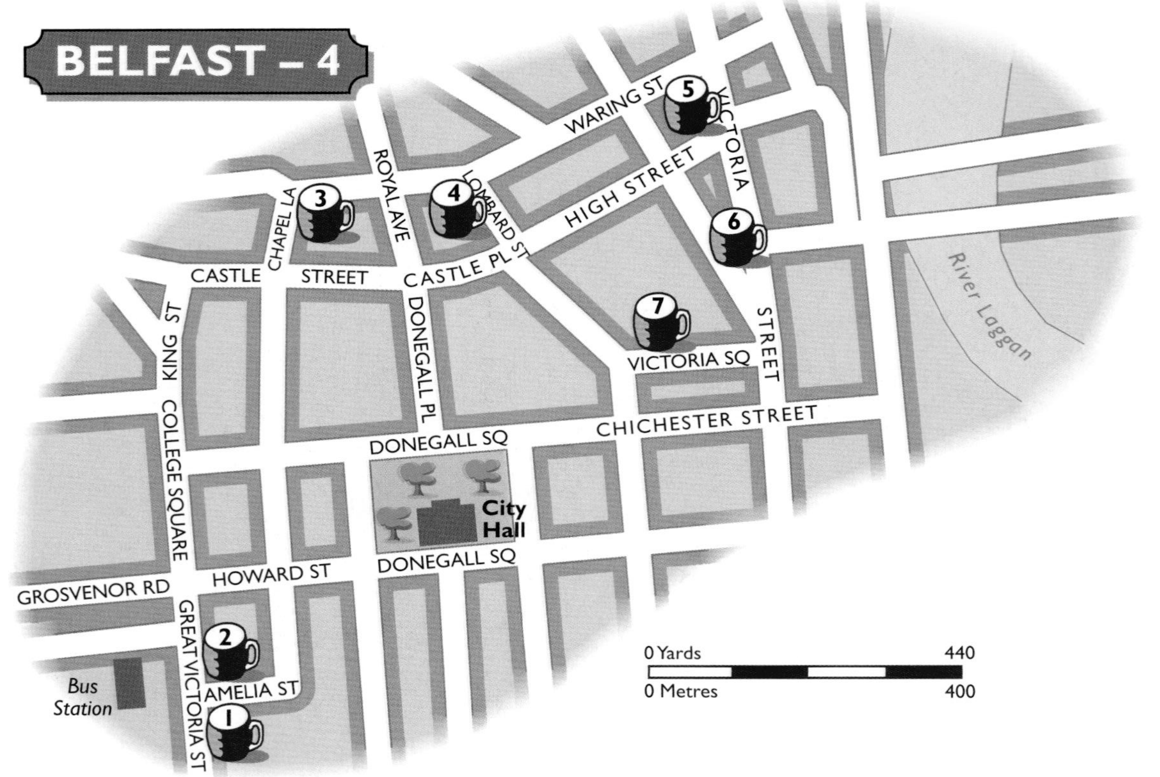
BELFAST – 4
WARING ST
VICTORIA
ROYAL AVE
LOMBARD ST
HIGH STREET
CHAPEL LA
CASTLE
STREET
CASTLE PL
KING ST
DONEGALL PL
VICTORIA SQ
STREET
River Laggan
CHICHESTER STREET
DONEGALL SQ
COLLEGE SQUARE
City
Hall
DONEGALL SQ
HOWARD ST
GROSVENOR RD
GREAT VICTORIA ST
AMELIA ST
Bus
Station
0 Yards
440
0 Metres
400
1
2
3
4
5
6
7

BRIDGNORTH – 5

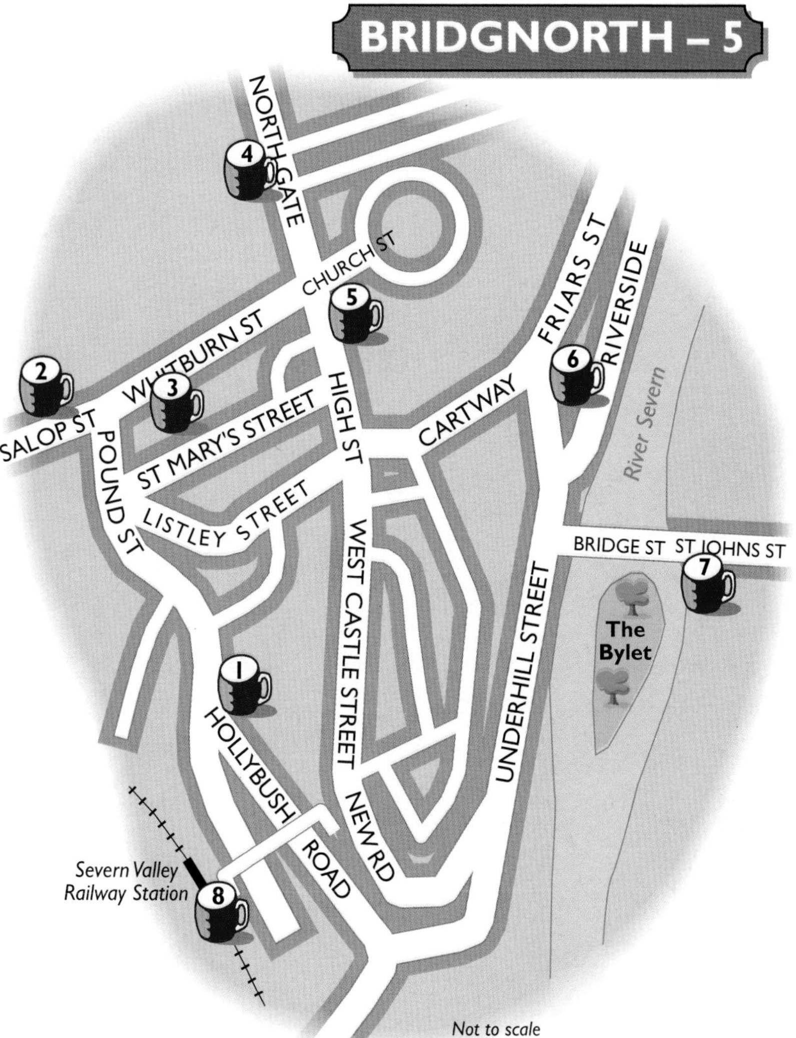

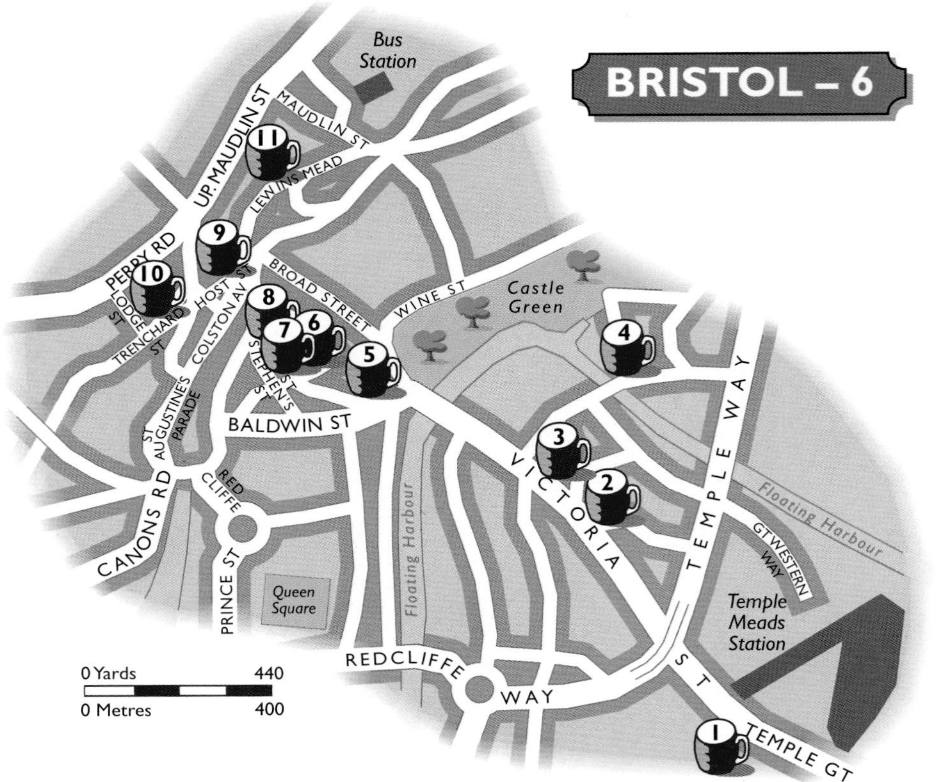

BRISTOL – 6
Bus Station
MAUDLIN ST
UP. MAUDLIN ST
LEWINS MEAD
PERRY RD
LODGE ST
TRENCHARD ST
HOST ST
COLSTON AV
BROAD STREET
WINE ST
Castle Green
ST STEPHEN'S ST
BALDWIN ST
ST AUGUSTINE'S PARADE
CANONS RD
RED CLIFFE
PRINCE ST
Queen Square
Floating Harbour
VICTORIA ST
TEMPLE WAY
GT WESTERN WAY
Floating Harbour
Temple Meads Station
REDCLIFFE WAY
TEMPLE GT
0 Yards 440
0 Metres 400
1
2
3
4
5
6
7
8
9
10
11

BURTON UPON TRENT – 7

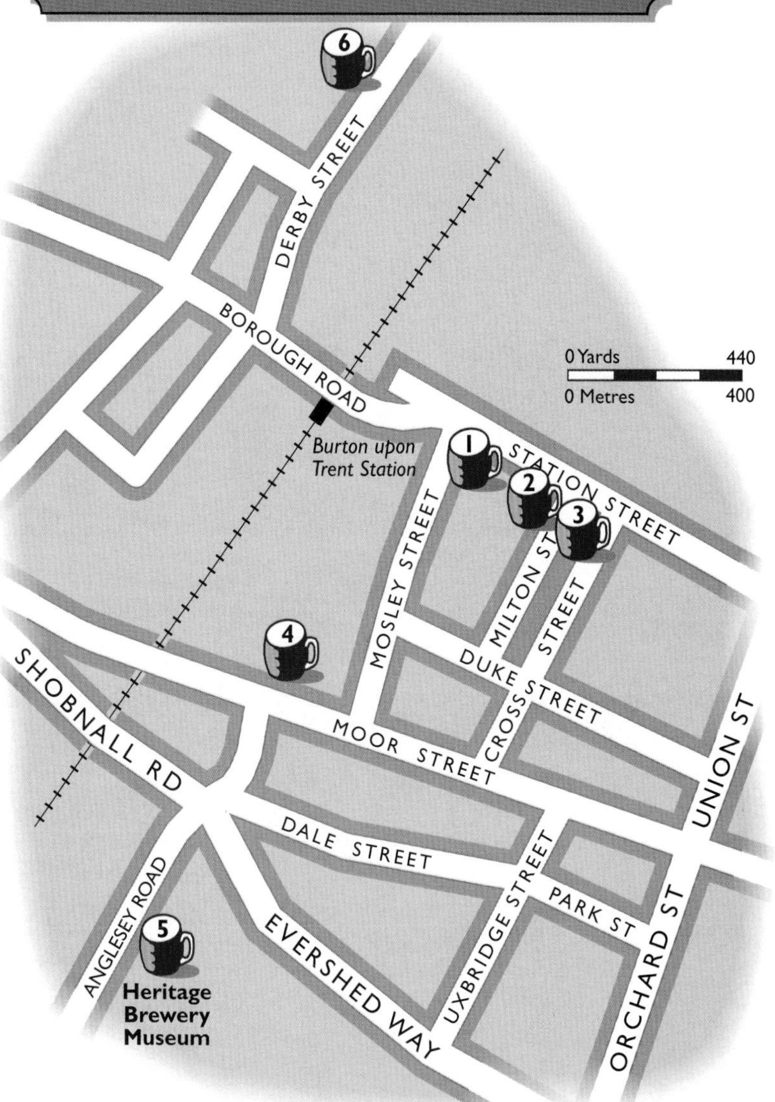

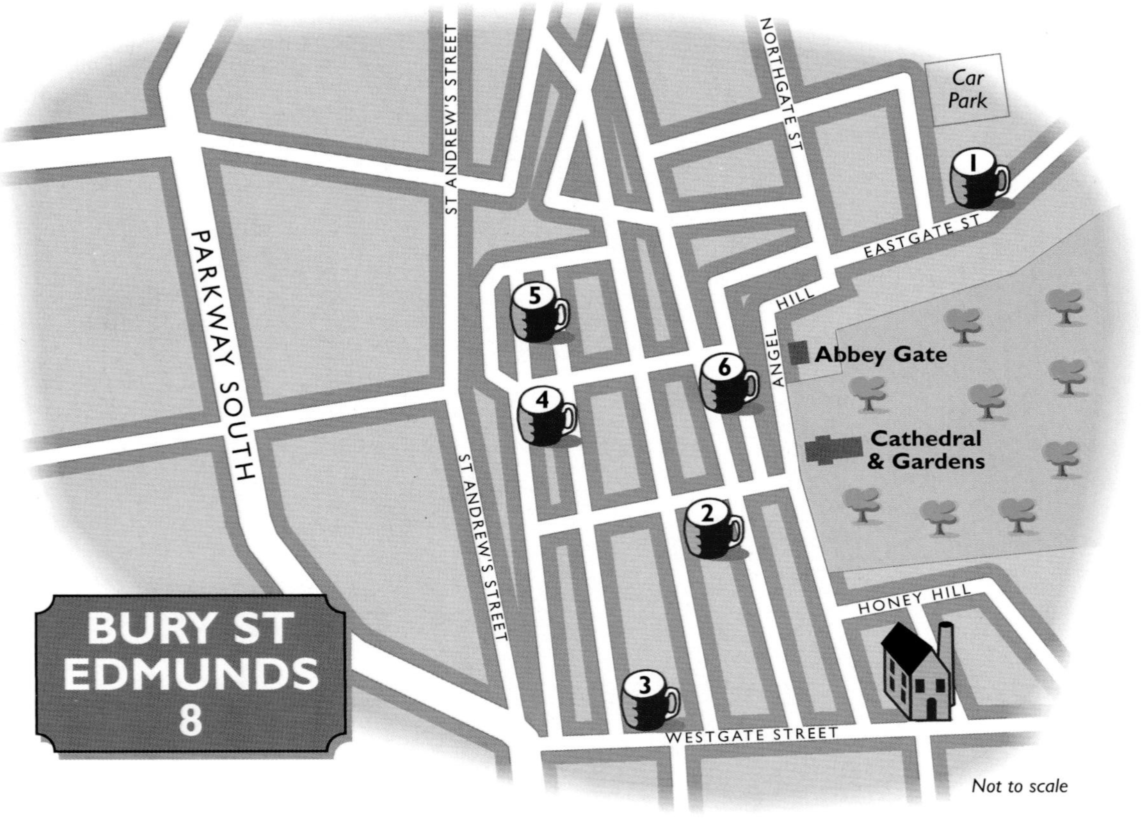

BURY ST EDMUNDS
8

Car Park
NORTHGATE ST
EASTGATE ST
ANGEL HILL
Abbey Gate
Cathedral & Gardens
HONEY HILL
WESTGATE STREET
ST ANDREW'S STREET
PARKWAY SOUTH
1
2
3
4
5
6

Not to scale

CAMBRIDGE – 9

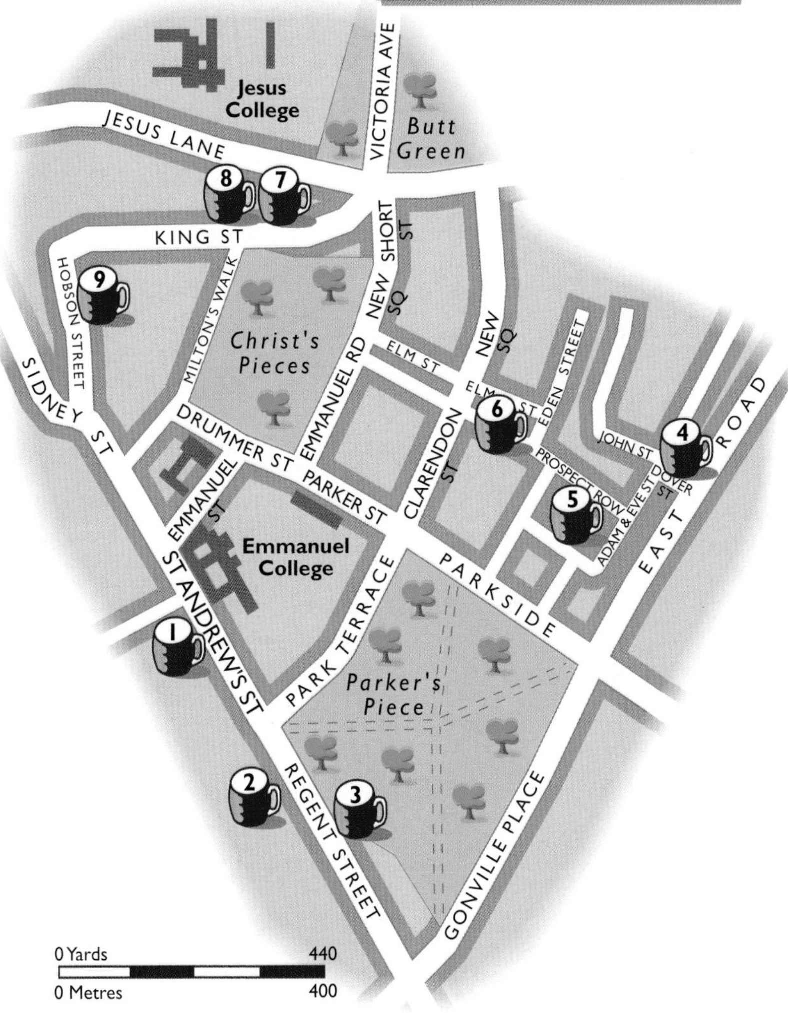

Jesus College
JESUS LANE
VICTORIA AVE
Butt Green
8
7
KING ST
NEW SHORT ST
HOBSON STREET
9
MILTON'S WALK
Christ's Pieces
NEW SQ
NEW SQ
EDEN STREET
ELM ST
ELM ST
SIDNEY ST
EMMANUEL RD
6
DRUMMER ST
CLARENDON ST
JOHN ST
4
ROAD
PROSPECT ROW
DOVER ST
ADAM & EVE ST
5
EMMANUEL ST
PARKER ST
Emmanuel College
EAST
PARKSIDE
ST ANDREW'S ST
1
PARK TERRACE
Parker's Piece
2
3
REGENT STREET
GONVILLE PLACE
0 Yards
440
0 Metres
400

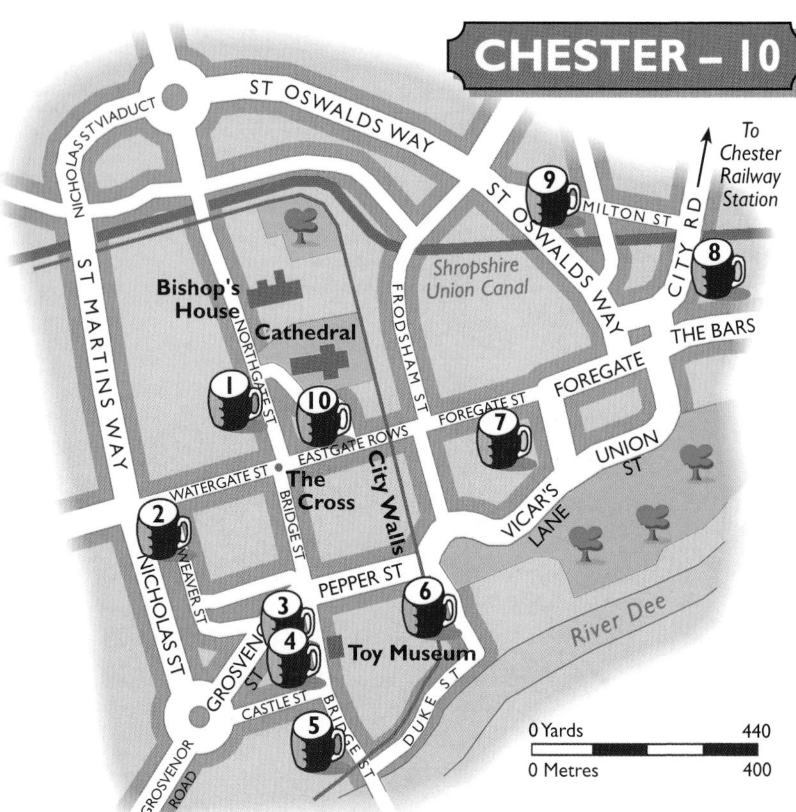
CHESTER – 10
ST OSWALDS WAY
NICHOLAS ST VIADUCT
To Chester Railway Station
ST MARTINS WAY
MILTON ST
CITY RD
Shropshire Union Canal
Bishop's House
Cathedral
NORTHGATE ST
FRODSHAM ST
THE BARS
FOREGATE
FOREGATE ST
EASTGATE ROWS
WATERGATE ST
The Cross
BRIDGE ST
City Walls
UNION ST
VICAR'S LANE
NICHOLAS ST
WEAVER ST
PEPPER ST
River Dee
GROSVENOR ST
Toy Museum
CASTLE ST
DUKE ST
GROSVENOR ROAD
0 Yards 440
0 Metres 400
1
2
3
4
5
6
7
8
9
10

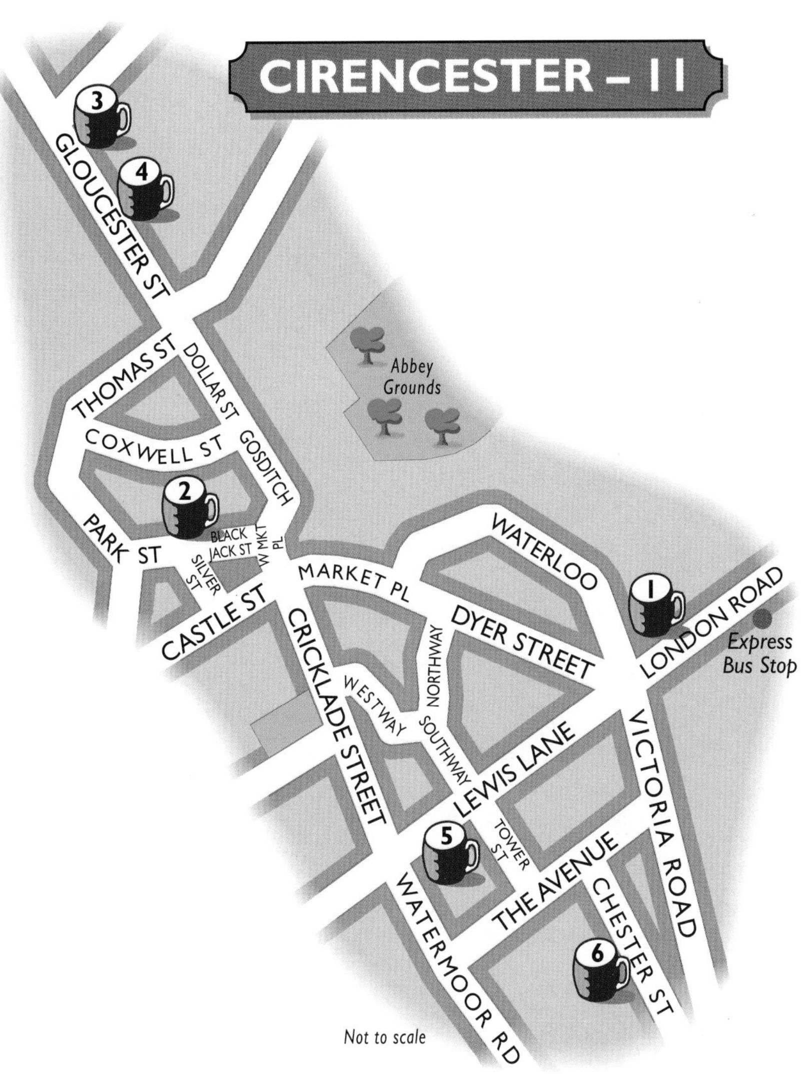
CIRENCESTER – 11
GLOUCESTER ST
THOMAS ST
DOLLAR ST
COXWELL ST
GOSDITCH
PARK ST
BLACK JACK ST
SILVER ST
W MKT PL
CASTLE ST
MARKET PL
CRICKLADE STREET
Abbey Grounds
WATERLOO
DYER STREET
NORTHWAY
WESTWAY
SOUTHWAY
LEWIS LANE
TOWER ST
LONDON ROAD
Express Bus Stop
VICTORIA ROAD
THE AVENUE
CHESTER ST
WATERMOOR RD
1
2
3
4
5
6
Not to scale

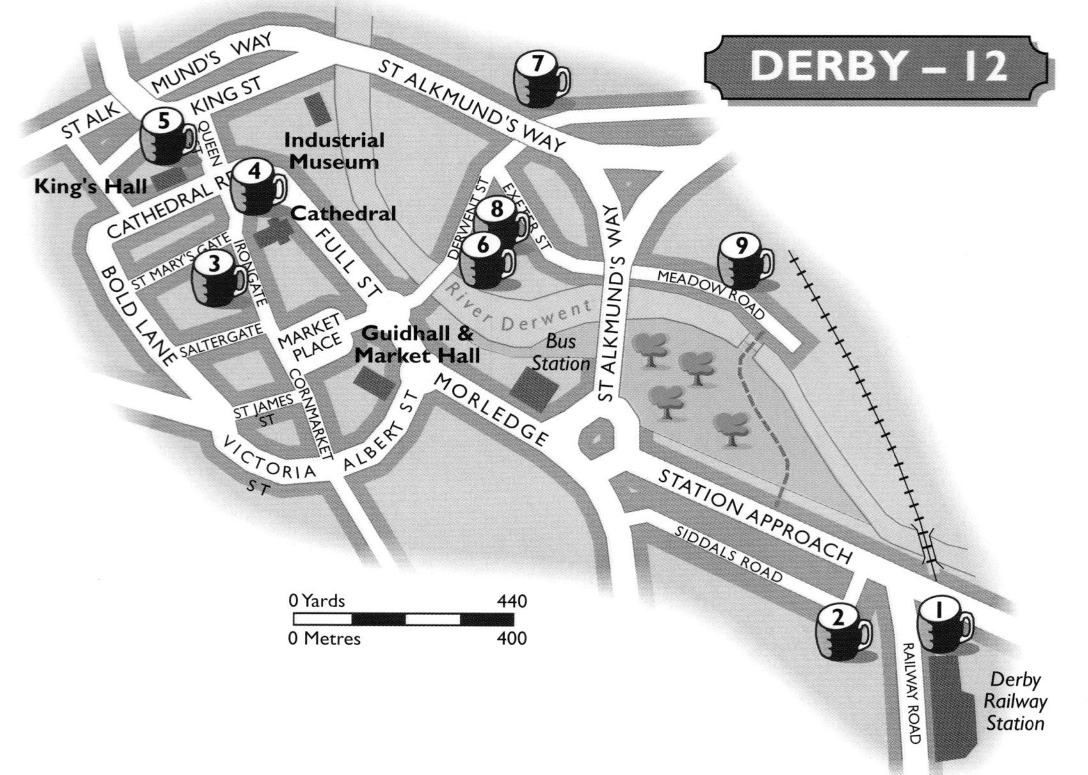
DERBY – 12
ST ALKMUND'S WAY
ST ALKMUND'S WAY
ST ALKMUND'S WAY
KING ST
QUEEN ST
CATHEDRAL RD
King's Hall
Industrial Museum
Cathedral
FULL ST
ST MARY'S GATE
IRONGATE
BOLD LANE
SALTERGATE
MARKET PLACE
CORNMARKET
ST JAMES ST
VICTORIA ST
ALBERT ST
MORLEDGE
Guidhall & Market Hall
DERWENT ST
EXETER ST
River Derwent
Bus Station
MEADOW ROAD
STATION APPROACH
SIDDALS ROAD
RAILWAY ROAD
Derby Railway Station
0 Yards
440
0 Metres
400
1
2
3
4
5
6
7
8
9

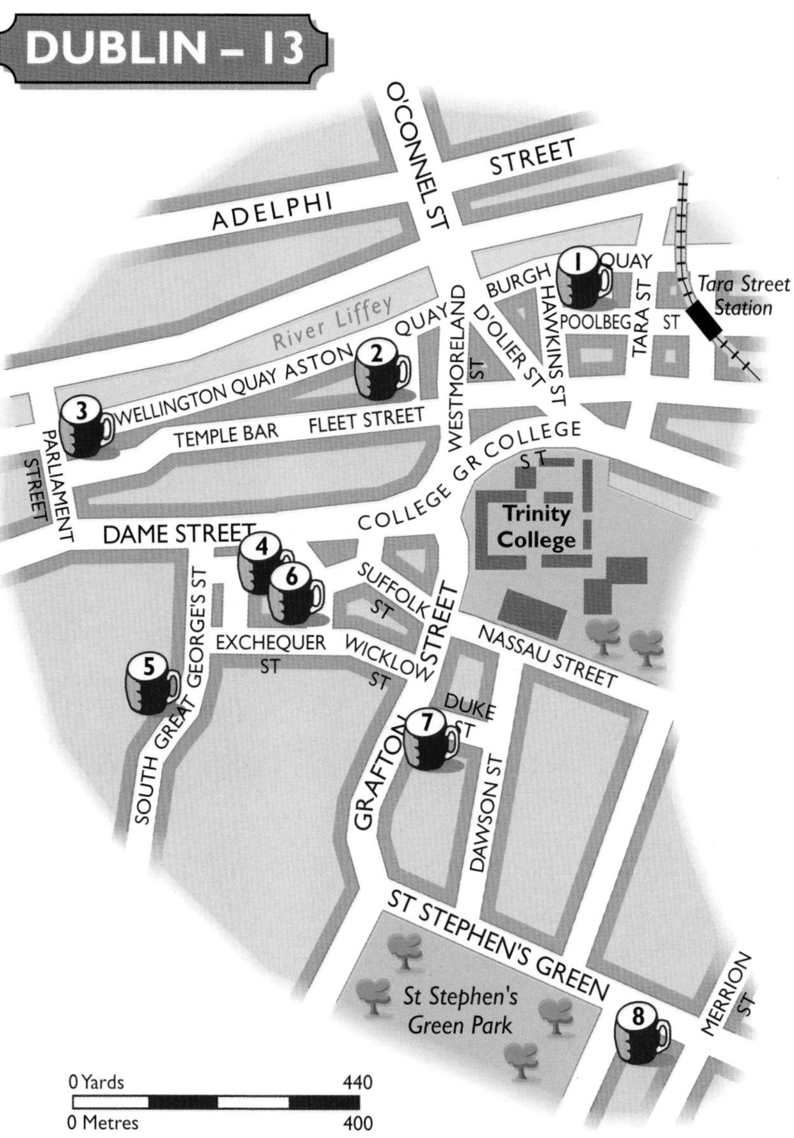

DUBLIN – 13
O'CONNEL ST
STREET
ADELPHI
QUAY
BURGH
HAWKINS ST
POOLBEG
TARA ST
ST
Tara Street Station
River Liffey
QUAY
ASTON
WELLINGTON QUAY
WESTMORELAND ST
D'OLIER ST
FLEET STREET
TEMPLE BAR
PARLIAMENT STREET
COLLEGE GR
COLLEGE ST
COLLEGE
Trinity College
DAME STREET
SUFFOLK ST
EXCHEQUER ST
WICKLOW ST
SOUTH GREAT GEORGE'S ST
GRAFTON STREET
NASSAU STREET
DUKE ST
DAWSON ST
ST STEPHEN'S GREEN
St Stephen's Green Park
MERRION ST
0 Yards
440
0 Metres
400

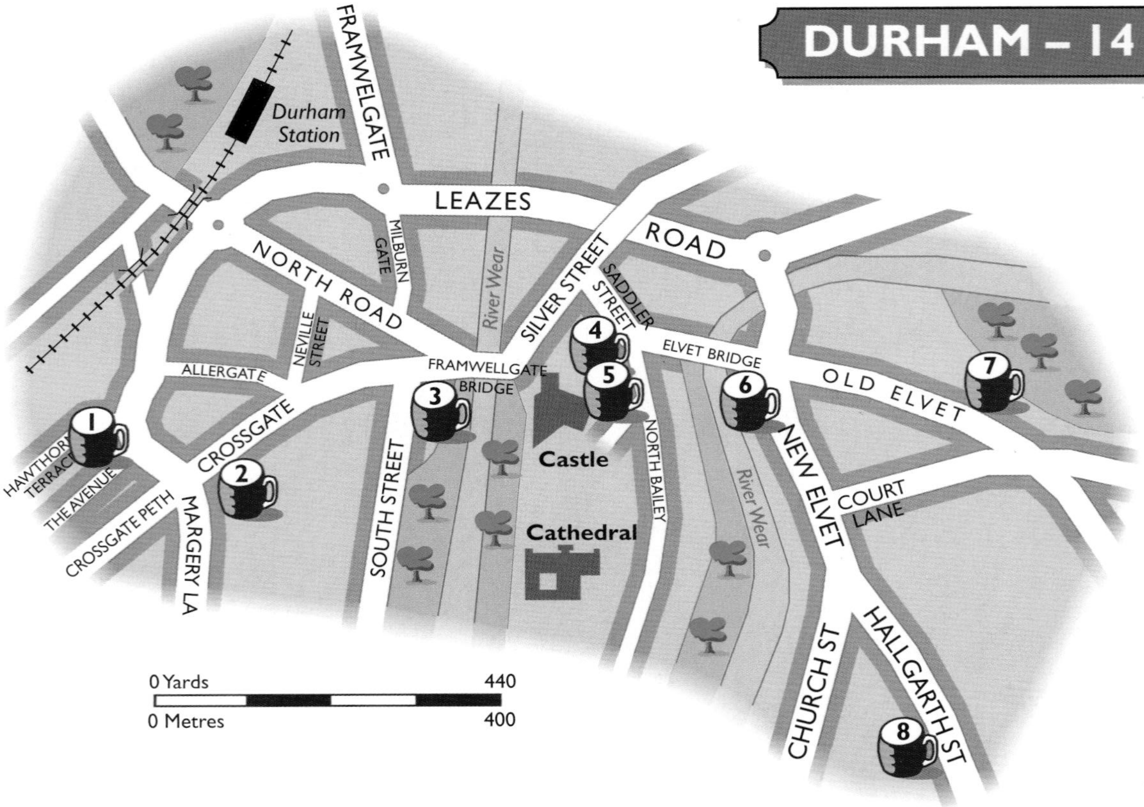

DURHAM – 14

Durham Station
FRAMWELGATE
LEAZES
ROAD
MILBURN GATE
NORTH ROAD
River Wear
SILVER STREET
SADDLER STREET
NEVILLE STREET
ALLERGATE
FRAMWELLGATE BRIDGE
ELVET BRIDGE
OLD ELVET
NORTH BAILEY
Castle
Cathedral
HAWTHORN TERRACE
THE AVENUE
CROSSGATE PETH
CROSSGATE
MARGERY LA
SOUTH STREET
NEW ELVET
COURT LANE
CHURCH ST
HALLGARTH ST
1
2
3
4
5
6
7
8
0 Yards
440
0 Metres
400

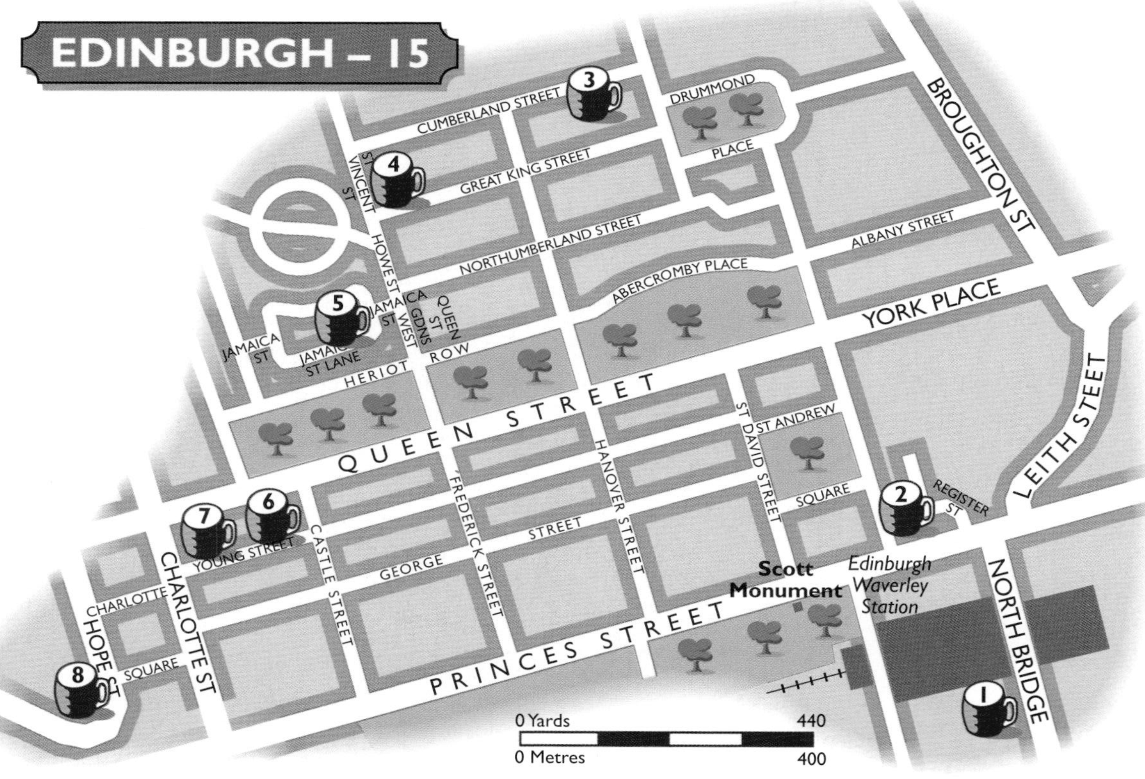

EDINBURGH – 15
CUMBERLAND STREET
DRUMMOND PLACE
BROUGHTON ST
ST VINCENT ST
GREAT KING STREET
HOWE ST
NORTHUMBERLAND STREET
ALBANY STREET
ABERCROMBY PLACE
YORK PLACE
JAMAICA ST
JAMAICA ST LANE
JAMAICA ST WEST
QUEEN ST GDNS
HERIOT ROW
QUEEN STREET
LEITH STEET
ST ANDREW SQUARE
ST DAVID STREET
REGISTER ST
HANOVER STREET
FREDERICK STREET
GEORGE STREET
CASTLE STREET
YOUNG STREET
CHARLOTTE ST
CHARLOTTE SQUARE
HOPE ST
PRINCES STREET
Scott Monument
Edinburgh Waverley Station
NORTH BRIDGE
0 Yards
440
0 Metres
400
1
2
3
4
5
6
7
8

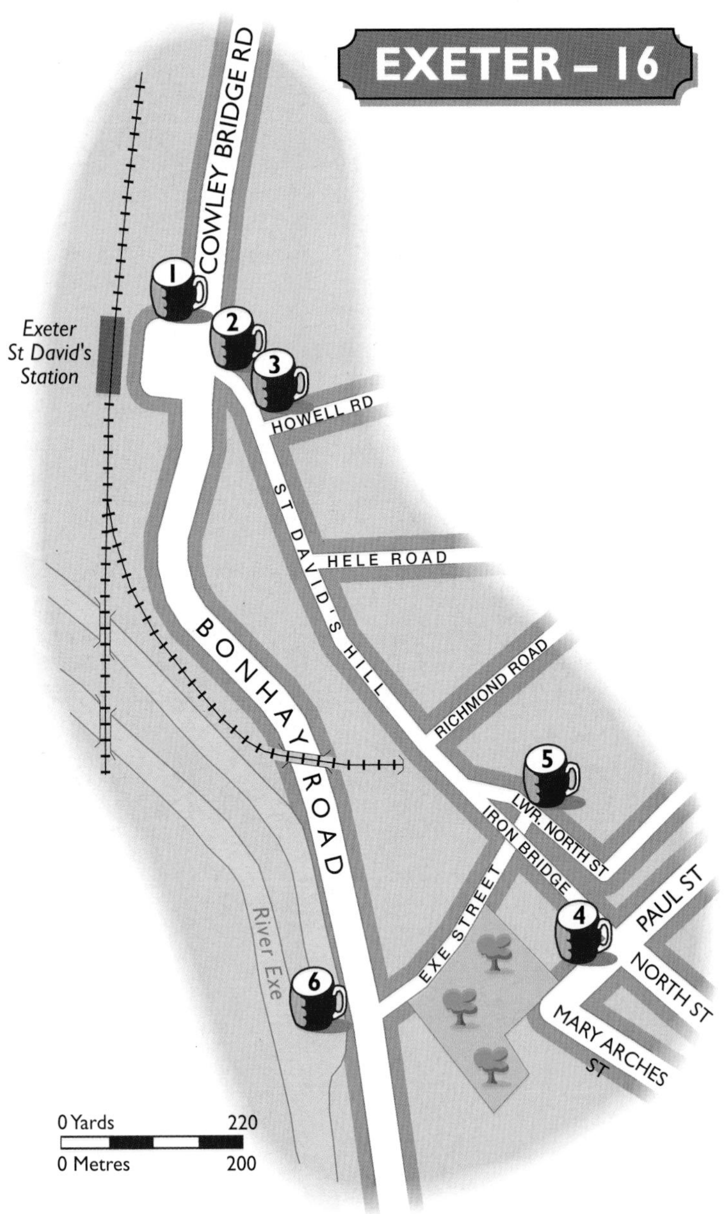
EXETER – 16
COWLEY BRIDGE RD
Exeter
St David's
Station
HOWELL RD
ST DAVID'S HILL
HELE ROAD
BONHAY ROAD
RICHMOND ROAD
LWR. NORTH ST
IRON BRIDGE
EXE STREET
PAUL ST
NORTH ST
MARY ARCHES
ST
River Exe
0 Yards
220
0 Metres
200
1
2
3
4
5
6

HISTORIC GREENWICH – 17

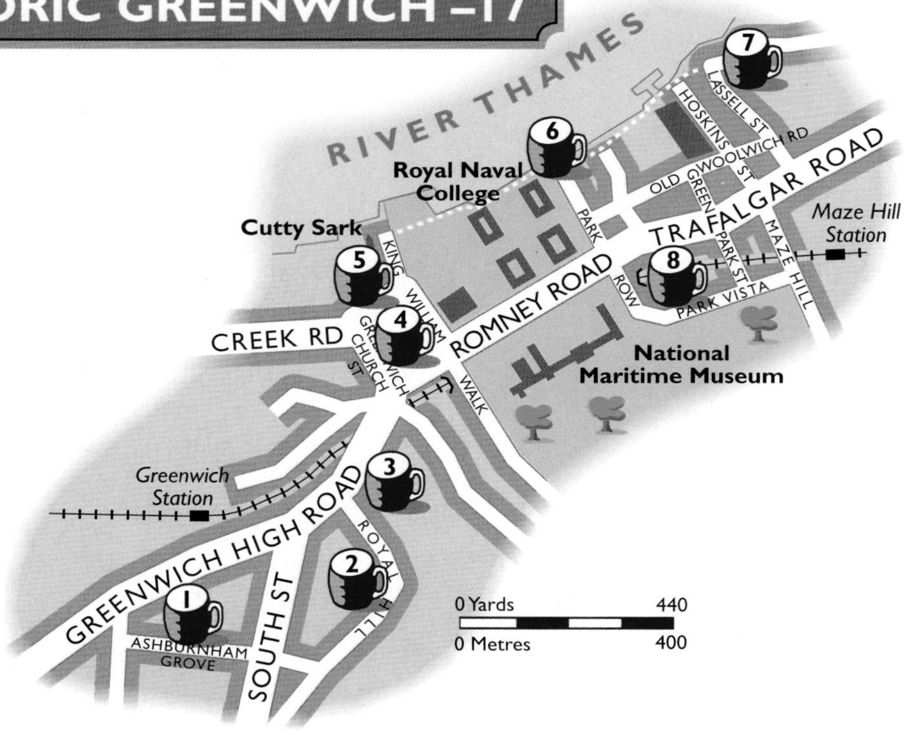

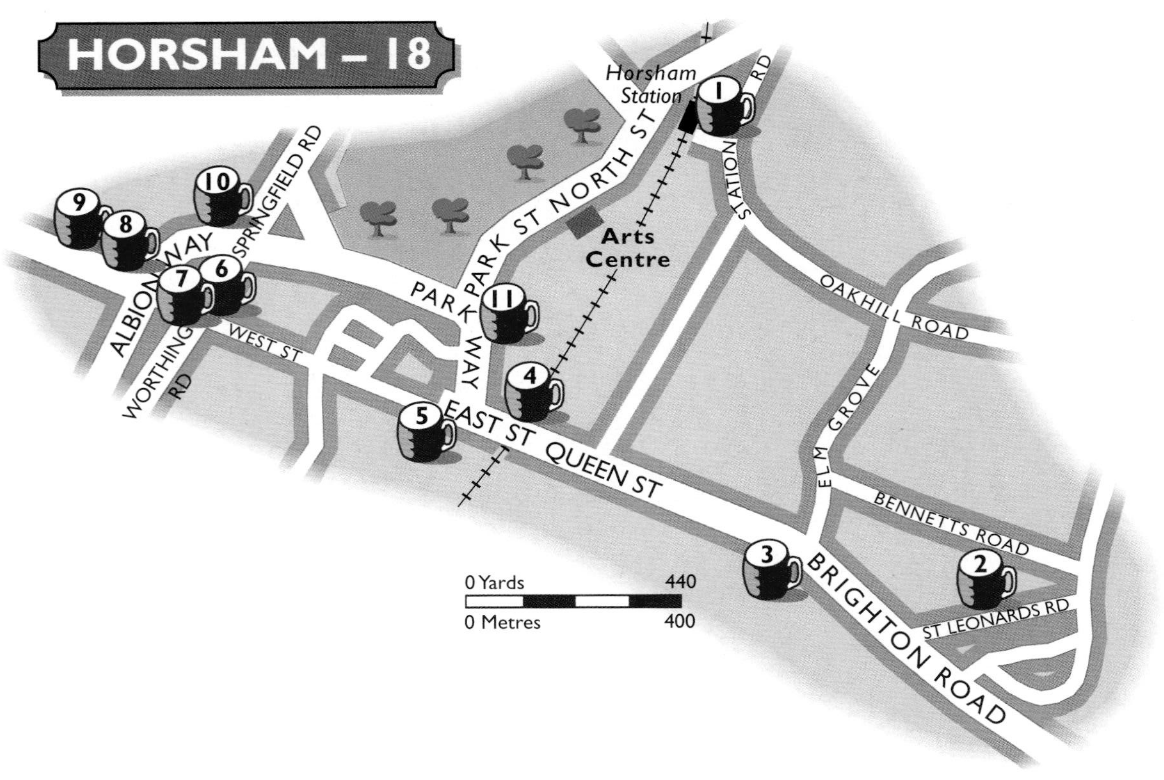
HORSHAM – 18
Horsham Station
Arts Centre
STATION RD
PARK ST
NORTH ST
PARK WAY
EAST ST
QUEEN ST
WEST ST
SPRINGFIELD RD
ALBION WAY
WORTHING RD
OAKHILL ROAD
ELM GROVE
BENNETTS ROAD
ST LEONARDS RD
BRIGHTON ROAD
0 Yards
440
0 Metres
400
1
2
3
4
5
6
7
8
9
10
11

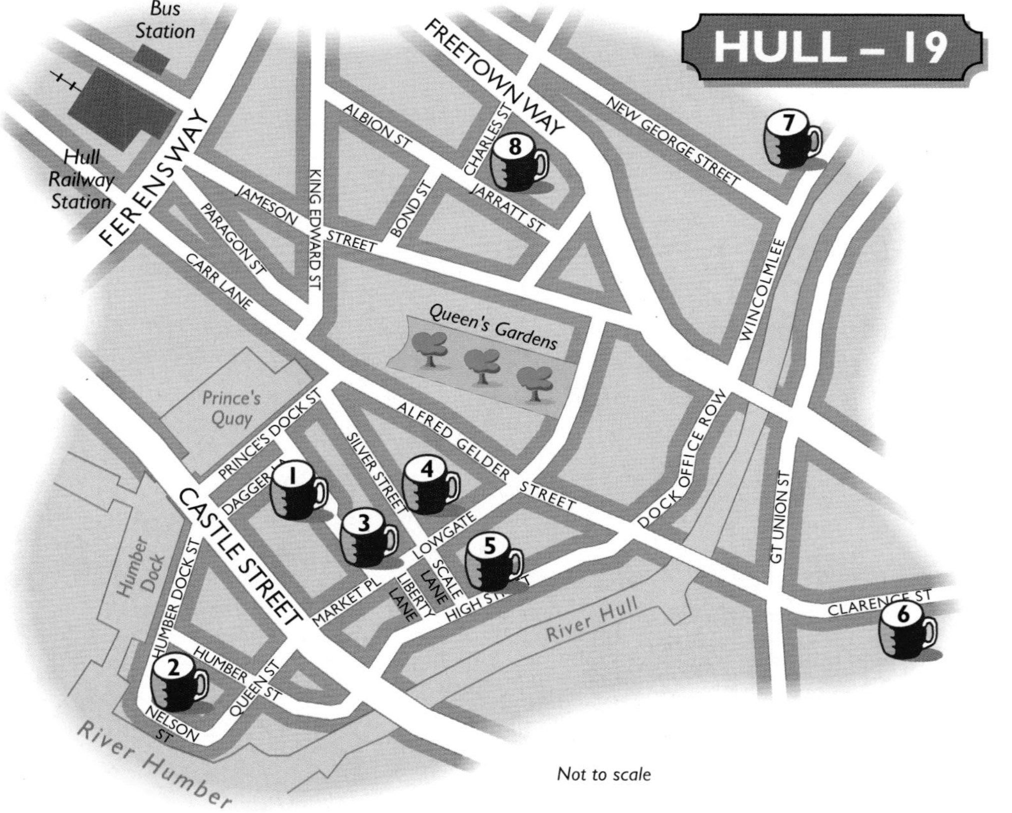
HULL – 19
Bus Station
Hull Railway Station
FERENSWAY
FREETOWN WAY
NEW GEORGE STREET
ALBION ST
CHARLES ST
JARRATT ST
BOND ST
JAMESON
STREET
KING EDWARD ST
PARAGON ST
CARR LANE
WINCOLMLEE
Queen's Gardens
Prince's Quay
PRINCE'S DOCK ST
ALFRED GELDER
STREET
SILVER STREET
DAGGER LA
DOCK OFFICE ROW
GT UNION ST
CASTLE STREET
LOWGATE
SCALE LANE
LIBERTY LANE
MARKET PL
HIGH STREET
Humber Dock
HUMBER DOCK ST
HUMBER ST
QUEEN ST
NELSON ST
River Hull
CLARENCE ST
River Humber
1
2
3
4
5
6
7
8
Not to scale

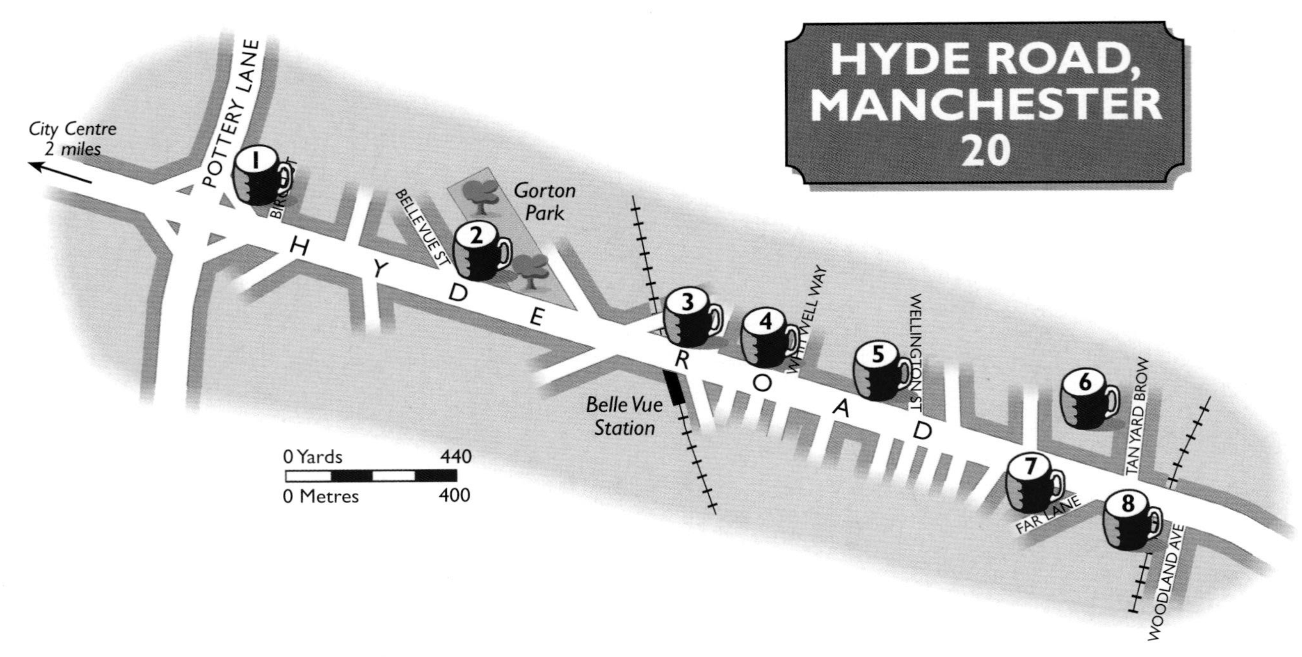
HYDE ROAD, MANCHESTER 20
City Centre 2 miles
POTTERY LANE
BELLEVUE ST
Gorton Park
HYDE ROAD
Belle Vue Station
WELLINGTON ST
TAN YARD BROW
FAR LANE
WOODLAND AVE
0 Yards 440
0 Metres 400
1
2
3
4
5
6
7
8

KENDAL – 21

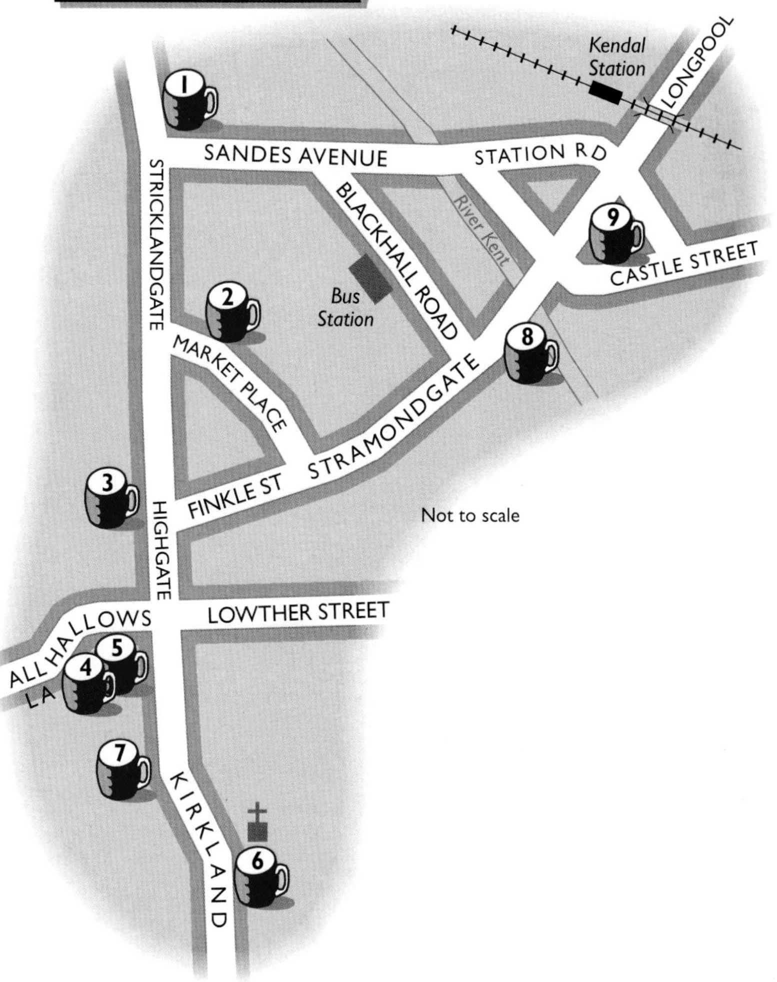
Kendal
Station
LONGPOOL
SANDES AVENUE
STATION RD
STRICKLANDGATE
BLACKHALL ROAD
River Kent
CASTLE STREET
Bus
Station
MARKET PLACE
STRAMONDGATE
FINKLE ST
HIGHGATE
Not to scale
ALLHALLOWS
LA
LOWTHER STREET
KIRKLAND
1
2
3
4
5
6
7
8
9

KINGTON – 22

A44

CHURCH ROAD

HIGH STREET

VICTORIA ROAD

B4359

BRIDGE STREET

A44

Not to scale

LANCASTER – 23

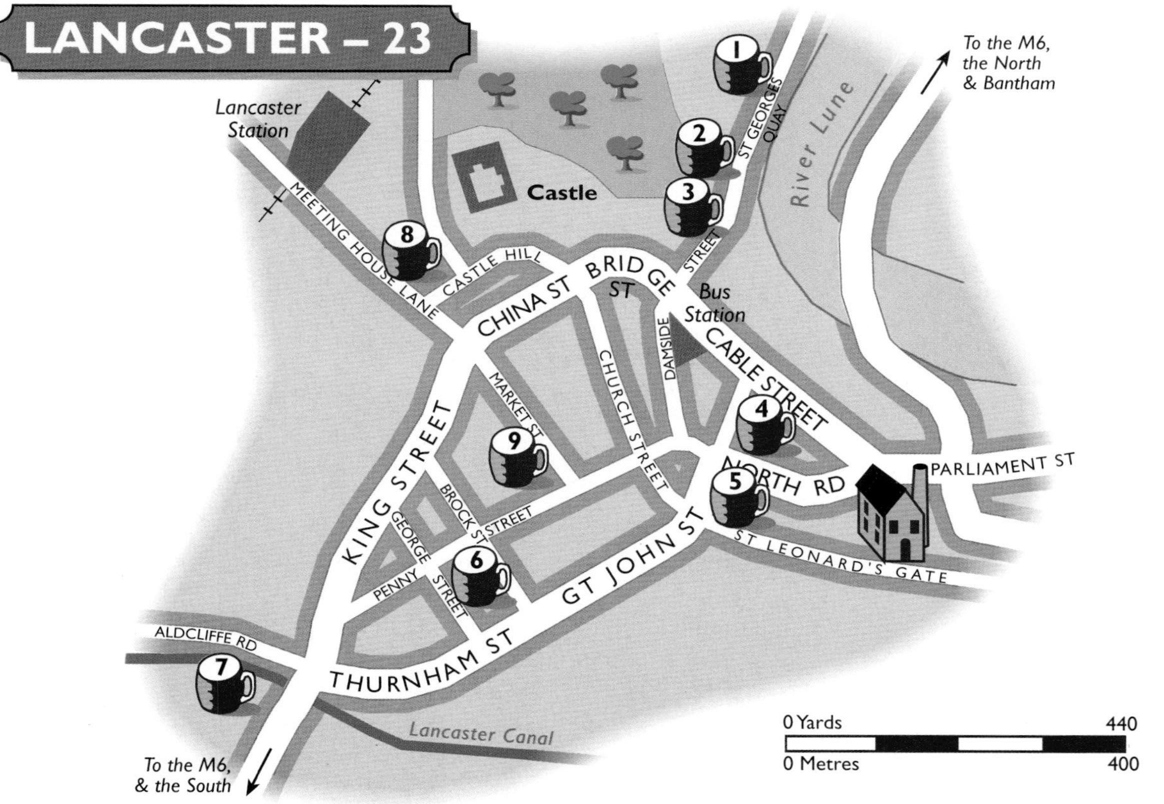

LEDBURY – 24

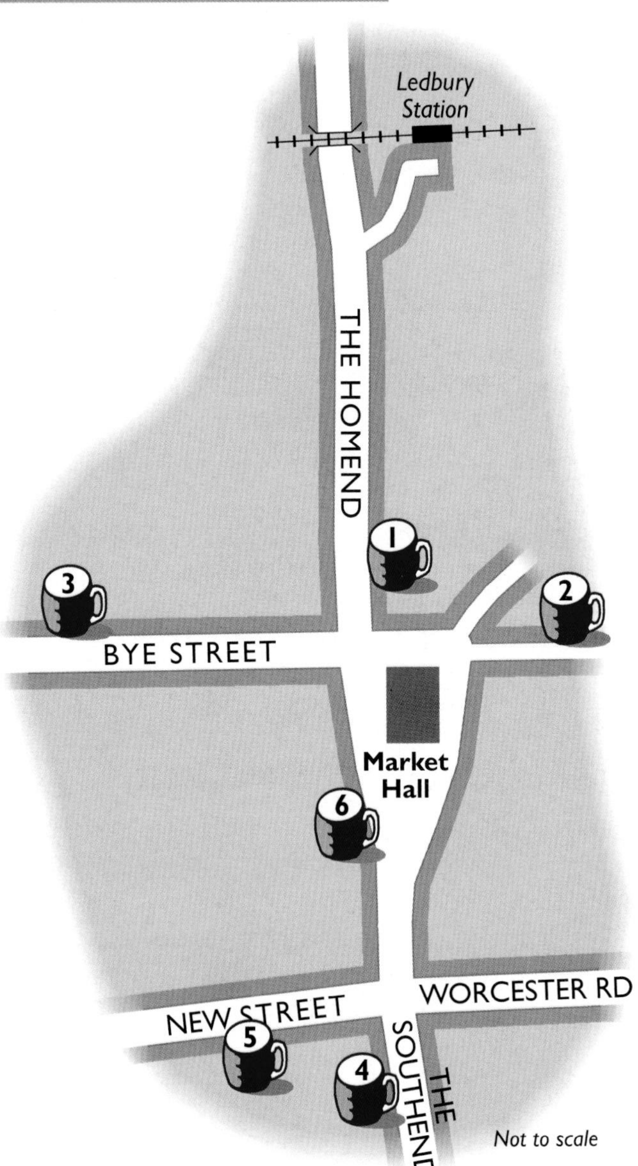

Ledbury Station
THE HOMEND
1
2
3
BYE STREET
Market Hall
6
NEW STREET
WORCESTER RD
5
4
THE SOUTHEND
Not to scale

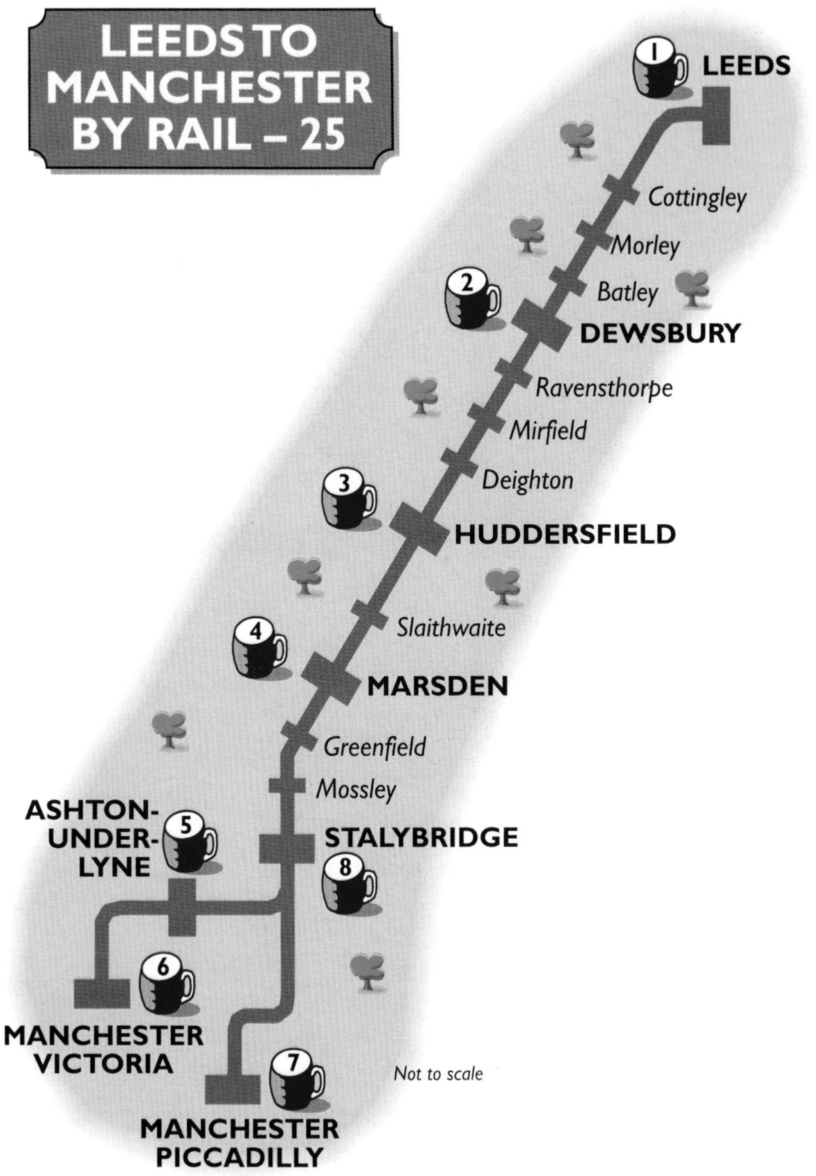
LEEDS TO
MANCHESTER
BY RAIL – 25
1
LEEDS
Cottingley
Morley
2
Batley
DEWSBURY
Ravensthorpe
Mirfield
3
Deighton
HUDDERSFIELD
Slaithwaite
4
MARSDEN
Greenfield
Mossley
ASHTON-
UNDER-
LYNE
5
STALYBRIDGE
8
6
MANCHESTER
VICTORIA
7
Not to scale
MANCHESTER
PICCADILLY

LEE VALLEY BY BOAT – 26

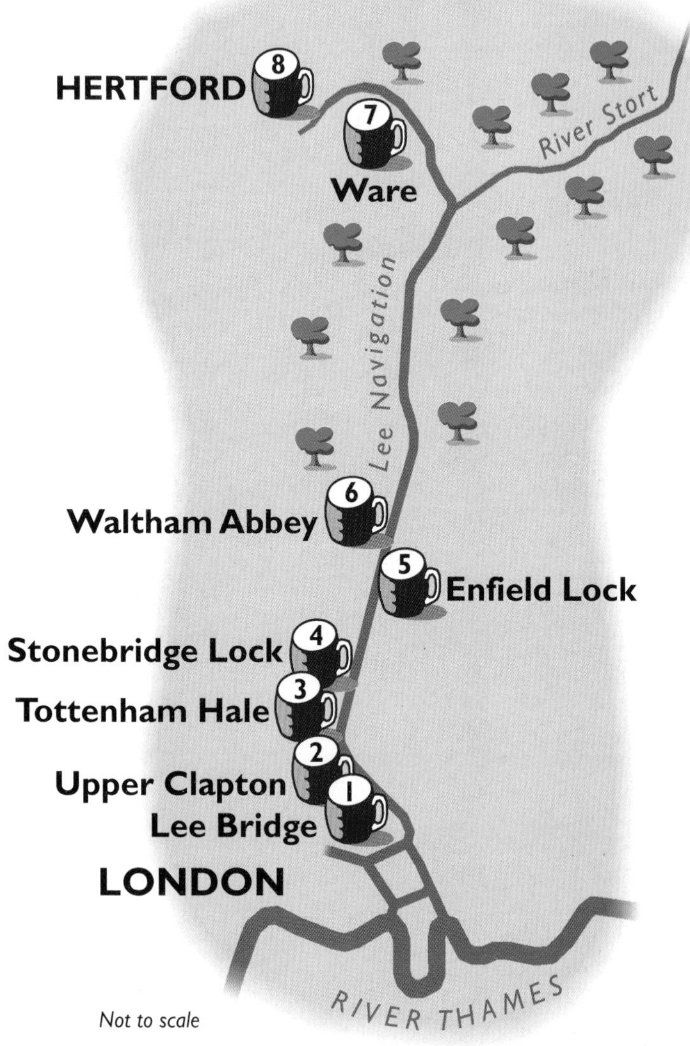

LINCOLN – 27

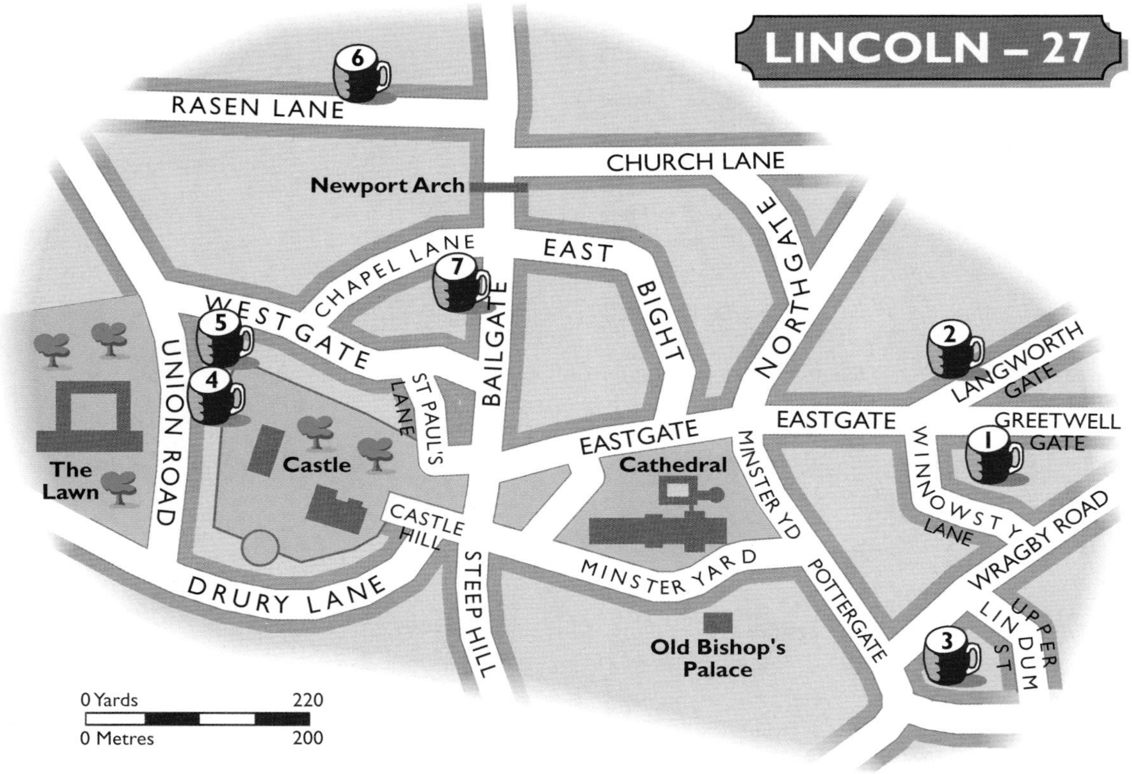

RASEN LANE
CHURCH LANE
Newport Arch
NORTHGATE
EAST
BIGHT
CHAPEL LANE
WESTGATE
BAILGATE
ST PAUL'S LANE
EASTGATE
EASTGATE
LANGWORTH GATE
GREETWELL GATE
WINNOWSTY LANE
WRAGBY ROAD
UPPER LINDUM ST
POTTERGATE
MINSTER YD
MINSTER YARD
Cathedral
Old Bishop's Palace
STEEP HILL
CASTLE HILL
Castle
UNION ROAD
DRURY LANE
The Lawn
1
2
3
4
5
6
7
0 Yards
220
0 Metres
200

LIVERPOOL – 28

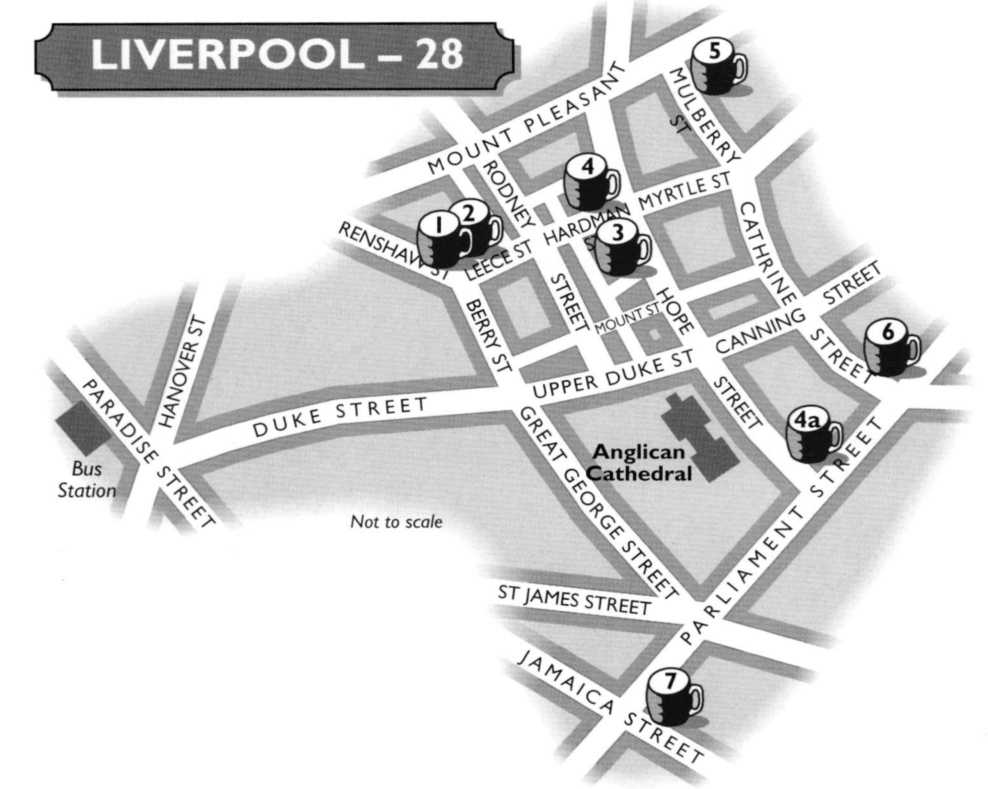

LLANDUDNO – 29

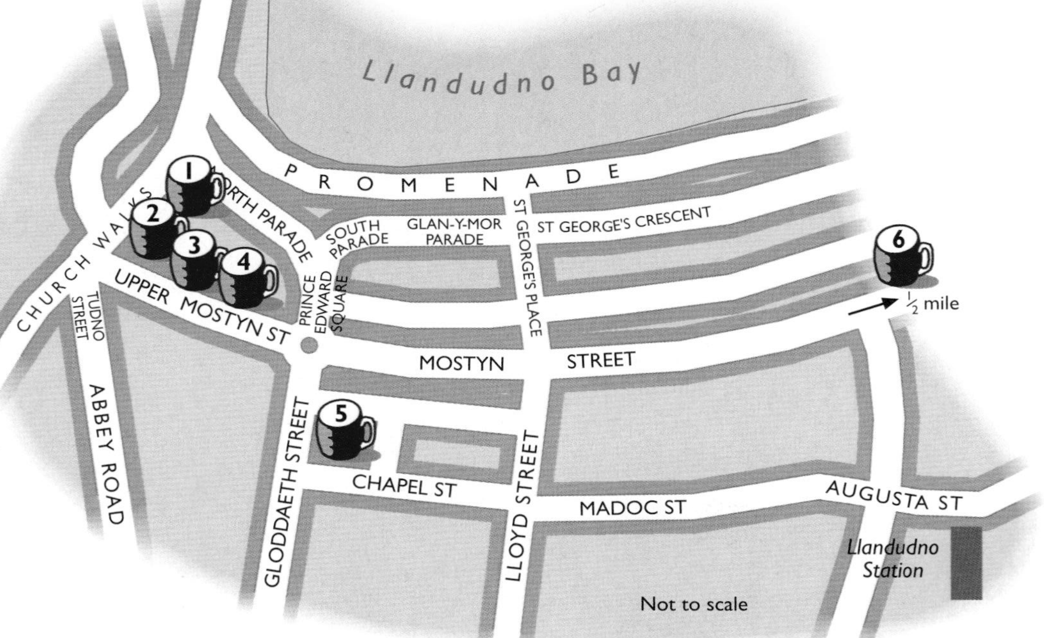

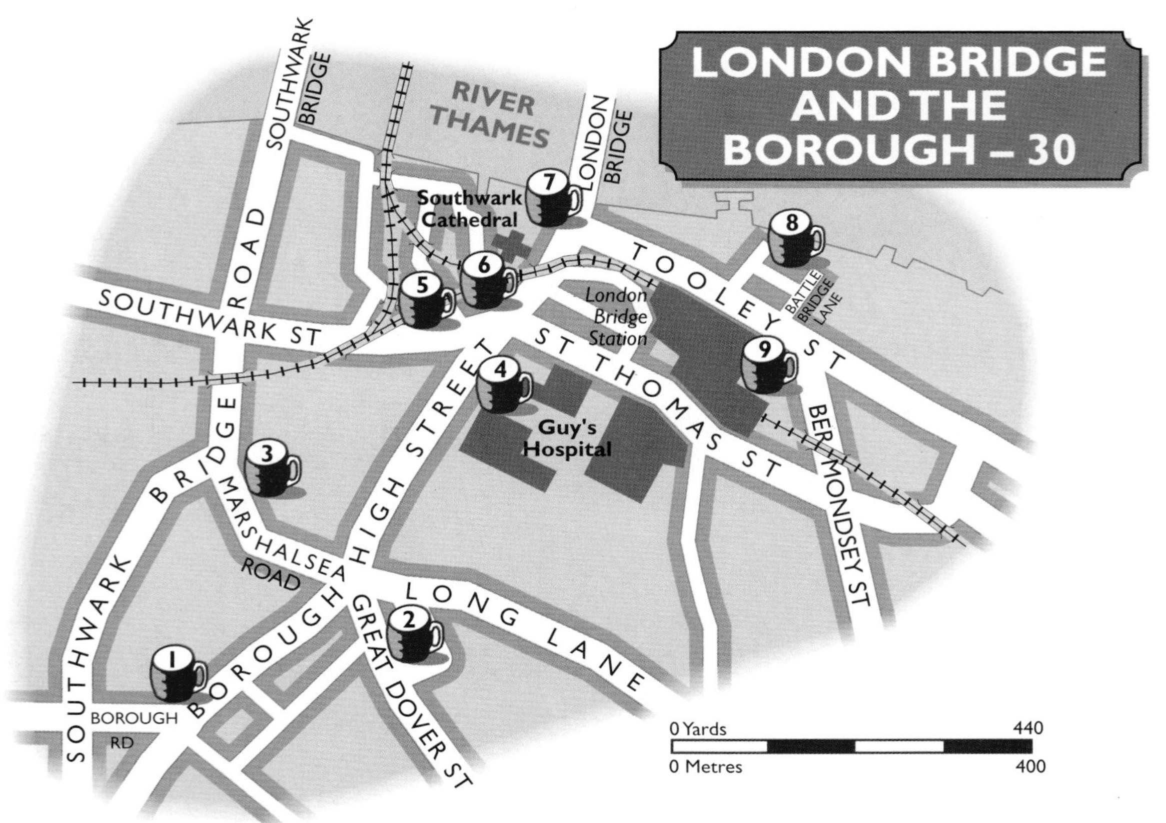
LONDON BRIDGE AND THE BOROUGH – 30
RIVER THAMES
SOUTHWARK BRIDGE
LONDON BRIDGE
Southwark Cathedral
TOOLEY ST
BATTLE BRIDGE LANE
London Bridge Station
SOUTHWARK ST
ROAD
ST THOMAS ST
HIGH STREET
Guy's Hospital
BERMONDSEY ST
SOUTHWARK BRIDGE
MARSHALSEA ROAD
LONG LANE
BOROUGH HIGH
GREAT DOVER ST
SOUTHWARK
BOROUGH RD
1
2
3
4
5
6
7
8
9
0 Yards
440
0 Metres
400

LOUTH – 31

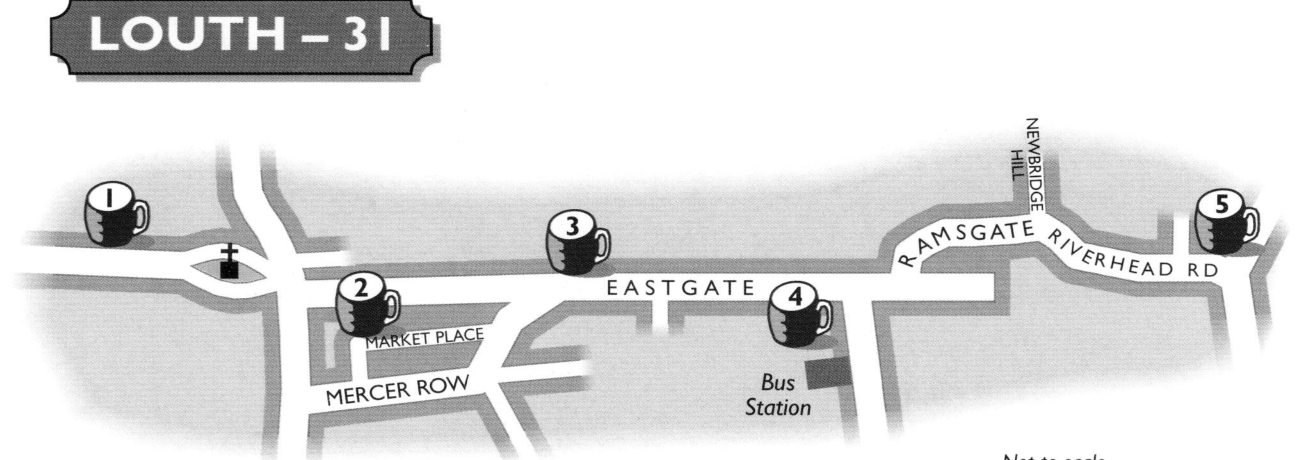
1
2
3
4
5
MARKET PLACE
MERCER ROW
EASTGATE
Bus Station
RAMSGATE
NEWBRIDGE HILL
RIVERHEAD RD
Not to scale

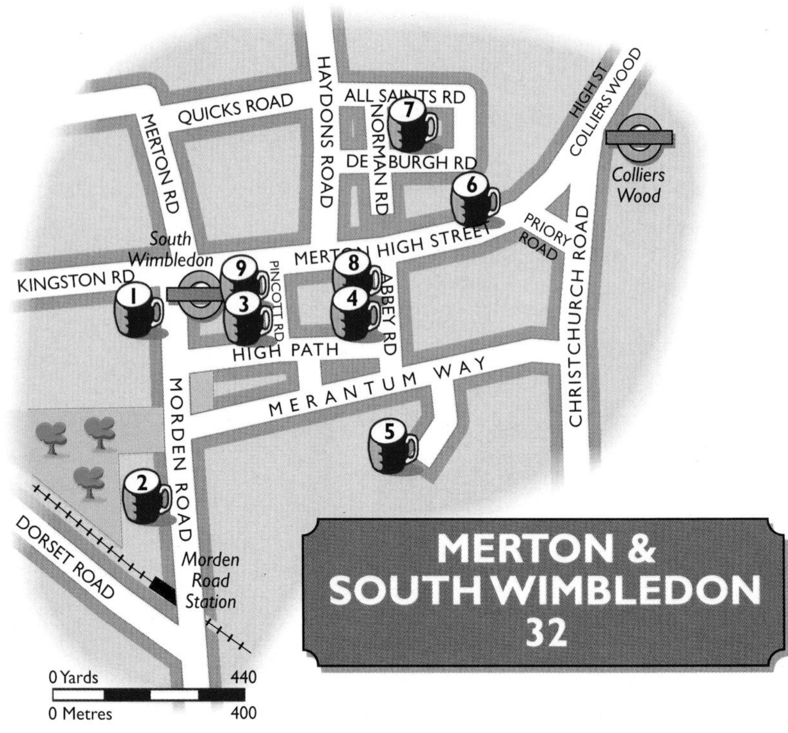
MERTON &
SOUTH WIMBLEDON
32
QUICKS ROAD
HAYDONS ROAD
ALL SAINTS RD
NORMAN RD
DE BURGH RD
HIGH ST
COLLIERS WOOD
Colliers
Wood
MERTON RD
South
Wimbledon
MERTON HIGH STREET
PRIORY
ROAD
KINGSTON RD
PINCOTT RD
ABBEY RD
CHRISTCHURCH ROAD
HIGH PATH
MERANTUM WAY
MORDEN ROAD
DORSET ROAD
Morden
Road
Station
1
2
3
4
5
6
7
8
9
0 Yards
440
0 Metres
400

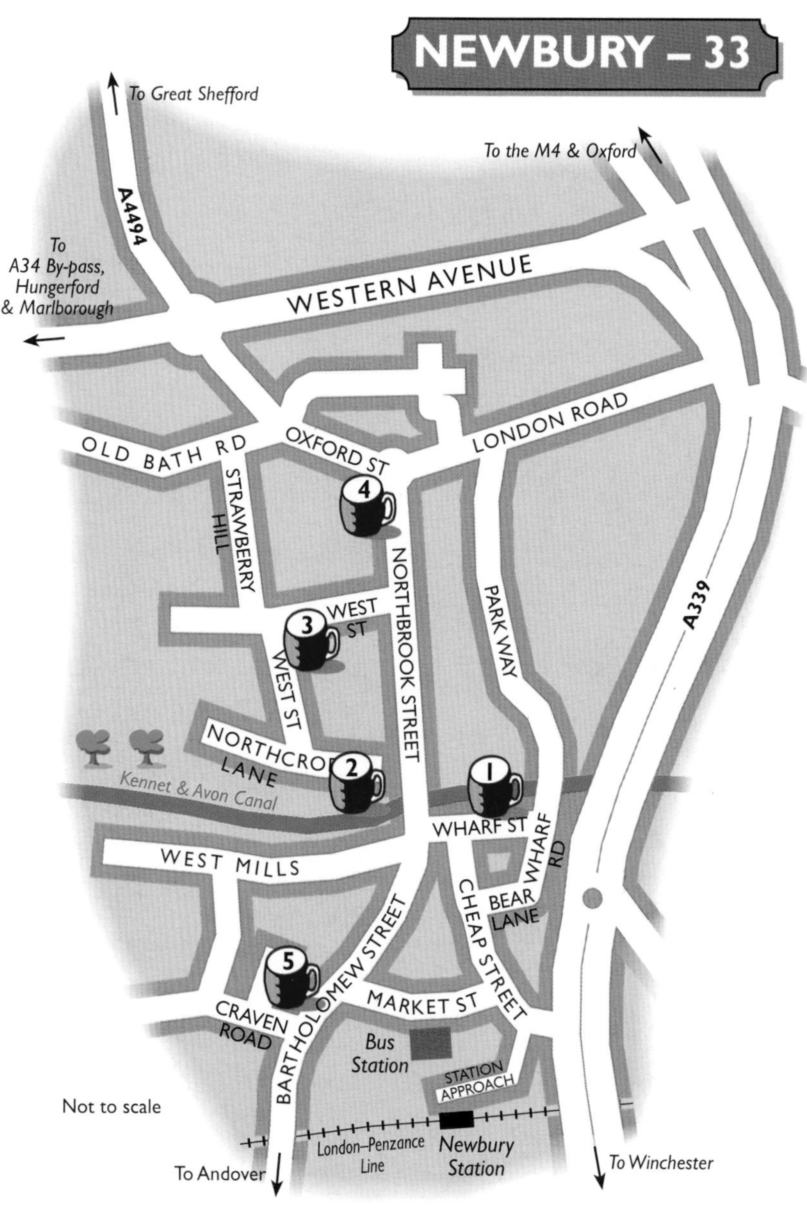

NEWBURY – 33
To Great Shefford
To the M4 & Oxford
A4494
To
A34 By-pass,
Hungerford
& Marlborough
WESTERN AVENUE
OLD BATH RD
OXFORD ST
LONDON ROAD
STRAWBERRY
HILL
NORTHBROOK STREET
PARK WAY
A339
WEST
ST
WEST ST
NORTHCROFT
LANE
Kennet & Avon Canal
WHARF ST
WHARF
RD
WEST MILLS
CHEAP STREET
BEAR
LANE
BARTHOLOMEW STREET
MARKET ST
CRAVEN
ROAD
Bus
Station
STATION
APPROACH
Not to scale
London–Penzance
Line
Newbury
Station
To Andover
To Winchester

NEWCASTLE – 34

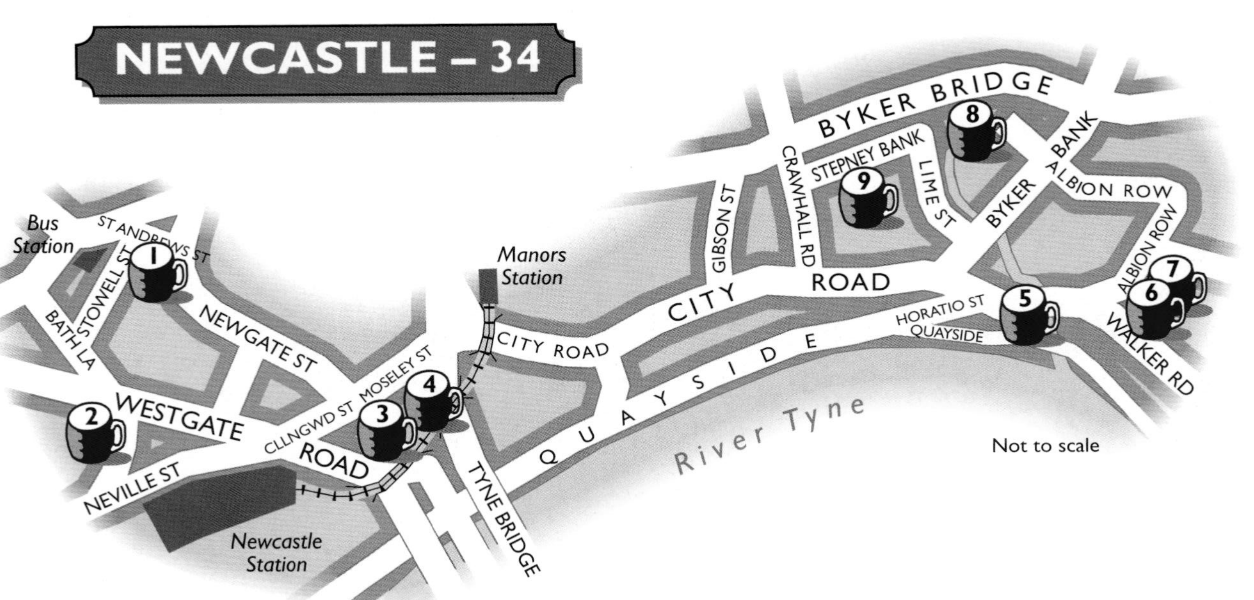

NOTTINGHAM – 35

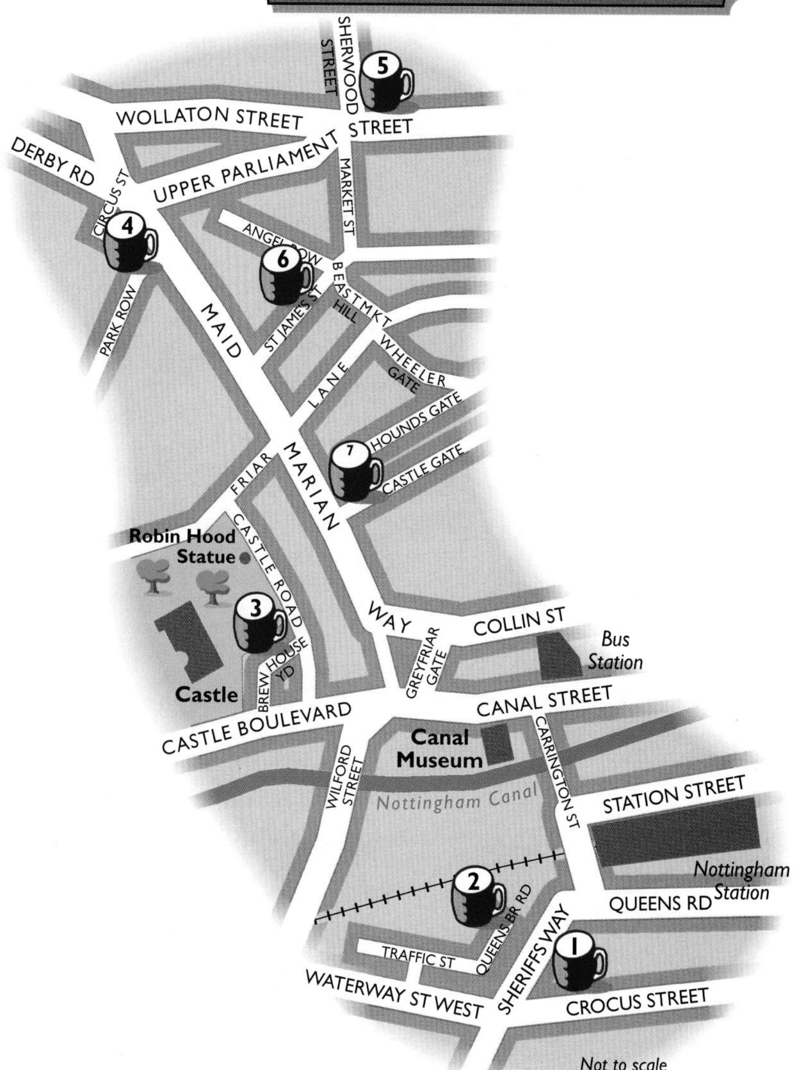

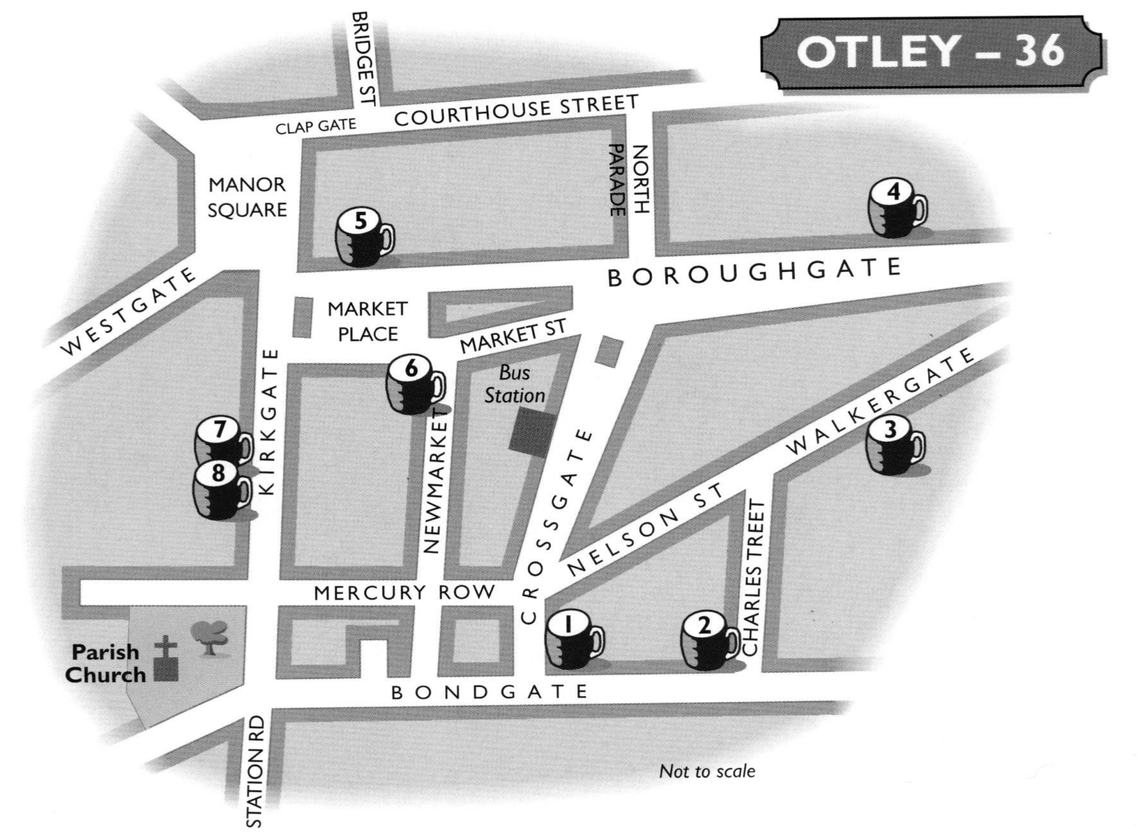
OTLEY – 36
BRIDGE ST
COURTHOUSE STREET
CLAP GATE
NORTH PARADE
MANOR SQUARE
BOROUGHGATE
WESTGATE
MARKET PLACE
MARKET ST
Bus Station
KIRKGATE
NEWMARKET
CROSSGATE
WALKERGATE
NELSON ST
CHARLES TREET
MERCURY ROW
Parish Church
BONDGATE
STATION RD
Not to scale
1
2
3
4
5
6
7
8

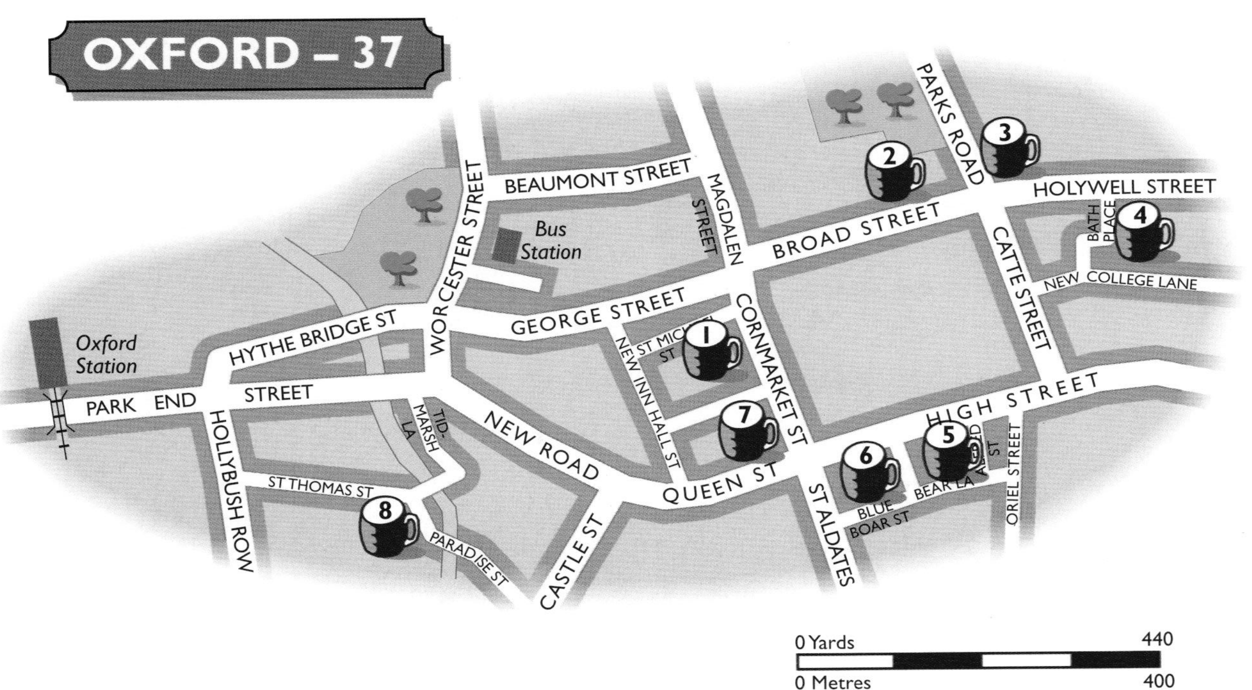

OXFORD – 37
PARKS ROAD
HOLYWELL STREET
BATH PLACE
NEW COLLEGE LANE
BEAUMONT STREET
MAGDALEN STREET
BROAD STREET
CATTE STREET
Bus Station
WORCESTER STREET
GEORGE STREET
CORNMARKET ST
NEW INN HALL ST
HYTHE BRIDGE ST
Oxford Station
PARK END STREET
HIGH STREET
ORIEL STREET
BEAR LA
BLUE BOAR ST
ST ALDATES
QUEEN ST
NEW ROAD
TID-MARSH LA
HOLLYBUSH ROW
ST THOMAS ST
PARADISE ST
CASTLE ST
1
2
3
4
5
6
7
8
0 Yards
440
0 Metres
400

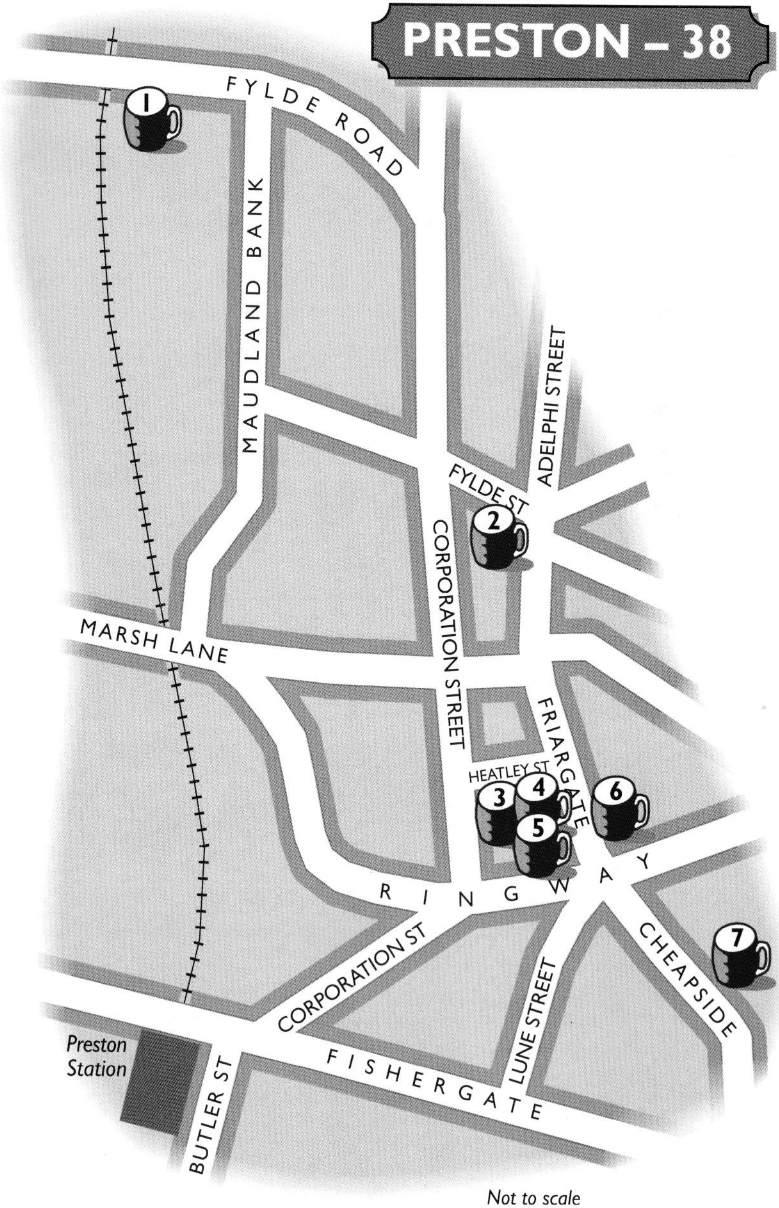

PRESTON – 38

FYLDE ROAD
MAUDLAND BANK
ADELPHI STREET
FYLDE ST
CORPORATION STREET
MARSH LANE
FRIARGATE
HEATLEY ST
RINGWAY
CORPORATION ST
LUNE STREET
CHEAPSIDE
Preston Station
BUTLER ST
FISHERGATE
1
2
3
4
5
6
7

Not to scale

ST ALBANS – 39

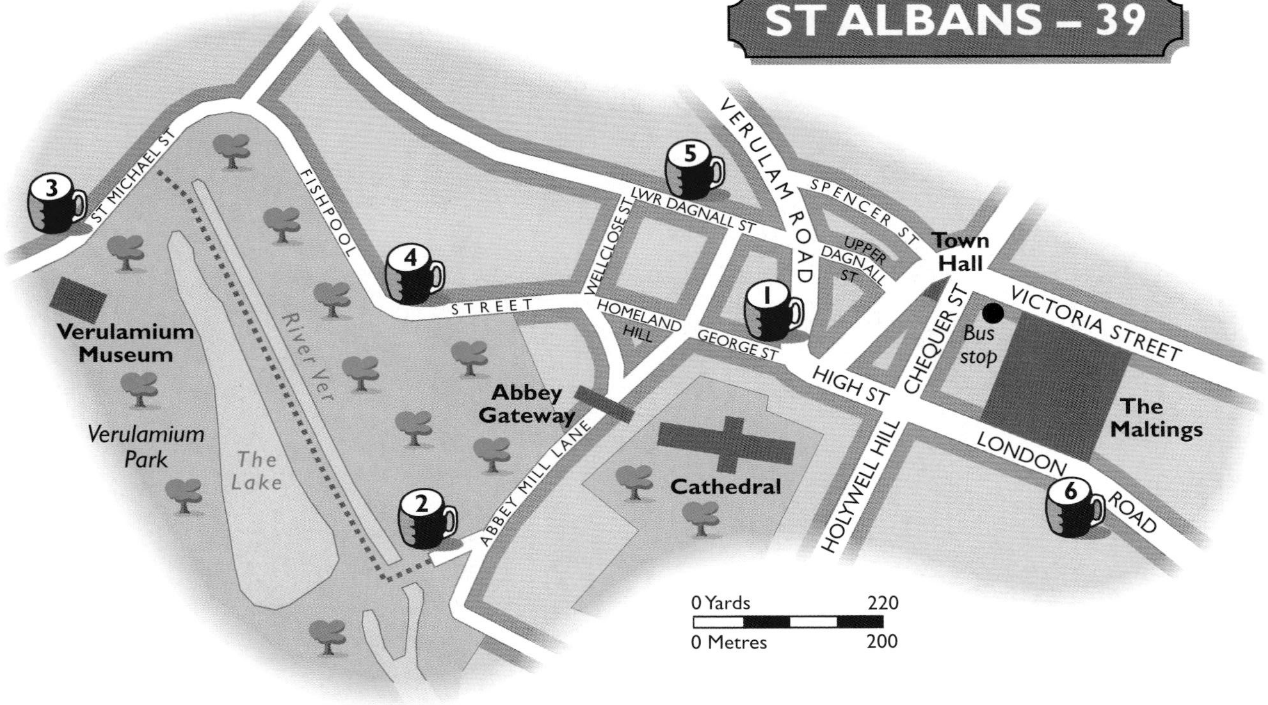

ST MICHAEL ST
FISHPOOL
STREET
Verulamium Museum
Verulamium Park
The Lake
River Ver
Abbey Gateway
ABBEY MILL LANE
LWR DAGNALL ST
WELLCLOSE ST
HOMELAND HILL
GEORGE ST
VERULAM ROAD
SPENCER ST
UPPER DAGNALL ST
Town Hall
CHEQUER ST
Bus stop
VICTORIA STREET
HIGH ST
HOLYWELL HILL
Cathedral
The Maltings
LONDON ROAD
1
2
3
4
5
6
0 Yards
220
0 Metres
200

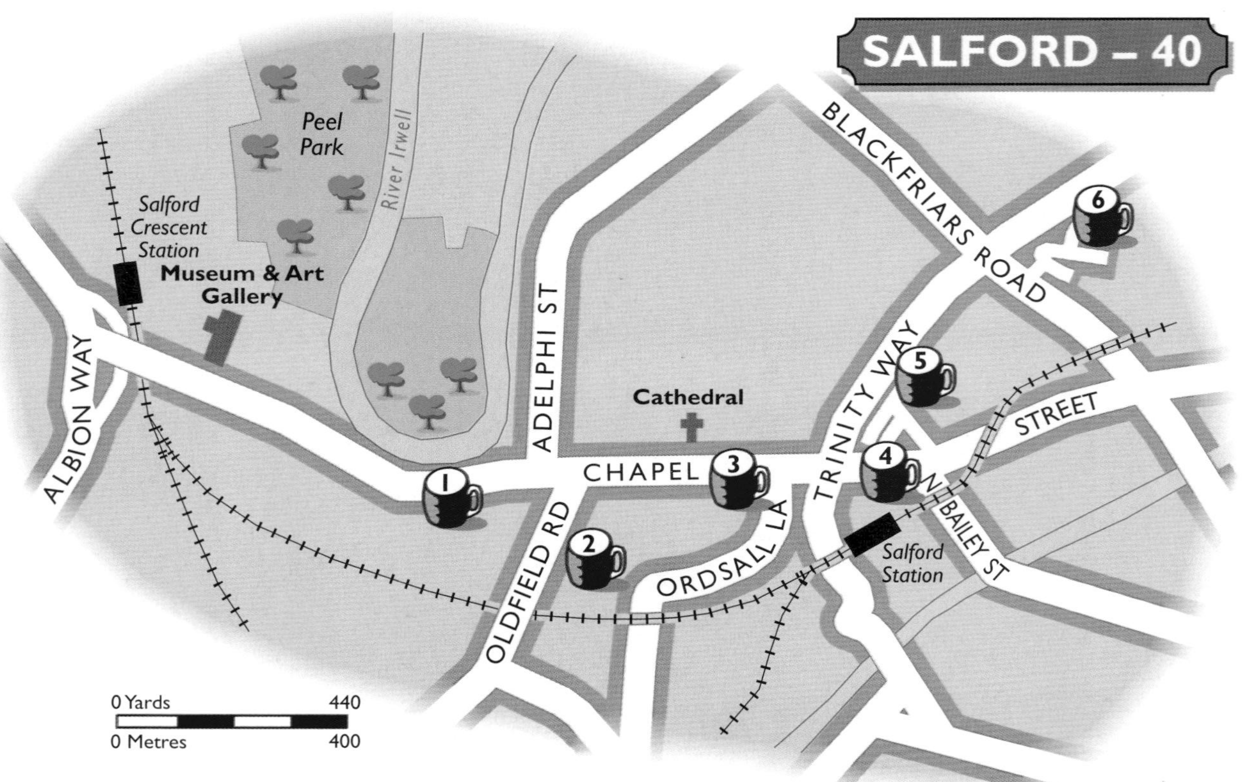
SALFORD – 40
Peel Park
River Irwell
Salford Crescent Station
Museum & Art Gallery
ALBION WAY
ADELPHI ST
Cathedral
BLACKFRIARS ROAD
TRINITY WAY
CHAPEL
STREET
N. BAILEY ST
Salford Station
ORDSALL LA
OLDFIELD RD
1
2
3
4
5
6
0 Yards
440
0 Metres
400

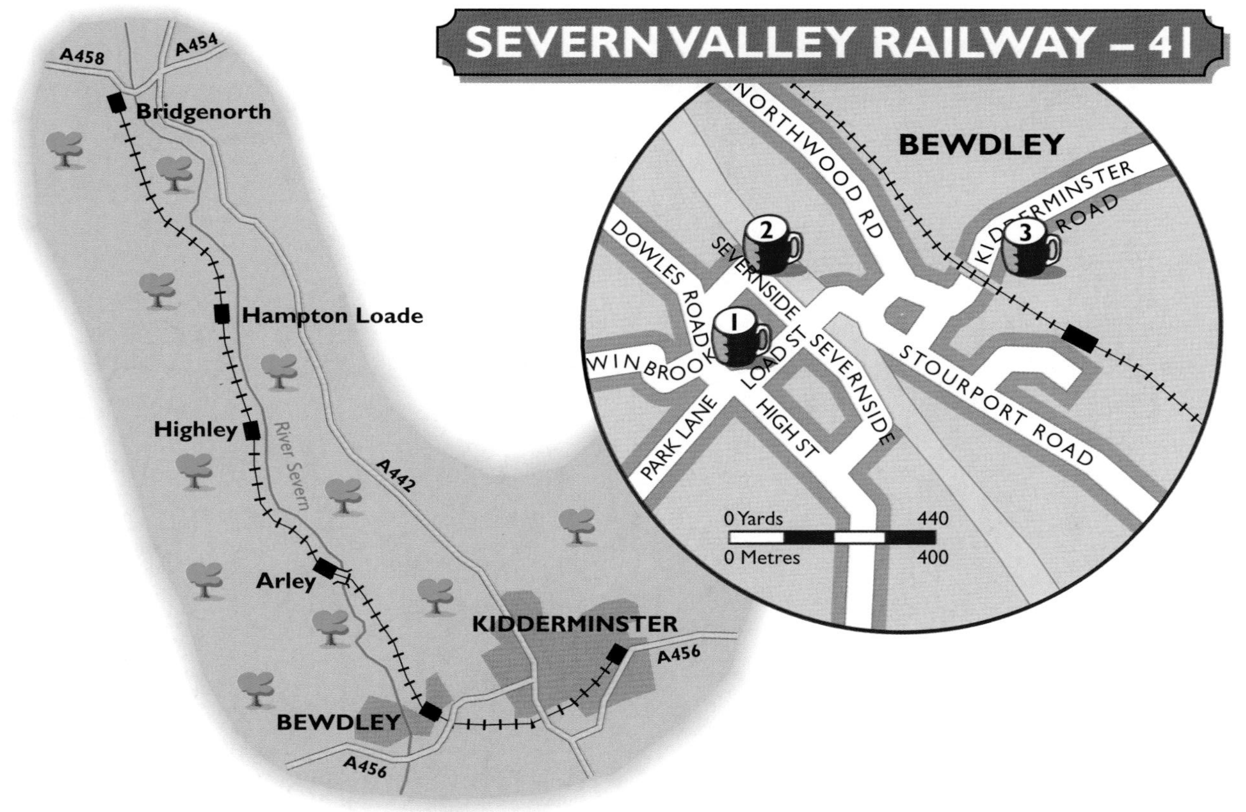

SEVERN VALLEY RAILWAY – 41
BEWDLEY
NORTHWOOD RD
KIDDERMINSTER ROAD
DOWLES ROAD
SEVERNSIDE
SEVERNSIDE
LOAD ST
WINBROOK
PARK LANE
HIGH ST
STOURPORT ROAD
1
2
3
0 Yards
440
0 Metres
400
A458
A454
Bridgenorth
Hampton Loade
Highley
River Severn
A442
Arley
KIDDERMINSTER
A456
BEWDLEY
A456

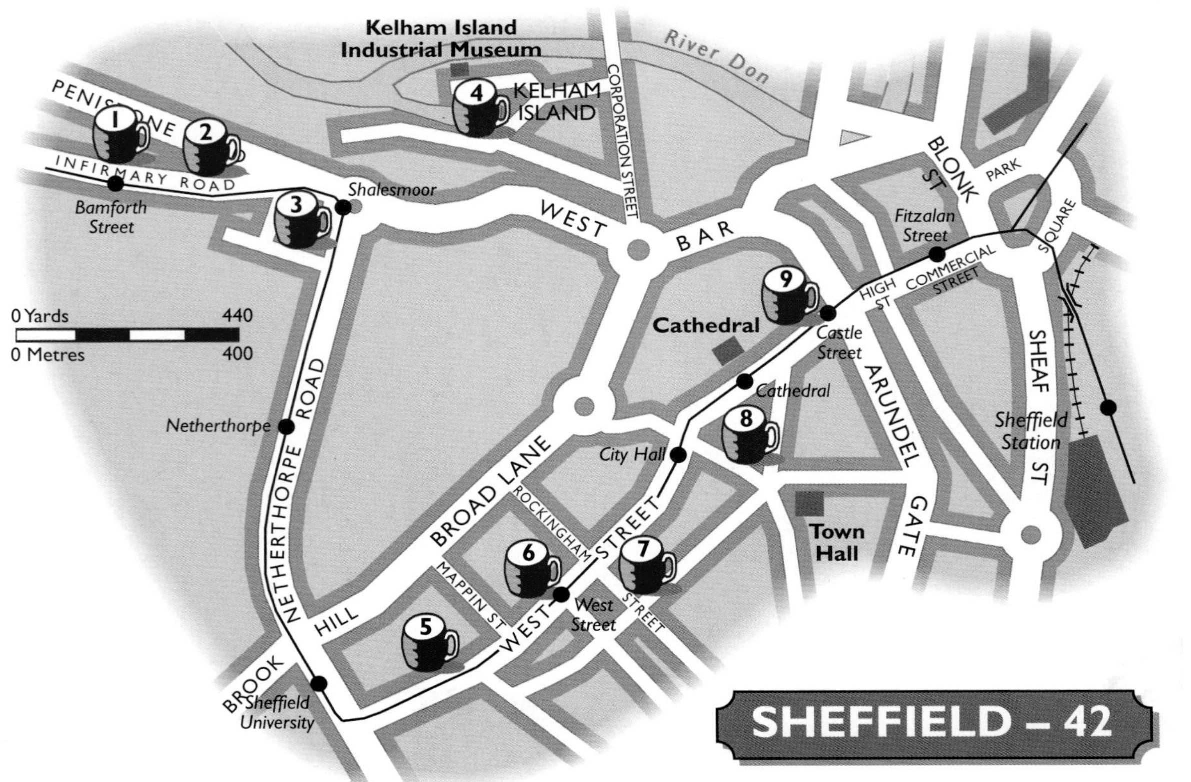
SHEFFIELD – 42
Kelham Island Industrial Museum
River Don
KELHAM ISLAND
PENISTONE
INFIRMARY ROAD
Bamforth Street
Shalesmoor
CORPORATION STREET
WEST BAR
BLONK ST
PARK
SQUARE
Fitzalan Street
HIGH ST
COMMERCIAL STREET
Cathedral
Castle Street
Cathedral
ARUNDEL GATE
SHEAF ST
Sheffield Station
Town Hall
City Hall
BROAD LANE
ROCKINGHAM
WEST STREET
STREET
West Street
MAPPIN ST
NETHERTHORPE ROAD
Netherthorpe
HILL
BROOK
Sheffield University
0 Yards
440
0 Metres
400
1
2
3
4
5
6
7
8
9

SOUTH SHIELDS – 43

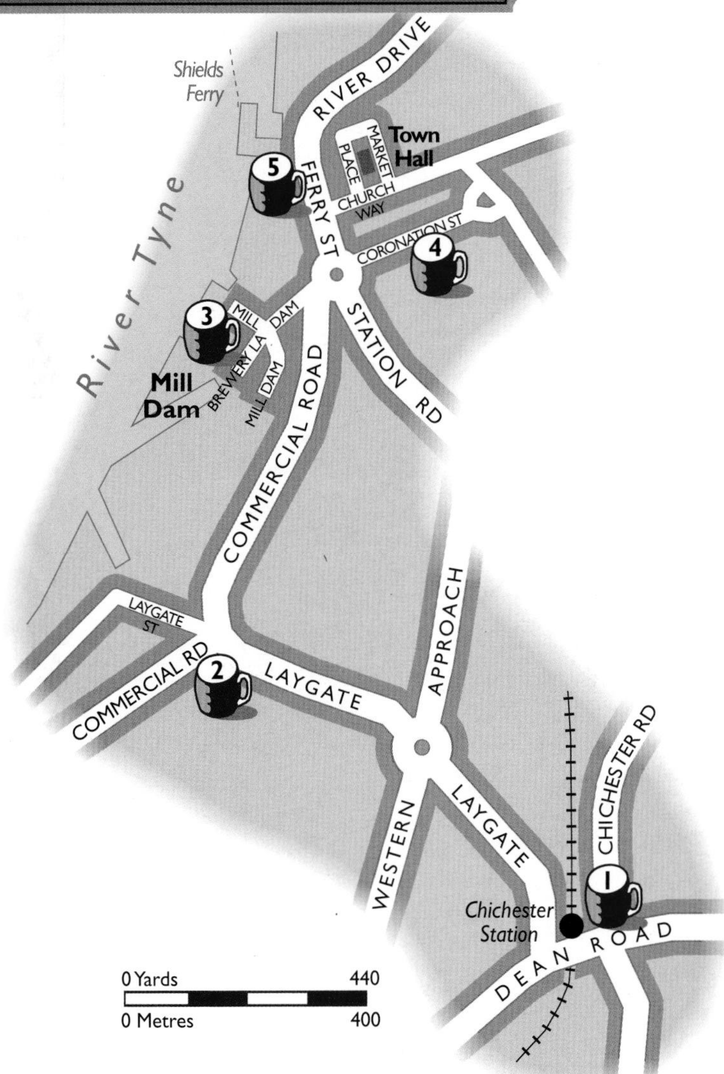

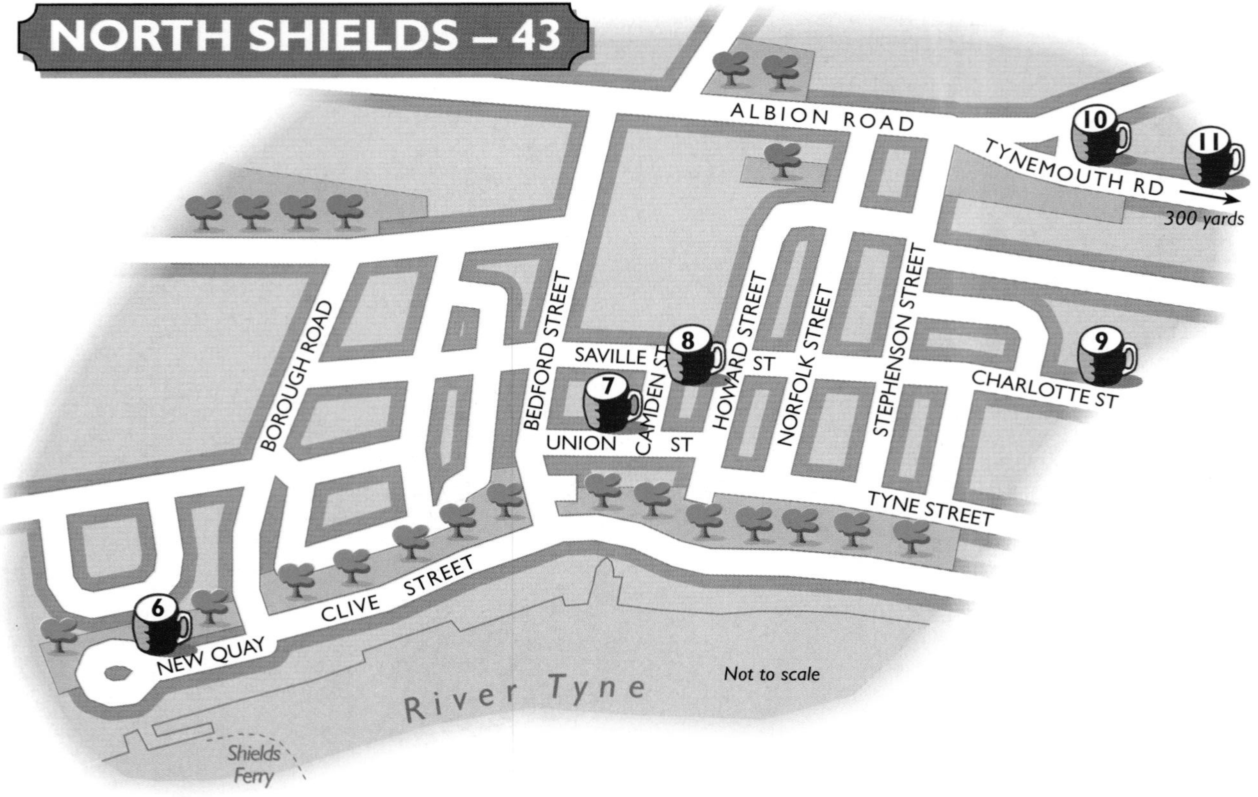

NORTH SHIELDS – 43

ALBION ROAD
TYNEMOUTH RD
300 yards
10
11
BOROUGH ROAD
BEDFORD STREET
SAVILLE ST
CAMDEN ST
HOWARD STREET
NORFOLK STREET
STEPHENSON STREET
CHARLOTTE ST
UNION ST
TYNE STREET
CLIVE STREET
NEW QUAY
6
7
8
9
River Tyne
Not to scale
Shields Ferry

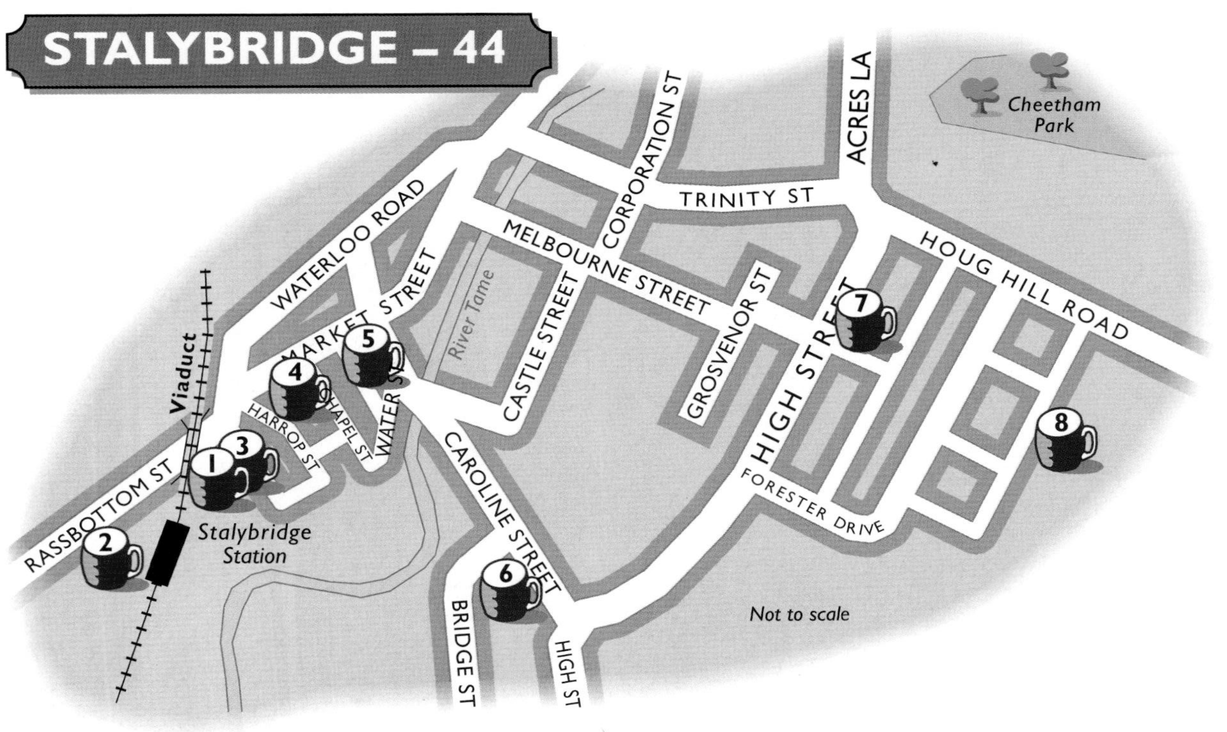
STALYBRIDGE – 44
Cheetham Park
ACRES LA
CORPORATION ST
TRINITY ST
WATERLOO ROAD
MELBOURNE STREET
HOUG HILL ROAD
MARKET STREET
River Tame
CASTLE STREET
GROSVENOR ST
HIGH STREET
Viaduct
HARROP ST
CHAPEL ST
WATER ST
RASSBOTTOM ST
Stalybridge Station
CAROLINE STREET
FORESTER DRIVE
BRIDGE ST
HIGH ST
Not to scale
1
2
3
4
5
6
7
8

STOCKPORT – 45

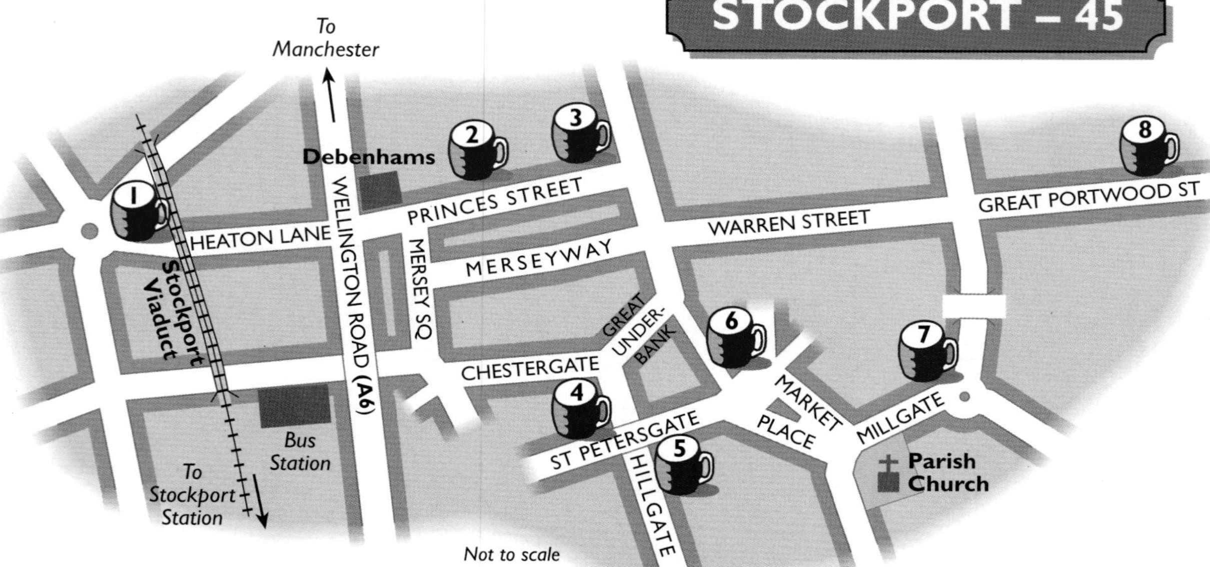

SWINDON – 46

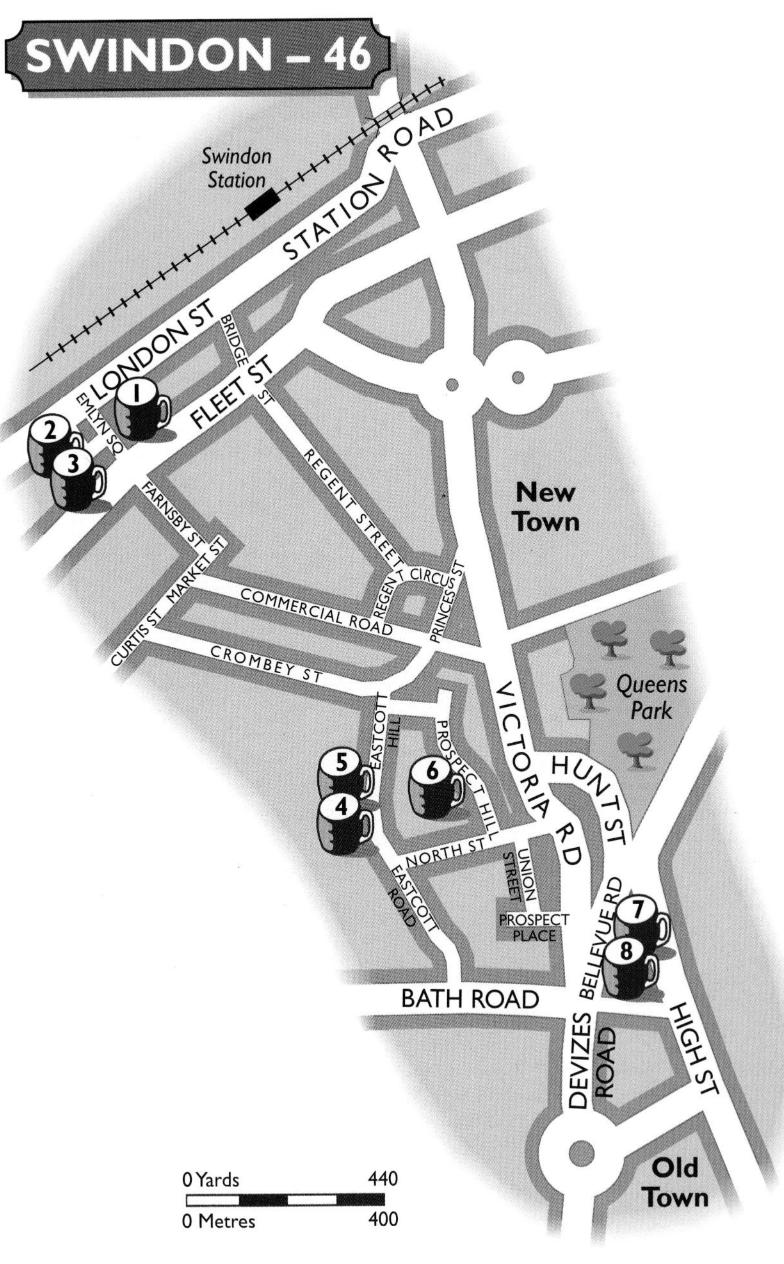

Swindon Station
STATION ROAD
LONDON ST
BRIDGE ST
EMLYN SQ
FLEET ST
REGENT STREET
FARNSBY ST
MARKET ST
CURTIS ST
COMMERCIAL ROAD
REGENT CIRCUS
PRINCES ST
CROMBEY ST
New Town
Queens Park
VICTORIA RD
HUNT ST
EASTCOTT HILL
PROSPECT HILL
NORTH ST
UNION STREET
EASTCOTT ROAD
PROSPECT PLACE
BELLEVUE RD
BATH ROAD
DEVIZES ROAD
HIGH ST
Old Town
0 Yards 440
0 Metres 400
1
2
3
4
5
6
7
8

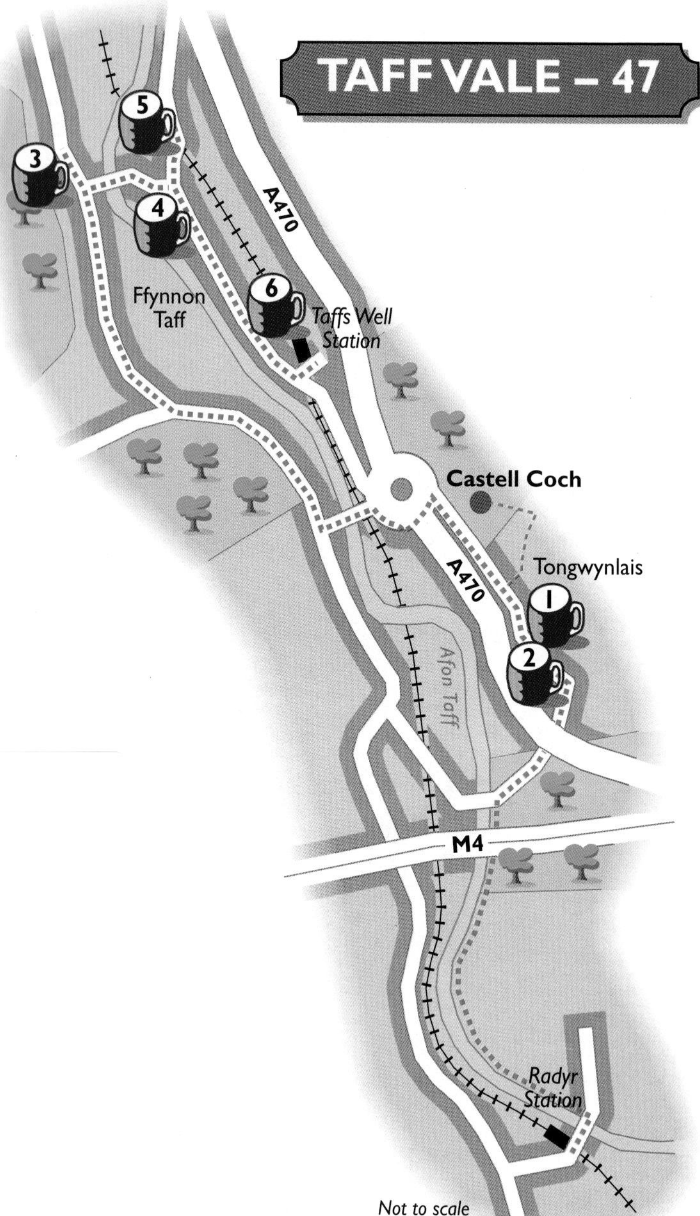

TAFF VALE – 47
A470
Ffynnon Taff
Taffs Well Station
Castell Coch
Tongwynlais
A470
Afon Taff
M4
Radyr Station
Not to scale

WALSALL – 48

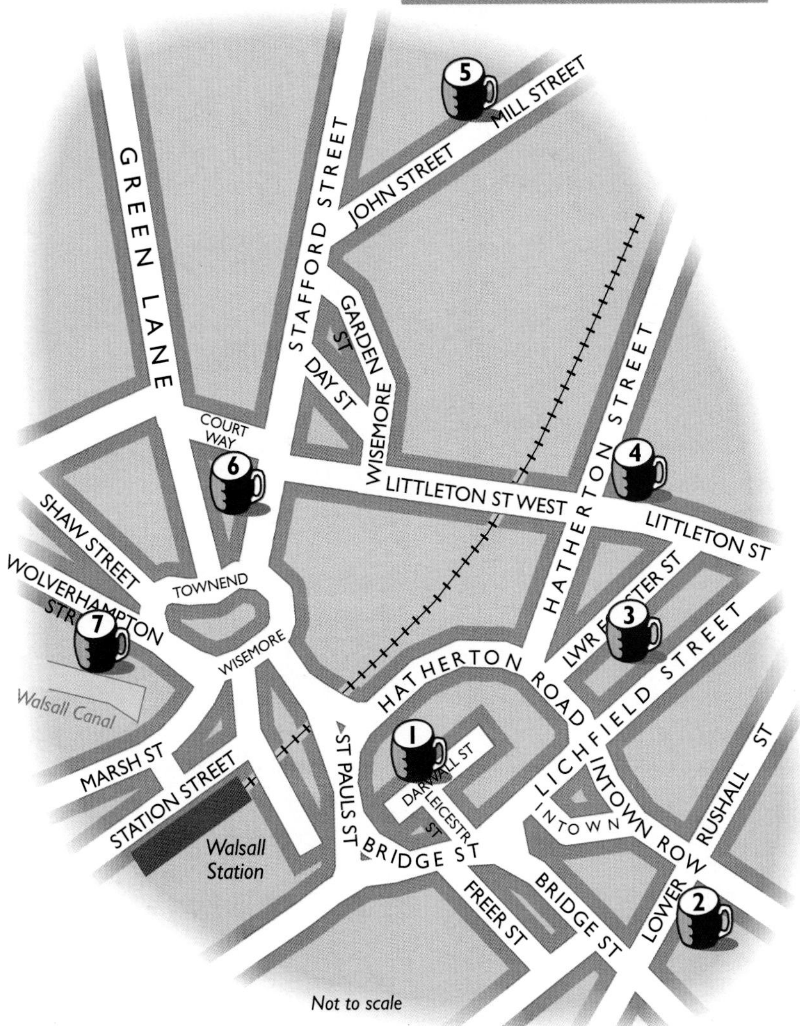

GREEN LANE
STAFFORD STREET
JOHN STREET
MILL STREET
GARDEN ST
DAY ST
WISEMORE
COURT WAY
LITTLETON ST WEST
LITTLETON ST
HATHERTON STREET
SHAW STREET
WOLVERHAMPTON STREET
TOWNEND
WISEMORE
HATHERTON ROAD
LICHFIELD STREET
Walsall Canal
MARSH ST
STATION STREET
ST PAULS ST
DARWALL ST
LEICESTER ST
BRIDGE ST
INTOWN
INTOWN ROW
RUSHALL ST
LOWER
FREER ST
BRIDGE ST
Walsall Station
Not to scale

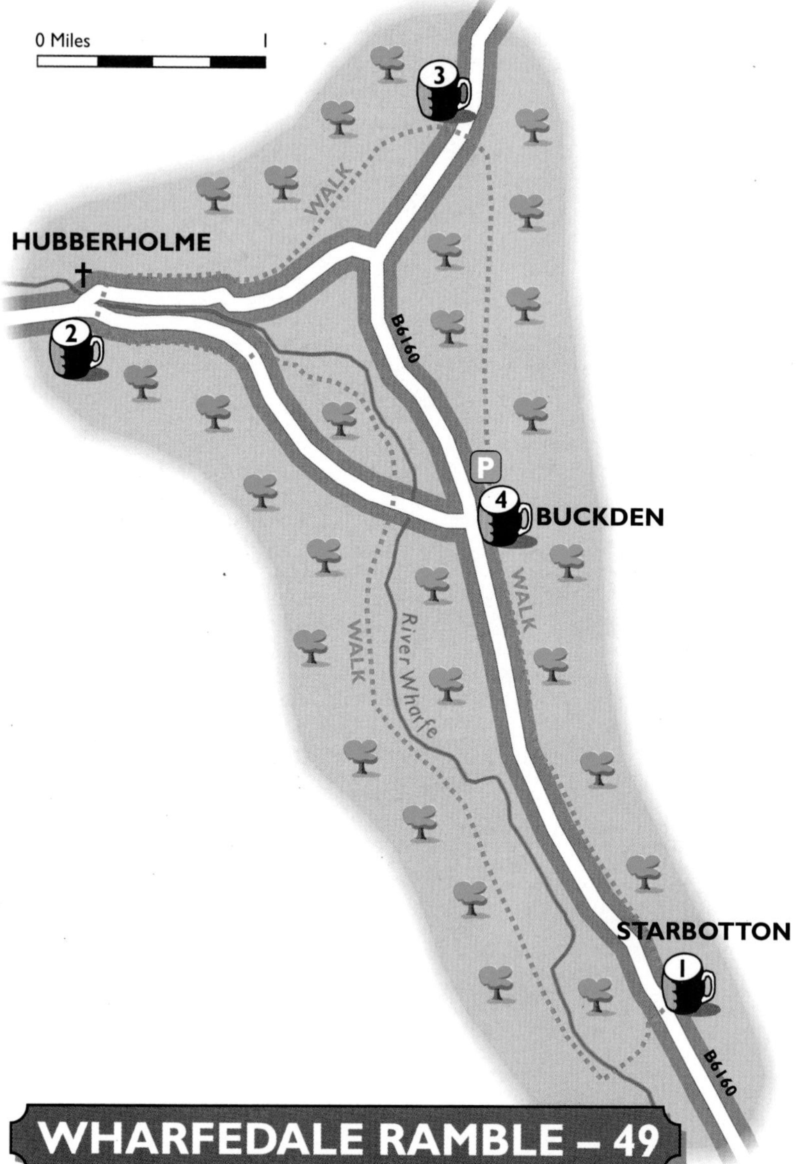

WHARFEDALE RAMBLE – 49

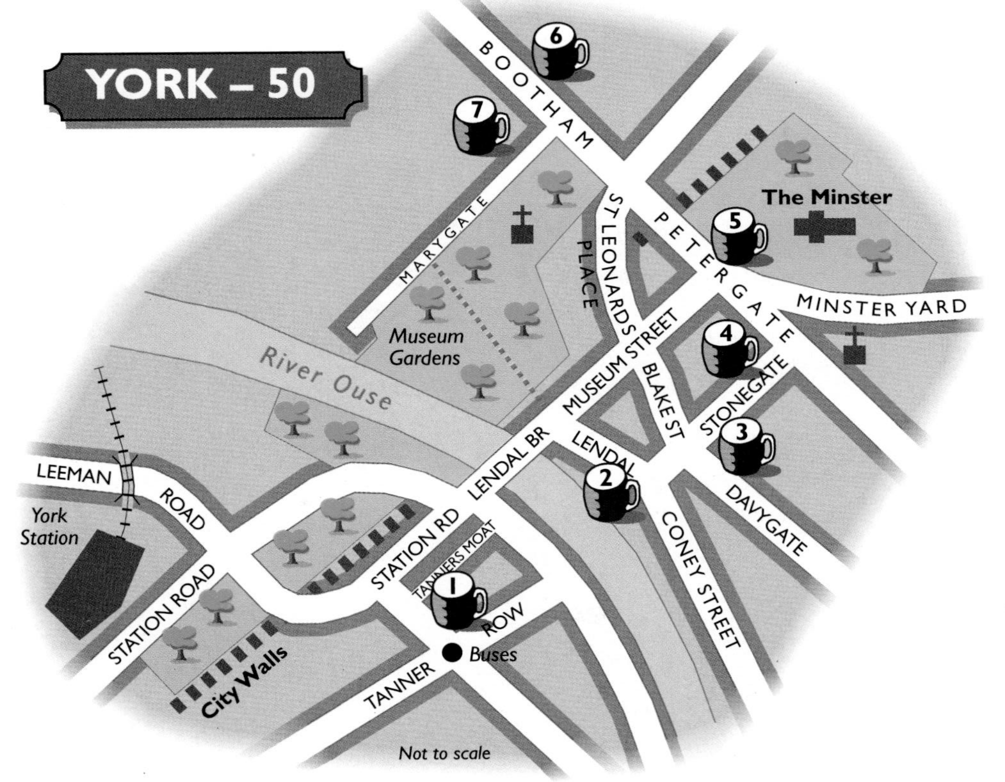
YORK – 50
BOOTHAM
MARYGATE
ST LEONARDS PLACE
PETERGATE
The Minster
MINSTER YARD
Museum Gardens
River Ouse
MUSEUM STREET
BLAKE ST
STONEGATE
LENDAL
LENDAL BR
DAVYGATE
CONEY STREET
STATION RD
TANNERS MOAT
ROW
Buses
TANNER
LEEMAN
ROAD
York Station
STATION ROAD
City Walls
Not to scale
1
2
3
4
5
6
7

Cupola House
Bury St Edmunds
Pub Crawl No. 8
starting on
page number 32.

middle
The Long Hall
Dublin
Pub Crawl
No. 13
starting
on page
number 50.

The Guildford Arms
Edinburgh
Pub Crawl No. 15
starting on
page number 58.

The Crown Bar
Belfast
Pub Crawl No. 4
starting on
page number 18

middle
Railwaymans Arms
Pub Crawl No. 5
starting on
page number 21

The Roebuck
Pub Crawl No. 5
starting on
page number 21

The Golden Cross
Cirencester
Pub Crawl No. 11
starting on
page number 43.

middle
The Head of Steam
Hull
Pub Crawl No. 19
starting on
page number 69.

Anchor and Hope
Lee Valley by Boat
Pub Crawl No. 26
starting on
page number 91.

The Bay Horse, Otley
Pub Crawl No. 36
starting on
page number 128.

middle
The Old Thirteenth Cheshire Astley Volunteer Rifleman Corps Inn
Stalybridge
Pub Crawl No. 44
starting on page number 158.

Kings Arms Hotel
Swindon
Pub Crawl
No. 46
starting on
page number

The Dispensary
Liverpool
Pub Crawl
No.28
starting on
page
number 97.

middle
Cooper's Arms
Newbury
Pub Crawl
No. 33
starting on
page
number 115.

The Lord Clyde
London Bridge and the Borough
Pub Crawl No. 30
starting on page number 103.